WASHINGTON'S COLUMBIA RIVER GORGE CAMPING & HIKING

TOM STIENSTRA & SCOTT LEONARD

How to Use This Book

ABOUT THE CAMPGROUND PROFILES

The campgrounds are listed in a consistent, easy-to-read format to help you choose the ideal camping spot. If you already know the name of the specific campground you want to visit, or the name of the surrounding geological area or nearby feature (town, national or state park, forest, mountain, lake, river, etc.), look it up in the index and turn to the corresponding page. Here is a sample profile:

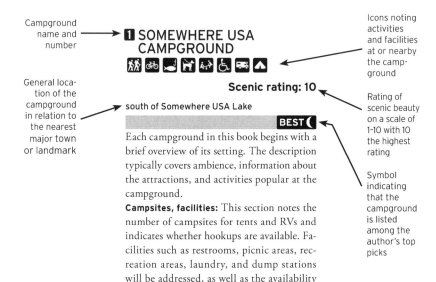

Campground name and number →

General location of the campground in relation to the nearest major town or landmark →

1 SOMEWHERE USA CAMPGROUND

Icons noting activities and facilities at or nearby the campground ←

Scenic rating: 10 ←

south of Somewhere USA Lake

BEST (←

Rating of scenic beauty on a scale of 1-10 with 10 the highest rating

Symbol indicating that the campground is listed among the author's top picks

Each campground in this book begins with a brief overview of its setting. The description typically covers ambience, information about the attractions, and activities popular at the campground.

Campsites, facilities: This section notes the number of campsites for tents and RVs and indicates whether hookups are available. Facilities such as restrooms, picnic areas, recreation areas, laundry, and dump stations will be addressed, as well as the availability of piped water, showers, playgrounds, stores, and other amenities. The campground's pet policy and wheelchair accessibility is also mentioned here.

Reservations, fees: This section notes whether reservations are accepted, and provides rates for tent sites and RV sites. If there are additional fees for parking or pets, or discounted weekly or seasonal rates, they will also be noted here.

Directions: This section provides mile-by-mile driving directions to the campground from the nearest major town or highway.

Contact: This section provides an address, phone number, and website, if available, for the campground.

ABOUT THE ICONS

The icons in this book are designed to provide at-a-glance information on activities, facilities, and services available on-site or within walking distance of each campground.

- 🚶 Hiking trails
- 🚲 Biking trails
- 🏊 Swimming
- 🎣 Fishing
- 🚣 Boating
- 🛶 Canoeing and/or kayaking
- ❄ Winter sports

- ♨ Hot springs
- 🐾 Pets permitted
- 🎠 Playground
- ♿ Wheelchair accessible
- 🚐 RV sites
- ⛺ Tent sites

ABOUT THE SCENIC RATING

Each campground profile employs a scenic rating on a scale of 1 to 10, with 1 being the least scenic and 10 being the most scenic. A scenic rating measures only the overall beauty of the campground and environs; it does not take into account noise level, facilities, maintenance, recreation options, or campground management. The setting of a campground with a lower scenic rating may simply not be as picturesque that of as a higher rated campground, however other factors that can influence a trip, such as noise or recreation access, can still affect or enhance your camping trip. Consider both the scenic rating and the profile description before deciding which campground is perfect for you.

ABOUT THE TRAIL PROFILES

Each hike in this book is listed in a consistent, easy-to-read format to help you choose the ideal hike. From a general overview of the setting to detailed driving directions, the profile will provide all the information you need. Here is a sample profile:

Map number and hike number

Round-trip mileage (unless otherwise noted) and the approximate amount of time needed to complete the hike (actual times can vary widely, especially on longer hikes)

❶ SOMEWHERE USA HIKE
9.0 mi/5.0 hrs 　　　　3　8

Difficulty and quality ratings

at the mouth of the Somewhere River

General location of the trail, named by its proximity to the nearest major town or landmark

BEST (

Symbol indicating that the hike is listed among the author's top picks

Each hike in this book begins with a brief overview of its setting. The description typically covers what kind of terrain to expect, what might be seen, and any conditions that may make the hike difficult to navigate. Side trips, such as to waterfalls or panoramic vistas, in addition to ways to combine the trail with others nearby for a longer outing, are also noted here. In many cases, mile-by-mile trail directions are included.

User Groups: This section notes the types of users that are permitted on the trail, including hikers, mountain bikers, horseback riders, and dogs. Wheelchair access is also noted here.

Permits: This section notes whether a permit is required for hiking, or, if the hike spans more than one day, whether one is required for camping. Any fees, such as for parking, day use, or entrance, are also noted here.

Maps: This section provides information on how to obtain detailed trail maps of the hike and its environs. Whenever applicable, names of U.S. Geologic Survey (USGS) topographic maps and national forest maps are also included; contact information for these and other map sources are noted in the Resources section at the back of this book.

Directions: This section provides mile-by-mile driving directions to the trailhead from the nearest major town.

Contact: This section provides an address and phone number for each hike. The contact is usually the agency maintaining the trail but may also be a trail club or other organization.

ABOUT THE ICONS

The icons in this book are designed to provide at-a-glance information on the difficulty and quality of each hike.

The **DIFFICULTY** rating (rated **1-5** with **1** being the lowest and **5** the highest) is based on the steepness of the trail and how difficult it is to traverse

The **QUALITY** rating (rated **1-10** with **1** being the lowest and **10** the highest) is based largely on scenic beauty, but also takes into account how crowded the trail is and whether noise of nearby civilization is audible

ABOUT THE DIFFICULTY RATINGS

Trails rated 1 are very easy and suitable for hikers of all abilities, including young children.

Trails rated 2 are easy-to-moderate and suitable for most hikers, including families with active children 6 and older.

Trails rated 3 are moderately challenging and suitable for reasonably fit adults and older children who are very active.

Trails rated 4 are very challenging and suitable for physically fit hikers who are seeking a workout.

Trails rated 5 are extremely challenging and suitable only for experienced hikers who are in top physical condition.

MAP SYMBOLS

Expressway	80	Interstate Freeway	✗	Airfield
Primary Road	101	U.S. Highway	✈	Airport
Secondary Road	21	State Highway	○	City/Town
Unpaved Road	66	County Highway	▲	Mountain
Ferry		Lake	♣	Park
National Border		Dry Lake	)(	Pass
State Border		Seasonal Lake	◉	State Capital

ABOUT THE MAPS

This book is divided into chapters based on major regions in the state. Each chapter begins with a map of the region, which is further broken down into detail maps. Sites are noted on the detail maps by number.

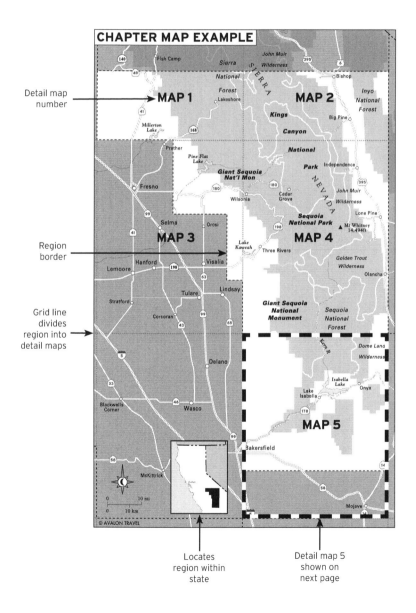

Locates detail
map within
region

Map
number ➝ **Map 5**

Sites shown
on detail map ➝ **Sites 106-119**

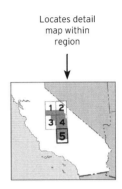

Site number ➝

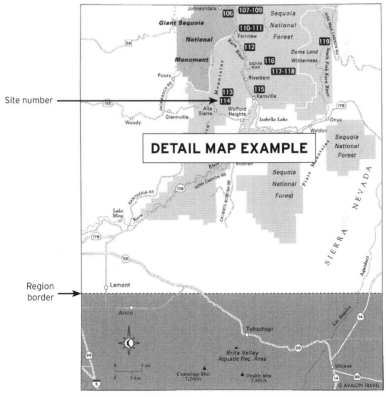

DETAIL MAP EXAMPLE

Region
border ➝

Camping and Hiking Tips

THE 10 ESSENTIALS

The 10 Essentials are just that—indispensable items that you should carry every time you hit the trail. No matter where you're headed, you never know what you're going to come across (or what's going to come across you); being prepared can help to prevent problems before they start.

Clothing

Here in Washington, the weather can turn at the drop of a hat. In every season, rain is an inevitability. We didn't get a reputation for wet weather for nothing. During the summer, sudden thundershowers or snowstorms can give even experienced hikers a surprise. So it's best to bring extra clothing for those unexpected weather fronts.

Clothing that can ward off the cold is extremely important. Most accidents in the wilderness are the result of, or complicated by, hypothermia, which can set in quickly and with little warning. Once a person starts getting cold, the ability to think and troubleshoot heads downhill. Symptoms of hypothermia include fatigue, drowsiness, unwillingness to go on, a feeling of deep cold or numbness, poor coordination, and mumbling. To avoid this, bring clothes that are easily layered. During the summer, that can be as simple as a warm fleece. During the winter, wool or synthetic fleeces are effective against the cold. A stocking cap is extremely helpful since a big chunk of body heat is lost through the head. Extra socks are helpful for keeping feet warm and comfortable. Remember that you can be vulnerable even in the summer—bitter July snowstorms are not unprecedented.

Rain gear, such as a waterproof jacket, pants, and a hat or hood, is equally important during all seasons, but especially during the fall and spring when it's practically impossible to head outdoors without rain. Even if there is no rain in the forecast, be prepared for it. (Local weather reporters are forecasting for the cities, not the mountains.) And short but serious rainstorms are the year-round norm, not the exception, in Washington.

When dressing for a hike, it's important to avoid cotton clothing, especially if rain is a possibility. Once cotton gets wet, it can draw off body heat, causing hypothermia to set in quickly. Wool and polypropylene are good alternatives. If you get wet wearing cotton, take it off if you have another layer that is not cotton.

Water

Be sure to drink lots of water, even if it's not that hot out. Staying properly hydrated can prevent heat exhaustion. Symptoms of heat exhaustion include excessive sweating, gradual weakness, nausea, anxiety, and eventually loss of consciousness. Usually, the skin becomes pale and clammy or cold, the pulse slows, and blood pressure may drop. Heat exhaustion is often unexpected but very serious; someone experiencing heat exhaustion will have difficulty getting out of a wilderness setting and will need assistance—not always an easy task.

When day hiking, you can probably carry from the trailhead all the water you'll need for the hike. Two liters per person is a good rule of thumb. Carrying water with you or having a method of filtering water is important—never drink untreated water in the

HIKING WITH KIDS

1. **Prepare, prepare, prepare.** Heading out on the trail with kids calls for extra preparation. The 10 Essentials are more important than ever. And be ready for the unexpected: Bring something extra to drink and eat, and bring proper rain/sun protection. And don't hesitate to involve them – kids often love to help pack.
2. **Pick the right hike.** Kids are much more likely to enjoy hiking if the trail is appropriate for their age and ability. And don't assume the trail will need to include peaks and summits for kids to enjoy the journey: From bugs and animals to streams and forests, kids will find something in nature to interest them (if they aren't wiped from the hike).
3. **Gear up.** Hiking with children doesn't mean you have to drop a week's pay at REI. But making sure you and your little hiker have the proper gear is important for safety and enjoyment. Comfortable footwear and weather-appropriate clothing are musts. A backpack for your child helps them feel involved in the "work" of hiking; just make sure it's not too heavy. And parents should be carrying extra water and food for all.
4. **Be flexible.** Hiking is not mandatory. Our parents may have insisted that discomfort builds character, but kids often know when enough is enough for their bodies. Accommodating a request to turn around before the intended destination can be rewarded by a request for another trip soon. Remember, the point is for each hiker to enjoy the journey.
5. **Be attentive.** When hiking with children, there are more factors to keep in mind. Kids may be getting wet or cold, sunburned or overheated. Many hikes have inherent danger, such as cliffs, snakes, poison oak, or slippery ground. Keep an eye on your little hikers and they will be around for many hikes to come.

wild. A stream may look crystal clear and be ice cold, but it can also be full of nasty parasites and viruses. If you catch a case of *giardia* or *cryptosporidia,* you could be incapacitated for a full week. Carrying a stove or a filter can be impractical on day hikes. The best back-up method is to carry iodine and chlorine tablets that quickly and easily purify water. They're lightweight and come in handy in a pinch. If you don't mind a strange taste in your water, these will do the trick.

Food

The lore of the backcountry is filled with tales of folks who head out for a quick day hike and end up spending a night (or more) in the wilderness. Planning on just an afternoon away from the kitchen, they don't bring enough food to last into the night or morning. Not only is an empty stomach a restless stomach, it can be dangerous, as well. A full stomach provides energy to help ward off hypothermia and keeps the mind clear for the task at hand: Not getting even more lost.

When packing food for an outing, include a little extra gorp or an extra energy bar. This will come in extremely handy if you find yourself wandering back to the trailhead later than planned. A grizzled old veteran of the backcountry once passed on a helpful tip for packing extra food. Extra food is meant for an emergency; the last thing you want to do is eat it in a nonemergency and then need it later. So, he packed something nutritious that he'd consider eating only in an emergency: canned dog food.

Fire Starter

Some people prefer matches while others choose to bring along a lighter. Either way, it's important to have something with which to start a fire. Don't think that you can start your fire by rubbing two sticks together. Even when it's dry, sticks don't like to start up easily. So be certain to purchase some quality waterproof matches (you can make your own with paraffin wax and wooden matches), or carry a couple of lighters. Regardless of your choice, keep them packed away in a safe and dry place (like a sandwich baggie). Besides a starter, bring along something to keep the fire going for a bit. Fire pellets are available at any outdoor store. Do-it-yourselfers will be glad to know that toilet paper is highly flammable, as are cotton balls dipped in Vaseline. Starting a fire when it's cold, dark, and wet can save your life.

Map and Compass

You need to carry a map and compass on your person *every* time you hit the trail, whether you're going up Mount Si with the rest of Seattle or venturing into the vacant backcountry of North Cascades National Park. No matter how familiar you think you are with a trail, you can get lost. Not only should you carry a map and compass, but you also need to know how to use them.

A map is not always a map. You can't rely on the map that AAA gave you out on the trail. Instead, it's best to purchase a quality topographic map for use on the trail. A quality topographic map allows hikers to follow their steps more accurately and is infinitely more helpful for figuring out where you are when you're lost. Green Trails of Seattle makes high-quality topo maps for 90 percent of Washington trails. The USGS and National Geographic also make good topo maps.

Now that it's the 21st century, GPS devices are becoming more popular. These are great toys to play with while out on the trail. Some folks even swear by them. But a GPS device often won't work in a thick forest canopy. A good old-fashioned

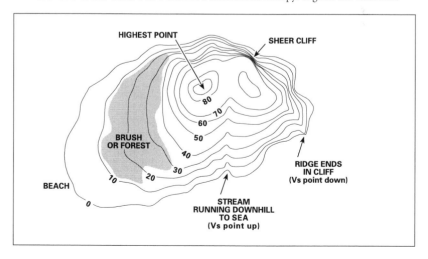

compass, on the other hand, is significantly cheaper and won't ever die on you when the batteries run out.

First-Aid Kit

A first-aid kit is an important essential to carry while out on the trail. With twigs, rocks, and bears lurking around every corner, hiking can be dangerous business. Injuries can range from small abrasions to serious breaks, and a simple but well-stocked first-aid kit can be a lifesaver. It's best to purchase a first-aid kit at an outdoors store. Kits come in different sizes, depending on intended use, and include the fundamentals. Also, a number of organizations provide medical training for backcountry situations. Courses run from one-day seminars in simple first aid all the way to month-long classes for wilderness EMT certification. Outdoors enthusiasts who venture out on a regular basis should consider a course in Wilderness First Aid (WOOFA) or Wilderness First Response (WOOFER).

Band-aids come in every kit but are only helpful for small, nonserious cuts or abrasions. Here are a few things that are especially important and can come in handy in an emergency:
• Ibuprofen: It works very well to combat swelling. Twist an ankle or suffer a nasty bruise and reducing the swelling quickly becomes an important consideration.
• Athletic tape and gauze: These are helpful in treating twisted or strained joints. A firm wrap with athletic tape will make the three-mile hobble to the car less of an ordeal.
• Travel-size supplies of general medicines: Items like Alka-Seltzer or NyQuil are multipurpose and practical.

Finally: The only thing better than having a first-aid kit on the trail is not needing one.

Sun Protection

Most hikers don't think that fierce sunburns are a serious concern in notoriously gray Washington. But during the summer, the sun can be extremely brutal, especially at higher altitudes where a few thousand feet of atmosphere can be sorely missed. A full day in the blazing sun is hard on the eyes as well.

Don't let the sun spoil an otherwise great day in the outdoors. Sunscreen is worth its weight in gold out on the trail. Be sure to apply it regularly, and keep kids lathered up as well. It helps to bring a hat and lightweight clothing with long sleeves, both of which can make sunscreen almost unnecessary. Finally, many hikers swear by a good pair of sunglasses. Perhaps obvious during the summer, sunglasses are also a snowshoer's best friend. Snow blindness is a serious threat on beautiful sunny days during the winter.

All of these measures will make a trip not only safer but more enjoyable as well. Avoiding sunburn is also extremely helpful in warding off heat stroke, a serious condition in the backcountry.

Light Source

Even veteran hikers who intend to go out only for a "quick" day hike can end up finishing in the dark. There were just too many things to see, too many lakes to swim in, and too many peaks to bag on that "short" hike. Often, getting back to the car or camp before it's dark requires the difficult task of leaving a beautiful place while it's still light out. Or perhaps while out on an easy forest hike, you're on schedule to get back before dark, but the thick forest canopy brings on night an hour or two early. There are lots of ways to get stuck in the outdoors in the dark. And what good are a map and compass if you can't see them? Plan ahead and bring an adequate light source. The market is flooded these days with cheap (and not so cheap) headlamps. Headlamps are basically small flashlights that fit around your head. They're great because they're bright and they keep your hands free, so you're better able to beat back brush on the trail or fend off hungry fellow campers around the dinner stove.

Multipurpose Knife

For outdoors enthusiasts, the multipurpose Swiss Army knife is one of the greatest things since sliced bread. Handy utility knives come in all shapes and sizes and are made by about a hundred different companies. A high-quality utility knife will come in handy in a multitude of situations. The features available include big knives and little knives, saws and scissors, corkscrews and screwdrivers, and about 30 other fun little tools. They are useful almost everywhere, except at the airport.

Emergency Kit

You'll probably have a hard time finding a pre-prepared emergency kit for sale at any store. Instead, this is something that you can quickly and inexpensively assemble yourself.
• Space blanket: Find these at any outdoor store or army surplus store. They're small, shiny blankets that insulate extremely well, are highly visible, and will make do in place of a tent when needed.
• Signal mirror: A signal mirror is handy when you're lost. Catch the glare of the sun, and you can signal your position to search-and-rescue hikers or planes. The small mirror that comes attached to some compasses works perfectly.
• Whistle: Again, if you get really lost, don't waste your breath screaming and hollering. You'll lose your voice quickly, and it doesn't carry far anyhow. Blow your whistle all day or night long, and you'll still be able to talk to the trees (or yourself).

ON THE TRAIL

It's Friday afternoon, work has been a trial all week, and there's only one thing on your mind: getting outdoors and hitting the trail for the weekend. For many of us, nature is a getaway from the confines of urban living. The irony of it all, however, is that the more people head to the backcountry, the less wild it truly is. That means that it takes a collective effort from all trail users to keep the outdoors as pristine as it was 100 years ago. This effort is so important, in fact, that the organization Leave No Trace has created an ideology for low-impact use of our wilderness. (For more information on the Leave No Trace Center for Outdoor Ethics and their values, check out their website at www.lnt.org.) Here are a few principles that we all can follow to ensure that the great outdoors continues to be great.

Planning Your Trip

A little careful planning and preparation not only makes your trip safer, but it also makes it easy to minimize resource damage. Make sure you know the regulations, such as group size limits or campfire regulations, before hitting the trail. Prepare for any special circumstances an area may have, such as the need for ice axes or water filters. Many

HIKING ETIQUETTE

1. **Leave no trace.** We love hiking for the opportunity to leave civilization behind and enjoy nature. Thus, we all need to leave the trail as nice – or nicer – than we found it. Pack all litter out (even litter that others may have left behind, if you're so inclined). Do not leave graffiti or other marks on trees or rocks. Let wildlife stay wild by not feeding or harassing animals. If you find something interesting, it's likely that someone else will also find it interesting: Be sure to leave rocks, flowers, and other natural objects where you find them.

2. **Stay on the trail.** Washington trails are heavily used. While just one person cutting a switchback or zipping off trail through a meadow has little consequence, the cumulative damage from many hikers wandering off trail is all too easy to spot. Avoid erosion and unsightly way-trails by hiking only on established trails.

3. **Yield to uphill hikers.** Hikers who are headed up an incline have the right-of-way. After all, uphill hikers have built up momentum and are working hard to put trail beneath their feet. Downhill hikers should find a safe place to step off the trail and allow others to pass.

4. **Keep dogs under control.** Yes, we all love to take our best friends out on the trail. But they need to stay on the trail. Out-of-control dogs can easily end up lost in the woods. While a leash is not always necessary, one should be carried at all times and used when on a busy trail. Where dogs are not permitted, it is bad form and even dangerous to take them along.

5. **Be respectful of others.** Be aware of your noise level, and make way for others. Common courtesy creates community on the trail and enhances everyone's experience. Remember, our public lands belong to no one and everyone at the same time.

places are used heavily during summer weekends. Schedule your trip for a weekday or off-season, and you'll encounter far fewer fellow bipeds.

Hiking and Camping

One of the most important principles for hikers and campers here in Washington is to minimize our impact on the land. Many of our greatest and most heavily used trails visit fragile environments, such as alpine meadows and lakeshores. These ecosystems are easily injured by hikers and campers. Take care to travel only on the main trail, never cut a switchback, and avoid the social trails—small, unofficial trails that are made over years by hikers cutting trails—that spiderweb through many a high meadow. When camping, pitch camp in already established sites, never on a meadow. Take care in selecting a site for a camp kitchen and when heading off for the bathroom. Being aware of your impact not only improves the experience for yourself but also for those who follow you.

Packing Out Your Trash

It goes without saying that trash does not belong in the great outdoors. That goes for all trash, regardless of whether it's biodegradable or not. From food packaging to the food itself, it has to go out the way it came in: on your back. Ditto for toilet paper. As far as human waste goes, dig a cat hole for your waste, and pack all toilet paper and hygiene products in bags. It may be nasty, but it's only fair for others.

Leaving What You Find

The old saying goes, "Take only photographs and leave only footprints." Well, if you're walking on durable surfaces such as established trails, you won't even leave footprints. And it's best to leave the artifacts of nature where they belong: in nature. By doing so, you ensure that others can enjoy them as well. If you see something interesting, remember that it is only there because the hiker in front of you left it for you to find. The same goes for attractive rocks, deer and elk antlers, and wildflowers. Avoid altering sites by digging trenches, building lean-tos, or harming trees.

Lighting Campfires

Thanks to Smokey the Bear, we all know the seriousness of forest fires. If you're going to have a fire, make sure it's out before going to sleep or leaving camp. But there are other important considerations for campfires. Here in Washington, many national forests and wildernesses have fire bans above 3,500 feet. At these higher altitudes, trees grow slowly and depend greatly on decomposition of downed trees. Burning downed limbs and trees robs the ecosystems of much-needed nutrients, an impact that lasts centuries. Carry a camp stove any time you plan on cooking while backpacking.

Encountering Wildlife

Hiking is all about being outdoors. Fresh air, colorful wildflowers, expansive mountain views, and a little peace and quiet are what folks are after as they embark on the trail. The great outdoors is also home to creatures big and small. Remember, you are in their home: No chasing the deer. No throwing rocks at the chipmunks. No bareback riding the elk. And no wrestling the bears. In all seriousness, the most important way we can respect wildlife is by not feeding them. Chipmunks may be cute, but feeding them only makes them fat and dependent on people for food. Keep a clean camp without food on the ground, and be sure to hang food anytime you're separated from it. A good bear hang is as much about keeping the bears out of the food as it is about keeping the mice and squirrels from eating it.

Nearly all wildlife around Seattle is completely harmless to hikers; bears and cougars are the only wildlife that pose a danger to us humans. Fortunately, the vast majority of encounters with these big predators result in nothing more than a memorable story. Coming across bears and cougars may be frightening, but these encounters don't need to be dangerous as long as you follow a few simple precautions.

Bears

Running into a bear is the most common worry of novice hikers when they hit the trail. Bears are big, furry, and naturally a bit scary at first sight. But in reality, bears want little to do with people and much prefer to avoid us altogether. The chance of getting into a fistfight with a bear is rare in Washington. In our state's history, there have only been three attacks and one fatality recorded. As long as you stay away from bear cubs and food, bears will almost certainly leave you alone.

What kind of bear will you see out on the trail? Most likely, you won't see one at all, but if you do, it will probably be a black bear, although Washington is home to grizzly bears as well. Black bears, whose thick coats range from light tan to cinnamon to black, are by far the most numerous, with approximately 25,000 spread throughout our state. Grizzly bears are much more rare, numbering less than 50, and are primarily located along the Canadian border in the Pasayten Wilderness and Selkirk Mountains. Grizzlies have a distinctive hump between their shoulders.

The old image of Yogi the Bear stealing picnic baskets is not that far off. Bears love to get a hold of human food, so proper food storage is an effective way to avoid an unwanted bear encounter. When camping, be sure to use a bear hang. Collect all food, toiletries, and anything else with scent; place it all in a stuff sack and hang the sack in a tree. The sack should be at least 12 feet off the ground and eight feet from the tree trunk.

Should you come across a bear on the trail, stay calm. It's okay to be scared, but with a few precautions, you will be completely safe. First, know that your objective is not to intimidate the bear but simply to let it know you are not easy prey. Make yourself look big by standing tall, waving your arms, or even holding open your jacket. Second, don't look it in the eye. Bears consider eye contact to be aggressive and an invitation to a confrontation. Third, speak loudly and firmly to the bear. Bears are nearsighted and can't make out objects from afar. But a human voice means humans, and a bear is likely to retreat from your presence. If a bear advances, it is very likely only trying to get a better look. Finally, if the bear doesn't budge, go around it in a wide circle. In case the unlikely should occur and the bear attacks, curl up in a ball, stay as still as possible, and wait for the attack to end. If the bear bites, take a cheap shot at the nose. Bears hate being hit on their sensitive noses. Trying to hit a bear from this position is difficult. It can work if you can cover your neck with one hand and swing with the other. Protecting yourself is first priority. If the bear is especially aggressive, it's necessary to fight back. Most important, don't let fear of bears prevent you from getting out there; it's rare to see a bear and even rarer to have a problem with one.

COUGARS

With millions of acres of wilderness, Washington is home to cougars, bobcats, and lynx. Bobcats and lynx are small and highly withdrawn. If you encounter one of these recluses, you're in a small minority. Cougars are also very shy, and encounters with these big cats are rare; only 2,500 cougars live in our state. Cougar attacks are extremely uncommon; there have been few in recent years and only one fatality ever in Washington. You're more likely to be struck by lightning than attacked by a cougar. In most circumstances, sighting a cougar will just result in having a great story to tell.

If you should encounter a cougar in the wild, make every effort to intimidate it. First, don't run! A cougar views something running from it as dinner. Second, make yourself bigger by waving your arms, jumping around, and spreading open a jacket. Cougars have very little interest in a tough fight. Third, don't bend down to pick up a rock; you'll only look smaller to the cougar. Fourth, stare the cougar down—a menacing stare-down is intimidating for a cougar. Finally, should a cougar attack, fight back with everything you have and as dirtily as possible.

Respecting Other Hikers

If you are considerate of others on the trail, they are likely to return the favor. This includes such simple things as yielding right-of-way to those who are trudging uphill, keeping noise to a minimum, and observing any use regulations, such as no mountain bikes and no fires. If possible, try to set up camp off trail and out of sight. Together, everyone can equally enjoy the beauties of hiking in Washington.

Hiking with Dogs

Though not everyone may have a dog, nearly everyone has an opinion about dogs on the trail. Hiking with canine friends can be a great experience, not only for us but for them, as well. What dog doesn't love being out on the trail, roaming the wild and in touch with his ancestral roots? That's great, but there are a few matters that must be considered before taking a dog on a hike.

First, be aware that national parks do not allow dogs on any trail at any time. However, dogs are allowed throughout national forests and any wildernesses contained within them. Second, dogs should remain on the trail at all times. Dogs can create an enormous amount of erosion when roaming off trail, and they're frequent switchback cutters. Third, dogs must be under control at all times. Leashes are not always mandatory because many dogs are obedient and do very well while unleashed. But if you're not going to use a leash, your dog should respond to commands well and not bother other hikers. Finally, be aware that dogs and wildlife don't mix well. Dogs love to chase chipmunks, rabbits, deer, and anything else that moves. But from the chipmunk's point of view, a big, slobbering beast chasing you is stressful and unequivocally bad. Not only that, but dogs can incite aggression in bears or cougars. An unleashed dog can quickly transform a peaceful bear into a raging assault of claws and teeth. Plus, bears and cougars find dogs to be especially tasty. Don't hesitate to bring your dog out on the trail as long as you take the dog's interests, as well as other hikers' interests, into consideration.

PERMITS

You've got your pack ready, done your food shopping, purchased the right maps, and even wrestled the kids into the car. But do you have the right permits? Here in Washington, there are several permits that you may need before you can hit the trail. Headed for a national forest? Read up on the Northwest Forest Pass. Driving down to Mount Rainier or the Olympics? You probably need a National Parks Pass. Backpacking in a national park? Don't forget your backcountry camping permit.

Northwest Forest Pass

The Northwest Forest Pass (NWFP) is the most widely used permit in our state. The pass is accepted at 680 day-use recreation sites in Washington and Oregon. Almost every trailhead in every national forest in Washington requires a NWFP for parking. Remarkably, a Northwest Forest Pass is all that is required in the North Cascades National Park. The Colville National Forest is the one agency that does not participate in the NWFP program; access to trailheads in the Colville is free. Senior citizens take note: In lieu of a NWFP, the federal Golden Eagle, Golden Access, and Golden Age passes are accepted.

The Northwest Forest Pass costs $30 and is valid for one year from date of purchase. It's interchangeable between vehicles in the same household. Day passes may also be purchased at a cost of $5 per day. More than 240 vendors across the northwest offer the pass, including all ranger stations, most outdoor stores, and many service stations in recreational areas. Passes can also be ordered online through Nature of the Northwest at www.naturenw.org. Proceeds from Northwest Forest Passes go toward improvements at recreational sites, including refurbishing trailheads, trail maintenance and construction, and environmental education. There is a lot of controversy over the pass, as critics contend that national forests are public lands and already paid for by federal taxes. They have a point, but the revenue serves to supplement ever-dwindling forest service budgets.

National Parks Passes and Permits

No question, the United States has the world's premier national park system. From Acadia National Park in Maine to Denali National Park in Alaska, the United States has taken care to preserve our most important ecosystems for future generations to enjoy. Here in Washington, we have the North Cascades, Olympic, and Mount Rainier National Parks to savor. This book includes coverage only of Mount Rainier National Park. The four hikes inside the park require fees for car access to the trailheads. Access to Carbon River Road and Mowich Lake Road require one of three passes: a Single Visit Vehicle Permit ($10 and good for seven days), a Mount Rainier National Park Annual Pass ($30 and good for one year), or any of the national parks passes, which are good for one year at all national parks in the United States. National parks passes include: the National Parks Pass ($50 and good at any national park in the United States for one year), the Golden Access Pass (available for people who are blind or permanently disabled and allows lifetime admittance to any national park for free), and the Golden Age Pass (available to people 62 years or older and allows lifetime admittance to any national park for a one-time fee of $10).

WASHINGTON'S COLUMBIA RIVER GORGE CAMPING

BEST CAMPGROUNDS

CAMPING

As you stand at the rim of the Mount St. Helens

volcano, the greatest natural spectacle anywhere on the planet is at your boot tips. The top 1,300 feet of the old mountain, along with the entire north flank, was blown clean off. The half-moon crater walls drop almost 2,100 feet straight down to a lava plug dome, a mile across and still building, where a wisp of smoke emerges from its center. At its edges, the rising plumes of dust from continuous rock falls can be deceptive — you may think a small eruption is in progress. It's like looking inside the bowels of the earth.

The plug dome gives way to the blast zone, where the mountain has completely blown out its side and spreads out across 230 square miles of devastation. From here, it's largely a moonscape but for Spirit Lake on the northeast flank, where thousands of trees are still floating, log-jammed from the eruption in May 1980. Beyond this scene rises 14,411-foot Mount Rainier to the north, 12,276-foot Mount Adams to the northeast, and 11,239-foot Mount Hood to the south, all pristine jewels in contrast to the nearby remains. I've hiked most of the Pacific Crest Trail and climbed most of the West's highest mountains, but no view compares to this. Though infrequent, the trail to the summit can be closed because of volcanic activity at the plug dome.

You could explore this sweeping panorama of a land for years. The most famous spots in this region are St. Helens, Rainier, and Adams; the latter are two of the three most beautiful mountains in the Cascade Range (Mount Shasta in Northern California is the third). All of them offer outstanding touring and hiking, with excellent camps of all kinds available around their perimeters. St. Helens provides the most eye-popping views and most developed visitors centers, Rainier the most pristine wilderness, and Adams some of the best lakeside camps, with trout fishing sometimes within casting range of your tent.

That's just the beginning. The Western Cascades span down-river canyons and up-mountain sub-ridges filled with streams and lakes. There are camps throughout. At the same time, the I-5 corridor and its network of linked highways provide many privately developed RV parks fully furnished with everything a vacationer could desire.

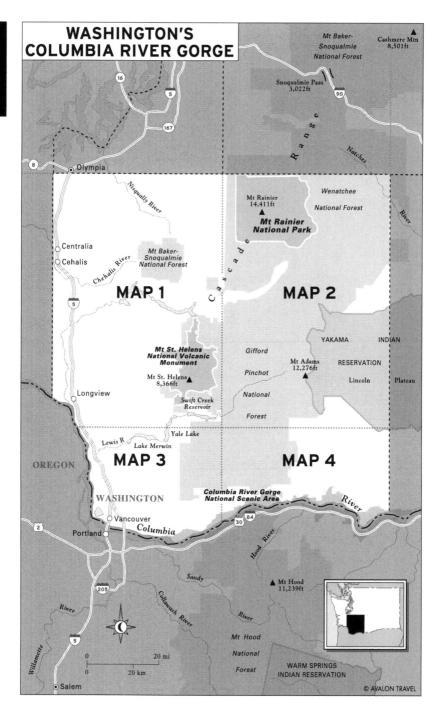

Map 1

Campgrounds 1-24

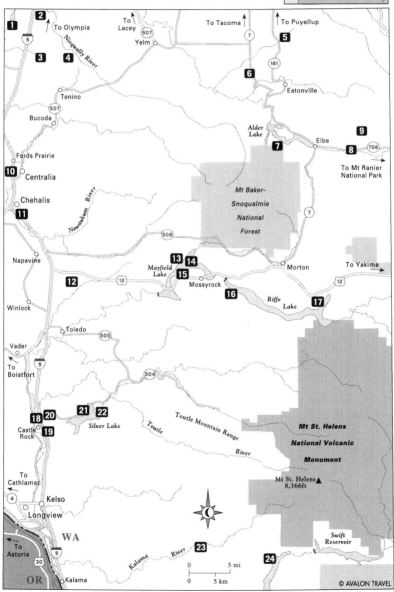

CAMPING

Map 2

Campgrounds 25-80

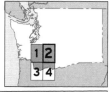

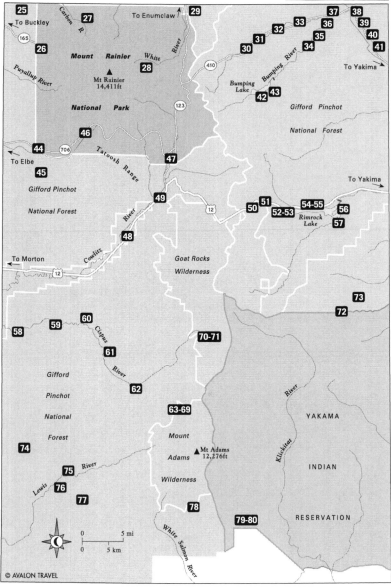

Map 3

Campgrounds 81-91

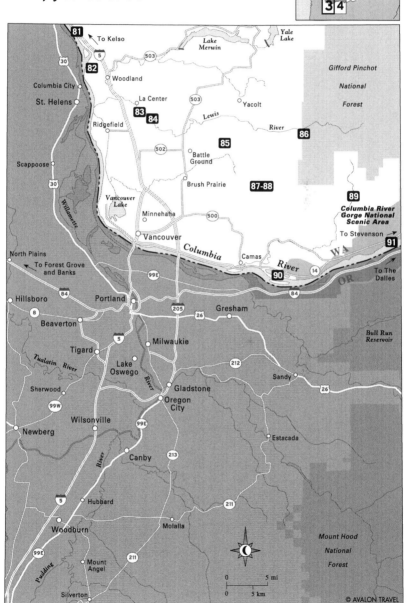

Map 4

Campgrounds 92-105

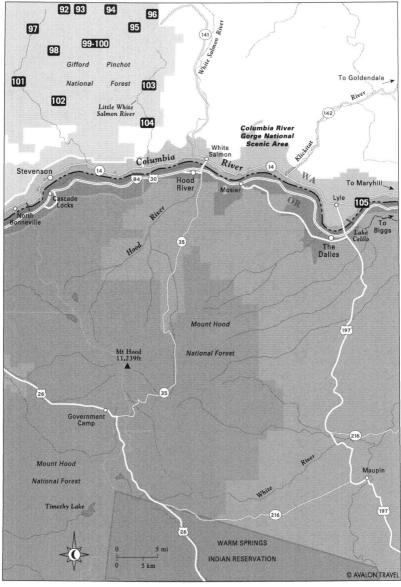

1 COLUMBUS PARK

Scenic rating: 8

on Black Lake

This spot along the shore of Black Lake is pretty enough for special events, such as weddings and reunions. The campsites are wooded, and a stream (no fishing) runs through the campground. Black Lake is good for fishing, however. An 18-hole golf course is nearby.

Campsites, facilities: There are 29 sites for tents or RVs up to 40 feet long (30 amp partial hookups) and one tent site. There are also 46 sites with full hookups that are usually rented by the month. Picnic tables are provided. Restrooms with flush toilets and showers, drinking water, a dump station, coin laundry, ice, firewood, a playground, volleyball, horseshoe pits, boat docks, and launching facilities are available. A picnic area for special events is nearby. Propane gas and a store are located within one mile; there is a restaurant within three miles. Some facilities are wheelchair accessible. Leashed pets are permitted, but not on the swimming beach.

Reservations, fees: Reservations are accepted and are recommended during summer. Sites are $22 per night, $6 per night per additional car. Open year-round.

Directions: From I-5 in Olympia, take Exit 104, which merges onto U.S. 101. Drive northwest on U.S. 101 for 1.7 miles to Black Lake Boulevard. Turn left (south) on Black Lake Boulevard and drive 3.5 miles to the park on the left.

Contact: Columbus Park, 360/786-9460 or 866/848-9460, www.columbuspark.net.

2 AMERICAN HERITAGE CAMPGROUND

Scenic rating: 6

near Olympia

This spacious, wooded campground situated just 0.5 mile off the highway is close to many activities, including an 18-hole golf course, hiking trails, marked bike trails, and tennis courts. The park features novelty cycle rentals, free wagon rides, and free nightly movies during the summer season. It's pretty and exceptionally clean, making for a pleasant layover on your way up or down I-5. The park has a 5,000-square-foot pavilion for special events or groups.

Campsites, facilities: There are 95 sites with full or partial hookups (30 amps) for tents or RVs of any length, 23 tent sites, and one cabin. Picnic tables and fire rings are provided. Restrooms with flush toilets and showers, drinking water, propane gas, dump station, recreation hall, group pavilion, seasonal recreation programs, a convenience store, coin laundry, ice, a playground, a seasonal heated swimming pool, and firewood are available. Leashed pets are permitted.

Reservations, fees: Reservations are accepted. Sites are $22–30 per night, plus $4 per person per night for more than two people. Some credit cards are accepted. Open year-round, with limited winter facilities.

Directions: From Olympia, drive five miles south on I-5 to Exit 99. Take that exit and drive 0.25 mile east to Kimmie Street. Turn right (south) on Kimmie Street and drive 0.25 mile to the end of the road to the campground on the left.

Contact: American Heritage Campground, 360/943-8778, www.americanheritagecampground.com.

CAMPING

🔳 MILLERSYLVANIA STATE PARK

🚶 🚴 ♨ 🎣 🚤 🏕 ♿ 🚐 ⛰

Scenic rating: 8

on Deep Lake

Millersylvania State Park is set on the shore of Deep Lake and features 3,300 feet of waterfront. The park has 8.6 miles of hiking trails amid an abundance of old-growth cedar and fir trees, of which 7.6 miles are open to bikes. Boating at Deep Lake is restricted to hand-launched boats, with a 5-mph speed limit. A fishing dock is available at the boat-launch area. Another highlight: a one-mile fitness trail. Look for the remains of a former railroad and skid trails dating from the 1800s, still present in the park.

Campsites, facilities: There are 120 developed tent sites, 48 sites with partial hookups (30 and 50 amps) for RVs up to 45 feet long, and four hike-in/bike-in sites. Picnic tables and fire grills are provided. Restrooms with flush toilets and coin showers, drinking water, a dump station, firewood boat docks and launching facilities, exercise trail, and amphitheater are available. A picnic area, boat rentals, summer interpretive activities, and horseshoe pits are nearby. A store, restaurant, and ice are located within one mile. Some facilities are wheelchair accessible. Leashed pets are permitted.

Reservations, fees: Reservations are accepted at 888/CAMP-OUT (888/226-7688) or www.parks.wa.gov/reservations ($6.50–8.50 reservation fee). Sites are $21–27 per night, $10 per night for hike-in/bike-in sites, $10 per extra vehicle per night. Some credit cards are accepted. Open year-round, with limited facilities mid-November–March.

Directions: From Olympia, drive south on I-5 for 10 miles to Exit 95 and Highway 121. Turn east on Maytown Road (Highway 121) and drive 2.7 miles to Tilley Road. Turn left (north) and drive 1.3 miles to the park.

Contact: Millersylvania State Park, 360/753-1519, fax 360/664-2180; state park information, 360/902-8844, www.parks. wa.gov.

🔳 OFFUT LAKE RESORT

♨ 🎣 🚤 🏕 🐕 ♿ 🚐 ⛰

Scenic rating: 8

on Offut Lake

BEST (

This wooded campground is set on Offut Lake, just enough off the beaten track to provide a bit of seclusion. Fishing, swimming, and boating are favorite activities here. Anglers will find everything they need, including tackle and boat rentals, at the resort. Boating is restricted to a 5-mph speed limit, and no gas motors are permitted on the lake. Several fishing derbies are held here every year.

Campsites, facilities: There are 31 sites with full hookups (30 and 50 amps) for RVs up to 40 feet long, 25 tent sites, and seven cabins. Picnic tables, fire rings, and cable TV are provided. Restrooms with flush toilets and coin showers, drinking water, modem access, a picnic shelter, dump station, firewood, a convenience store, bait and tackle, propane gas, coin laundry, ice, a playground, basketball, and horseshoe pits are available. Boat rentals and docks are available; no gas motors are permitted. Some facilities are wheelchair accessible. Leashed pets are permitted.

Reservations, fees: Reservations are accepted. Sites are $20–30 per night, plus $5 per person per night for more than two adults and two children, $2 per extra vehicle per night, and $2 per pet per night. Some credit cards are accepted. Open year-round.

Directions: From Olympia, drive south on I-5 for seven miles to Exit 99. Take that exit and turn east on 93rd Avenue; drive four miles to Old Highway 99. Turn right (south) and drive four miles to Offut Lake Road. Turn left (east) and drive 1.5 miles to the resort.

Contact: Offut Lake Resort, 360/264-2438, www.offutlakeresort.com.

5 RAINBOW RV RESORT

Scenic rating: 8

on Tanwax Lake

This wooded park along the shore of Tanwax Lake has spacious sites with views of mountains, forest, and lake. Highlights include good fishing for trout, perch, crappie, bass, bluegill, catfish, and bullhead. Powerboating and waterskiing are popular on hot summer weekends.

Campsites, facilities: There are about 50 sites with full hookups for RVs up to 40 feet long and eight tent sites. Picnic tables are provided at most sites, and portable fire pits are available. Restrooms with flush toilets and coin showers, drinking water, propane gas, recreation hall, convenience store, coin laundry, a café, ice, cable TV, boat docks and launch, boat rentals, and boat moorage are available. Leashed pets are permitted.

Reservations, fees: Reservations are accepted. RV sites are $25–28 per night, and tent sites are $15 per night. Some credit cards are accepted. Open year-round.

Directions: From Tacoma, drive south on I-5 to Exit 127 and Highway 512. Turn east on Highway 512 and drive to Highway 161. Turn right (south) on Highway 161 and drive to Tanwax Drive. Turn left (east) on Tanwax Drive and continue 200 yards to the resort.

Contact: Rainbow RV Resort, 360/879-5115, fax 360/879-5116, www.rainbowrvresort.com.

6 HENLEY'S SILVER LAKE RESORT

Scenic rating: 8

on Silver Lake

BEST (

Silver Lake is a 150-acre, spring-fed lake that can provide good trout fishing. This full-facility resort is set up as a family vacation destination. A rarity, this private campground caters both to tent campers and RVers. Silver Lake is beautiful and stocked with trout. Highlights include a 250-foot fishing dock and rental rowboats.

Campsites, facilities: There are 36 sites with full hookups, including two pull-through, for RVs, a very large area for dispersed tent camping, and six cabins. Picnic tables are provided, and fire pits are available at most sites. Restrooms with flush toilets, drinking water, snacks, bait and tackle, boat rentals, a boat ramp, and a dock are available. No showers are available. A grocery store, gasoline, and supplies are available within 3.5 miles. Leashed pets are permitted except in the cabins.

Reservations, fees: Reservations are accepted. RV sites are $20–27 per night, and tent sites are $18 per night. Open the first day of fishing season in late April through October, weather permitting.

Directions: From Tacoma, drive south on I-5 for five miles to Exit 127 and Highway 512. Turn east on Highway 512 and drive two miles to Highway 7. Turn right (south) on Highway 7 and drive 19 miles (two miles straight beyond the blinking light) to Silver Lake Road on the right (well marked). Turn right and drive 0.25 mile to the resort entrance on the left.

Contact: Henley's Silver Lake Resort, 360/832-3580, www.henleyssilverlakeresort.zoomshare.com.

7 ALDER LAKE PARK

Scenic rating: 6

on Alder Lake

The 161-acre recreation area at Alder Lake features four camping areas and a group camp; one of the camps is located four miles east of the main park entrance. Alder Lake is a 3,065-acre lake (7.5 miles long) often with

CAMPING

good fishing for kokanee salmon, rainbow trout, and cutthroat trout. Rocky Point features a sunny beach and is set near the mouth of feeder streams, often the best fishing spots on the lake. At the west end of the lake, anglers can catch catfish, perch, and crappie. The campsites have lots of trees and shrubbery. On clear, warm summer weekends, these camps can get crowded. The camps are always booked full for summer holiday weekends as soon as reservations are available in January. Another potential downer, the water level fluctuates here. Powerboating, waterskiing, and personal watercraft are allowed at this lake. Mount Rainier Scenic Railroad leaves from Elbe regularly and makes its way through the forests to Mineral Lake. It features open deck cars, live music, and restored passenger cars.

Campsites, facilities: There are four camping areas with approximately 111 sites with full or partial hookups (30 and 50 amps) for tents or RVs up to 40 feet, 62 tent sites, and one group area of 20 sites for tents or RVs (full hookups). Picnic tables and fire rings are provided. Restrooms with flush toilets and coin showers, drinking water, vault toilets, and a dump station are available. Boat docks and launching facilities are available nearby. A swimming beach, picnic area, playground, and fishing dock are also available nearby. Some facilities are wheelchair accessible. Leashed pets are permitted.

Reservations, fees: Reservations are accepted at 888/CAMP-OUT (888/226-7688) or www.mytpu.org/tacomapower ($6.50–8.50 reservation fee). For group reservations, phone 360/569-2778 ($15 group reservation fee). Sites are $19–26 per night, $10 per extra vehicle per night. The group camp is $26 per site per night, with a five-site minimum. Some credit cards are accepted. Open year-round, excluding December 20–January 1.

Directions: From Chehalis, drive south on I-5 for six miles to U.S. 12. Turn east and drive 31 miles to Morton and Highway 7. Turn north on Highway 7 and drive 17 miles to Elbe.

Bear left on Highway 7 and drive to the park entrance road on the left (on the east shore of Alder Lake). Turn left and drive 0.2 mile to the park entrance gate.

Contact: Alder Lake Park, Tacoma Power, 360/569-2778, fax 253/502-8631, www.mytpu.org/tacomapower.

8 SAHARA CREEK HORSE CAMP

🏃 ❄ 🐴 🚙 ⛺

Scenic rating: 6

near Elbe

While this camp is called a "horse camp," it is actually a multiple-use camp open to campers without horses. This pretty camp is set near the foot of Mount Rainier and features multiple trailheads and a camp host on-site. Note that no motorized vehicles or mountain bikes are allowed on trails. In winter, miles of groomed cross-country ski trails are available in the area.

Campsites, facilities: There are 18 sites for tents or RVs up to 25 feet long. Picnic tables and fire pits are provided. Drinking water, stock water, a covered pavilion, vault toilets, high lines, and hitching posts are available. Garbage must be packed out. Leashed pets are permitted.

Reservations, fees: Reservations are not accepted. There is no fee for camping. Open year-round.

Directions: From Chehalis, drive south on I-5 for six miles to U.S. 12. Turn east and drive 31 miles to Morton and Highway 7. Turn north on Highway 7 and drive 17 miles to Elbe and Highway 706. Turn right (east) and drive five miles to the campground on the left.

Contact: Department of Natural Resources, South Puget Sound Region, 360/825-1631, fax 360/825-1672, www.dnr.wa.gov.

9 ELBE HILLS
🚴 ❄️ 🐴 🚐 ⛰️

Scenic rating: 6

near Elbe

Elbe Hills is not an official, designated campground, but rather a trailhead with room for three campsites for four-wheelers, equestrians, or hikers. The Department of Natural Resources manages this wooded campground and provides eight miles of trails for short-wheelbase four-wheel-drive vehicles. The area features a technical obstacle course. In some places, you must have a winch to make it through the course. In winter, groomed cross-country ski trails are available in the area. Note: The area is always gated, and arrangements for access must be made in advance.

Campsites, facilities: There are three primitive sites for tents or RVs up to 25 feet long. Picnic tables and fire grills are provided. Vault toilets and a group shelter are available. There is no drinking water, and garbage must be packed out. Leashed pets are permitted.

Reservations, fees: Reservations are not accepted. There is no fee for camping. Open year-round, weather permitting.

Directions: From Chehalis, drive south on I-5 for six miles to U.S. 12. Turn east and drive 31 miles to Morton and Highway 7. Turn north on Highway 7 and drive 17 miles to Elbe and Highway 706. Turn right (east) and drive six miles to Stoner Road (a Department of Natural Resources access road). Turn left and drive 2.5 miles to The 9 Road. Bear right on The 9 Road and drive one mile; look for a spur road on the left. Turn left and drive about 100 yards to the four-wheel-drive trailhead.

Contact: Department of Natural Resources, South Puget Sound Region, 360/825-1631, fax 360/825-1672, www.dnr.wa.gov.

10 PEPPERTREE WEST MOTOR INN & RV PARK
👫 🚐 🐴 🚐 ⛰️

Scenic rating: 5

in Centralia

If you're driving I-5 and looking for a stopover, this spot is a good choice for tent campers and RVers. Surrounded by Chehalis Valley farmland, it's near an 18-hole golf course, hiking trails, and tennis courts.

Campsites, facilities: There are 42 sites with full or partial hookups (30 amps) for RVs of any length, a grassy area for tents, and 26 motel rooms. Most sites are pull-through. Restrooms with flush toilets and coin showers, drinking water, cable TV, a dump station, coin laundry, and ice are available. Boat-launching facilities are nearby. A store, propane, and a café are also nearby. Leashed pets are permitted.

Reservations, fees: Reservations are accepted. RV sites are $20 per night, and tent sites are $6 per night. Some credit cards are accepted. Open year-round.

Directions: From Centralia on I-5, take Exit 81 to Melon Street. Turn west and then take the first right (Alder Street) to the park (located in the southeast corner of Centralia).

Contact: Peppertree West Motor Inn & RV Park, 360/736-1124, fax 360/807-9779.

11 STAN HEDWALL PARK
👫 🚲 🐴 🎣 🚐 ⛰️

Scenic rating: 5

on the Newaukum River

This park is set along the Newaukum River, and its proximity to I-5 makes it a good layover spot for vacation travelers. Recreational opportunities include fishing, hiking, and golf; an 18-hole course and hiking trails are nearby.

Campsites, facilities: There are 29 sites with partial hookups (30 and 50 amps) for tents or RVs of any length. Picnic tables are provided, and some sites have fire pits. Restrooms with flush toilets and coin showers, drinking water, a dump station, satellite TV, and a playground are available. Propane gas, a store, café, and coin laundry are located within one mile. Leashed pets are permitted.

Reservations, fees: Reservations are accepted. Sites are $15 per night. Open April–November, weather permitting.

Directions: From Chehalis on I-5, take Exit 76 to Rice Road. Turn south and drive 0.13 mile to the park.

Contact: Stan Hedwall Park, City of Chehalis, 360/748-0271, fax 360/748-6993, www.ci.chehalis.wa.us.

12 LEWIS AND CLARK STATE PARK

Scenic rating: 8

near Chehalis

The highlight of this state park is an immense old-growth forest that contains some good hiking trails and a 0.5-mile nature trail. This famous grove lost half of its old-growth trees along the highway when they were blown down in the legendary 1962 Columbus Day storm. This was a cataclysmic event for this one of the last major stands of old-growth forest in the state. The park covers 621 acres and features primarily Douglas fir and red cedar, wetlands, and dense vegetation. There are eight miles of trails, including five miles of horse trails. June is Youth Fishing Month, when youngsters age 14 and younger can fish the creek. Jackson House tours, in which visitors can see a pioneer home built in 1845 north of the Columbia River, are available year-round by appointment.

Campsites, facilities: There are 25 sites for tents or self-contained RVs (no hookups), eight sites with full hookups (30 amps) for RVs up to 35 feet long, five equestrian sites, and two group camps for up to 50 people each. A bunkhouse is also available. Picnic tables and fire

grills are provided. Restrooms with flush toilets and coin showers, drinking water, a small store, firewood, a picnic area, an amphitheater, day-use area that can be reserved, playground, horseshoe pits, volleyball, and badminton, and interpretive activities are available. Leashed pets are permitted.

Reservations, fees: Reservations are not accepted for family sites but are required for the bunkhouse at 360/902-8600 or 800/360-4240. Sites are $21 per night, equestrian sites are $14 per night, $10 per extra vehicle per night. The bunkhouse is $13.95 per person with a 15-person minimum. Group sites are $2.15 per person per night with a 20-person minimum. Open April–September.

Directions: From Chehalis, drive south on I-5 six miles to Exit 68 and U.S. 12. Turn east on U.S. 12 for three miles to Jackson Highway. Turn right and drive three miles to the park entrance on the right.

Contact: Lewis and Clark State Park, 360/864-2643, fax 360/864-2515; state park information, 360/902-8844, www.parks.wa.gov.

13 IKE KINSWA STATE PARK

Scenic rating: 8

on Mayfield Lake

This state park is set alongside the north shore of Mayfield Lake. The park features 8.5 miles of shore, forested campsites, 2.5 miles of hiking trails, and two miles of bike trails. Mayfield Lake is a treasure trove of recreational possibilities. Fishing is a year-round affair here, with trout and tiger muskie often good. Boating, waterskiing, swimming, and driftwood collecting are all popular. The park is named after a prominent member of the Cowlitz tribe. Two fish hatcheries are located nearby. A spectacular view of Mount St. Helens can be found at a vista point 11 miles east. This popular campground often fills on summer weekends. Be sure to reserve well in advance.

Campsites, facilities: There are 31 developed tent sites, 72 sites with full or partial hookups (30 amps) for RVs up to 36 feet long, two primitive tent sites, and five cabins. Picnic tables and fire grills are provided. Restrooms with flush toilets and coin showers, drinking water, a dump station, store, playground, picnic area, horseshoe pits, and firewood are available. Boat docks and launching facilities are nearby. Some facilities are wheelchair accessible. Leashed pets are permitted.

Reservations, fees: Reservations are accepted at 888/CAMP-OUT (888/226-7688) or www. parks.wa.gov/reservations ($6.50–8.50 reservation fee). Sites are $21 per night for tent sites, $27–28 per night for RV sites, $14 per night for primitive sites, $10 per extra vehicle per night, and cabins are $55 per night. Some credit cards are accepted. Open year-round.

Directions: From Chehalis, drive south on I-5 six miles to Exit 68 and U.S. 12. Turn east on U.S. 12 and drive 14 miles to Silver Creek Road (State Route 122). Turn left (north) and drive 1.9 miles to a Y intersection. Bear right on State Route 122/Harmony Road and drive 1.6 miles to the park entrance.

Contact: Ike Kinswa State Park, 360/983-3402, fax 360/983-3332; state park information, 360/902-8844, www.parks.wa.gov.

14 HARMONY LAKESIDE RV PARK

Scenic rating: 6

on Mayfield Lake

This park fills up on weekends in July, August, and September. It is set on Mayfield Lake, a 10-mile-long lake with numerous recreational activities, including fishing, boating, riding personal watercraft, and waterskiing. Some sites feature lake views. Nearby Ike Kinswa State Park is a side-trip option.

Campsites, facilities: There are 80 sites with full hookups (30 and 50 amps) for RVs of any length; some sites are pull-through. Picnic tables and fire grills are provided. Restrooms with drinking water and coin showers, drinking water, a dump station, ice, firewood, a pay phone, boat docks, and launching facilities are available. Group facilities, including a banquet and meeting room, are also available. Leashed pets are permitted.

Reservations, fees: Reservations are recommended. Sites are $32–52.50 per night, and $2.50 per pet per night. Winter and monthly rates are available. Some credit cards are accepted. Open year-round.

Directions: From Chehalis, drive south on I-5 for six miles to Exit 68 and U.S. 12. Turn east on U.S. 12 and drive 21 miles to Mossyrock (Highway 122). Turn left (north) and drive 3.5 miles to the park on the left.

Contact: Harmony Lakeside RV Park, 360/983-3804, fax 360/983-8345, www. mayfieldlake.com.

15 MAYFIELD LAKE PARK

Scenic rating: 7

on Mayfield Lake

Mayfield Lake is the centerpiece of this 50-acre park. Insider's tip: Campsites 42–54 are set along the lake's shoreline. The camp has a relaxing atmosphere and comfortable, wooded sites. Fishing is primarily for trout, bass, and silver salmon. Other recreational activities include waterskiing, swimming, and boating. For a great side trip, tour nearby Mount St. Helens.

Campsites, facilities: There are 55 sites with partial hookups for tents or RVs of any length and a group camp (12 sites) for tents or RVs up to 45 feet long. Picnic tables and fire rings are provided. Restrooms with flush toilets and coin showers, drinking water, a pay phone, dump station, and a day-use area with a picnic shelter that can be reserved, playground, horseshoe pits, and a volleyball court are

CAMPING

available. Some facilities are wheelchair accessible. Leashed pets are permitted.

Reservations, fees: Reservations are accepted at 888/CAMP-OUT (888/226-7688) or www. mytpu.org/tacomapower ($6.50–8.50 reservation fee, $15 group reservation fee). Sites are $25–27 per night, $10 per extra vehicle per night. The group camp is $150 per night. Open mid-April–mid-October; the group camp is open Memorial Day weekend–mid-October.

Directions: From Longview, drive north on I-5 to Exit 68 and U.S. 12. Turn east on U.S. 12 and drive approximately 17 miles to Beach Road. Turn left and drive 0.25 mile to the park entrance.

Contact: Mayfield Lake Park, 360/985-2364, fax 360/985-7825, www.mytpu.org/tacomapower.

16 MOSSYROCK PARK

Scenic rating: 8

on Riffe Lake

BEST (

This park is located along the southwest shore of Riffe Lake. It is an extremely popular campground. For anglers, it provides the best of both worlds: a boat launch on Riffe Lake, which offers coho salmon, rainbow trout, and bass, and nearby Swofford Pond, a 240-acre pond stocked with rainbow trout, brown trout, bass, catfish, and bluegill. Swofford Pond is located south of Mossyrock on Swofford Road; no gas motors are permitted. This campground provides access to a 0.5-mile loop nature trail. Bald eagles and osprey nest on the north side of the lake in the 14,000-acre Cowlitz Wildlife Area.

Campsites, facilities: There are 152 sites with partial hookups for tents or RVs of any length, 12 walk-in sites, one group camp (60 sites) with partial hookups for tents or RVs of any length, and a primitive group camp (10 sites) for tents or RVs of any length. Picnic tables and fire rings are provided. Restrooms with flush toilets and coin showers, drinking

water, a dump station, seasonal convenience store, seasonal snack bar, coin laundry, fish-cleaning stations, boat launch, playground, picnic area that can be reserved, a swimming area, horseshoe pit, volleyball net, BMX track, camp host, and interpretive displays are available. Some facilities are wheelchair accessible. Leashed pets are permitted.

Reservations, fees: Reservations are accepted at 888/CAMP-OUT (888/226-7688) or www. mytpu.org/tacomapower ($6.50–8.50 reservation fee, $15 group reservation fee). Sites are $19–25 per night, $10 per extra vehicle per night. The primitive group camp is $150 per night, and the other group camp is $23 per site per night with a minimum of five sites. Some credit cards are accepted in summer. Open year-round, excluding December 20–January 1.

Directions: From Chehalis, drive south on I-5 six miles to Exit 68 and Highway 12 East. Take Highway 12 East and drive 21 miles to Williams Street (flashing yellow light). Turn right and drive several blocks in the town of Mossyrock to a T intersection with State Street. Turn left and drive 3.5 miles (becomes Mossyrock Road East, then Ajlune Road) to the park. Ajlune Road leads right into the park.

Contact: Mossyrock Park, Tacoma Power, 360/983-3900, fax 360/983-3906, www. mytpu.org/tacomapower.

17 TAIDNAPAM PARK

Scenic rating: 8

on Riffe Lake

This 50-acre park is located at the east end of Riffe Lake. Nestled in a cover of Douglas fir and maple, it is surrounded by thousands of acres of undeveloped greenbelt. Fishing is permitted year-round at the lake, with coho salmon, rainbow trout, and bass available. This camp was named after the Upper Cowlitz Indians, also known as Taidnapam.

Campsites, facilities: There are 52 sites with full

or partial hookups for tents or RVs of any length, 16 walk-in sites, and two group camps (one with 22 sites and one with 12 primitive sites) with full or partial hookups for tents or RVs or any length. Picnic tables and fire rings are provided. Restrooms with flush toilets and coin showers, drinking water, dump station, a fishing bridge, fish-cleaning stations, boat launch, picnic shelter, playground, swimming beach, horseshoe pit, volleyball net, and interpretive displays are available. Some facilities are wheelchair accessible. Leashed pets are permitted.

Reservations, fees: Reservations for individual sites are accepted at 888/CAMP-OUT (888/226-7688) or www.mytpu.org/tacomapower ($6.50–8.50 reservation fee, $15 fee for group reservation). Group reservations are accepted at 360/497-7707 ($15 group reservation fee). Sites are $25–26 per night, $10 per extra vehicle per night, and walk-in sites are $14 per night. The developed group camp is $25–26 per site per night with a minimum of 10 sites; the primitive group camp is $180 per night for all 12 sites. Some credit cards are accepted in summer season. Open year-round, excluding December 20–January 1.

Directions: From Chehalis, drive south on I-5 to Exit 68 and Highway 12 East. Take Highway 12 East and drive 37 miles (five miles past Morton) to Kosmos Road. Turn right and drive 200 yards to No. 100 Champion Haul Road. Turn left and drive four miles to the park entrance on the right.

Contact: Taidnapam Park, Tacoma Power, 360/497-7707, fax 360/497-7708, www. mytpu.org/tacomapower.

18 RIVER OAKS RV PARK & CAMPGROUND

Scenic rating: 8

on the Cowlitz River

This camp is set right on the Cowlitz River, with opportunities for boating and fishing

for sturgeon, steelhead, and salmon in season. Swimming is not recommended because of the cold water. The park provides nearby access to Mount St. Helens. Note that some sites are filled with monthly renters.

Campsites, facilities: There are 30 sites with full hookups (30 and 50 amps) for RVs of any length; some sites are pull-through. Picnic tables and fire rings are provided. Restrooms with flush toilets and showers, drinking water, firewood, and horseshoe pits are available. Propane gas, bait and tackle, a store, and a café are located within 0.3 mile. Boat-launching facilities, mooring buoys, and a fishing shelter are nearby. Leashed pets are permitted.

Reservations, fees: Reservations are accepted. Sites are $15–25 per night, $2.50 per person per night for more than two people. Weekly and monthly rates available. Open year-round.

Directions: From Castle Rock on I-5, take Exit 59 for Highway 506. Turn west on Highway 506 and drive 0.3 mile to the park on the left.

Contact: River Oaks RV Park & Campground, 360/864-2895, www.riveroaksrvpark.com.

19 PARADISE COVE RESORT & RV PARK

Scenic rating: 7

near the Toutle River

This wooded park is situated about 400 yards from the Toutle River and 0.5 mile from the Cowlitz River. Take your pick: Seaquest State Park and Silver Lake to the east provide two excellent, activity-filled side-trip options. This is a major stopover for visits to Mount St. Helens.

Campsites, facilities: There are 48 sites for tents or RVs of any length (20, 30, and 50 amp full hookups) and a large dispersed tent camping area. Some sites are pull-through. Picnic tables are provided. Restrooms, drinking water, flush toilets, showers, coin laundry, a general store with video rentals, and ice are available. Boat-launching facilities are nearby. Leashed pets are permitted.

Reservations, fees: Reservations are accepted. Sites are $12–30 per night. Some credit cards are accepted. Open year-round.

Directions: From Longview, drive 10 miles north on I-5 to Castle Rock and Exit 52. Take Exit 52 and turn right on the frontage road and drive a short distance to Burma Road. Turn left and drive a short distance to the resort, just off the freeway (within view of the freeway).

Contact: Paradise Cove Resort & RV Park, 360/274-6785, fax 360/274-4031.

20 MOUNT ST. HELENS RV PARK

Scenic rating: 6

near Silver Lake

This RV park is located just outside Castle Rock, only three miles from the Mount St. Helens Visitor Center. It is close to the highway. Fishing and boating are available nearby on Silver Lake. Note that some sites are filled with monthly renters.

Campsites, facilities: There are 88 sites with full or partial hookups (20 and 30 amps) for tents or RVs up to 45 feet long. Picnic tables are provided. Restrooms with flush toilets and coin showers, drinking water, cable TV, modem access, coin laundry, horseshoe pits, a meeting room, and dump station are available. A convenience store and gasoline are nearby. Some facilities are wheelchair accessible. Leashed pets are permitted.

Reservations, fees: Reservations are recommended in the summer. RV sites are $20–30 per night, tent sites are $20 per night, $2 per person per night for more than two people. Some credit cards are accepted. Open year-round.

Directions: From Longview, drive 10 miles

north on I-5 to Castle Rock and Exit 49 and Highway 504. Take Exit 49 and drive east on Highway 504 for two miles to Tower Road. Turn left (well signed) and drive a short distance to a Y intersection and Schaffran Road. Bear right and drive approximately 300 yards to the park on the right

Contact: Mount St. Helens RV Park, 360/274-8522, fax 360/274-4529, www.mtsthelensrv-park.com.

21 SEAQUEST STATE PARK

Scenic rating: 6

near Silver Lake

This camp fills nightly because it is set along the paved road to the awesome Johnston Ridge Observatory, the premier lookout of Mount St. Helens. This state park is adjacent to Silver Lake, one of western Washington's finest fishing lakes for bass and trout. But that's not all: The Mount St. Helens Visitor Center is located across the road from the park entrance. This heavily forested, 475-acre park features more than one mile of lake shoreline and 5.5 miles of trails for hiking and biking. The park is popular for day use as well as camping. No hunting or fishing is allowed.

The irony of the place is that some out-of-towners on vacation think that this park is located on the ocean because of its name, Seaquest. The park has nothing to do with the ocean, of course; it is named after Alfred L. Seaquest, who donated the property to the state for parkland. One interesting fact: He stipulated in his will that if liquor were ever sold on the property that the land would be transferred to Willamette University.

Campsites, facilities: There are 93 sites, including 33 with partial hookups (30 amps) for tents or RVs, four hike-in/bike-in sites, and five yurts. Picnic tables and fire grills are provided. Restrooms with flush toilets and coin showers, drinking water, a picnic area, playground, horseshoe pits, dump station, firewood, and a volleyball court are available. A store is within three miles. Some facilities are wheelchair accessible. Leashed pets are permitted.

Reservations, fees: Reservations are accepted at 888/CAMP-OUT (888/226-7688) or www.parks.wa.gov/reservations ($6.50–8.50 reservation fee). Sites are $21–28 per night, $12 per night for hike-in/bike-in sites, $10 per extra vehicle per night, and yurts are $55 per night. Some credit cards are accepted. Open year-round.

Directions: From Longview, drive 10 miles north on I-5 to Castle Rock and Exit 49 and Highway 504. Take Exit 49 and drive east on Highway 504 for 5.5 miles to the park.

Contact: Seaquest State Park, 360/274-8633, fax 360/274-0962; state park information, 360/902-8844, www.parks.wa.gov.

22 SILVER LAKE MOTEL AND RESORT

🏊 🚣 🚤 🏠 🎣 🚐 ⛺

Scenic rating: 8

on Silver Lake

BEST (

This park is set near the shore of Silver Lake and features a view of Mount St. Helens. One of Washington's better lakes for largemouth bass and trout, Silver Lake also has perch, crappie, and bluegill. Powerboating, personal watercraft riding, and waterskiing are popular. This spot is considered a great anglers' camp. The sites are set along a horseshoe-shaped driveway on grassy sites. Access is quick to Mount St. Helens, nearby to the east.

Campsites, facilities: There are 19 sites with full or partial hookups (30 amps) for RVs of any length, 11 tent sites, five cabins, and six motel rooms. Picnic tables are provided. Restrooms with flush toilets and coin showers, drinking water, a convenience store, bait and tackle, fish-cleaning station, ice, boat docks, boat rentals, launching facilities, and

a playground are available. A dump station is within one mile, and a café is within four miles. Leashed pets are permitted in the campground.

Reservations, fees: Reservations are accepted. RV sites are $23–27 per night, tent sites are $13–17 per night, $5 per extra vehicle per night. Cabins are $70–125. Some credit cards are accepted. Open mid-March–mid-November.

Directions: From Longview, drive 10 miles north on I-5 to Castle Rock and Exit 49 and Highway 504. Take Exit 49 and drive east on Highway 504 for six miles to the resort on the right.

Contact: Silver Lake Motel and Resort, 360/274-6141, fax 360/274-2183, www.silverlake-resort.com.

23 KALAMA HORSE CAMP

🚶 🏠 ♿ 🚐 ⛺

Scenic rating: 8

near Mount St. Helens

The most popular horse camp in the area, Kalama Horse Camp receives the enthusiastic volunteer support of local equestrians. The camp fills on weekends partly because of a network of 53 miles of horse trails accessible from camp. It is located very near Mount St. Helens.

Campsites, facilities: There are 17 sites for tents or RVs up to 25 feet long and two double sites. Picnic tables and fire grills are provided. Vault toilets are available. No drinking water is provided. Garbage must be packed out. Horse facilities include 10- by 10-foot corrals, a staging and mounting assist area, stock water, a stock-loading ramp, hitching rails, and manure disposal bins. A 24- by 36-foot log cabin shelter with a picnic area with horseshoe pits is also available. Boat-launching facilities are located on Lake Merrill. Some facilities are wheelchair accessible. Leashed pets are permitted.

CAMPING

Reservations, fees: Reservations are not accepted. Sites are $12 per night, $16 per night for double sites, $5 per night per extra vehicle. Open April–mid-December, weather permitting.

Directions: From Woodland on I-5, take Exit 21 for Highway 503. Drive east on Highway 503 for 23 miles to the Highway 503 spur. Continue northeast on the Highway 503 spur to Forest Road 81 (at Yale Lake, one mile south of Cougar). Turn left on Forest Road 81 and drive about eight miles to the camp on the right.

Contact: Gifford Pinchot National Forest, Mount St. Helens National Volcanic Monument, 360/449-7800, fax 360/449-7801, www.fs.fed.us/gpnf/recreation.

24 MERRILL LAKE

Scenic rating: 7

near Mount St. Helens

Campers seeking a quiet setting will enjoy this site, which has a reputation as the top fly-fishing area of Western Washington. Due to its popularity, there is a three-day stay limit. The campground is nestled in old-growth Douglas fir on the shore of Lake Merrill, very near Mount St. Helens. It's free and provides an alternative to the more developed parks in the area, especially those along the main access roads to viewing areas of the volcano. The lake provides fishing for brown trout and cutthroat trout but is restricted to fly-fishing only, with no gas motors permitted. These restrictions make it ideal for fly fishers with prams or float tubes.

Campsites, facilities: There are eight tent sites. Picnic tables, fire grills, and tent pads are provided. Vault toilets are available. There is no drinking water, and garbage must be packed out. Boat-launching facilities are located on Lake Merrill. Some facilities are wheelchair accessible. Leashed pets are permitted.

Reservations, fees: Reservations are not accepted. There is no fee for camping. Open May–October, weather permitting.

Directions: From Woodland on I-5, take Exit 21 for Highway 503. Drive east on Highway 503 for 23 miles to the Highway 503 spur. Continue northeast on the Highway 503 spur to Forest Road 81 (at Yale Lake, one mile south of Cougar). Turn left on Forest Road 81 and drive 4.5 miles to the campground access road on the left.

Contact: Department of Natural Resources, Pacific Cascade Region, South, 360/577-2025 or 360/274-4196, www.dnr.wa.gov; Pacific Cascade Region information, 360/274-2055.

25 LONE FIR RESORT

Scenic rating: 4

near Yale Lake

This private campground is located near Yale Lake (the smallest of four lakes in the area) and, with grassy sites and plenty of shade trees, is designed primarily for RV use. Mount St. Helens provides a side-trip option. The trailhead for the summit climb is located nearby at Climber's Bivouac on the south flank of the volcano; a primitive campground with dispersed sites for hikers only is available there. Note: This trailhead is the only one available for the summit climb. Though infrequent, the trail to the summit can be closed because of volcanic activity at the plug dome.

Campsites, facilities: There are 38 sites with full hookups (30 and 50 amps) for RVs of any length, a grassy area for tents, six cabins, and 12 motel rooms. Some sites are pull-through. Picnic tables are provided, and fire pits are at some sites. Restrooms with flush toilets and coin showers, satellite TV, drinking water, coin laundry, clubhouse, playground, Wi-Fi, community fire pit, horseshoe pits, ice, a snack bar, snowshoe rentals, restaurant, and a seasonal heated swimming pool are available. Propane gas, a store, boat docks, and launching facilities are nearby. Leashed pets are permitted.

Reservations, fees: Reservations are accepted. RV sites are $27 per night, and tent sites are $15 per night. Some credit cards are accepted. Open year-round.

Directions: In Woodland on I-5, take Exit 21 for Highway 503. Drive east on Highway 503 for 29 miles to Cougar and the resort turnoff (marked, in town, with the park visible from the road) on the left.

Contact: Lone Fir Resort, 360/238-5210, fax 360/238-5120, www.lonefirresort.com.

26 EVANS CREEK

Scenic rating: 7

on Evans Creek in Mount Baker-Snoqualmie National Forest

This primitive campground is located close to Evans Creek in an off-road-vehicle area near the northwestern corner of Mount Rainier National Park. If you're looking for a quiet, secluded spot, this isn't it. The two nearby roads that lead into the park are secondary or gravel roads and provide access to several other primitive campgrounds and backcountry trails in the park. A national forest map details the back roads and hiking trails.

Campsites, facilities: There are 26 tent sites. Picnic tables and fire grills are provided. Drinking water and vault toilets are available. Downed wood can be gathered for campfires. Garbage must be packed out. Leashed pets are permitted.

Reservations, fees: Reservations are not accepted. There is no fee. A Northwest Forest Pass ($5 daily fee or $30 annual fee per parked vehicle) is required to park at the trailhead. Open year-round, weather permitting.

Directions: From Tacoma on I-5, turn east on Highway 167 and drive nine miles to Highway 410. Continue 11 miles east on Highway 410 to the town of Buckley and Highway 165.

Turn south on Highway 165 and drive 11 miles to Forest Road 7920. Turn left and drive 1.5 miles to the campground on the right.

Contact: Mount Baker–Snoqualmie National Forest, White River Ranger District, 360/825-6585, fax 360/825-0660, www.fs.fed.us.

27 MOWICH LAKE WALK-IN

Scenic rating: 8

near the Carbon River in Mount Rainier National Park

This walk-in camp features campsites set adjacent to and above Mowich Lake, with a lake view from some of the sites. A 200-yard walk is required to reach the campsites. Some backpackers use the camp as a launch point for trips into the Mount Rainier Wilderness. The Wonderland Trail can be accessed at this campground. Fishing is poor for trout at Mowich Lake because it is not stocked and lacks a habitat for natural spawning.

Campsites, facilities: There are 30 walk-in tent sites. Picnic tables are available at some sites. Pit toilets and garbage bins are available. No drinking water is provided. No campfires are permitted; use a backpacking stove. Leashed pets are permitted in camp, but not on trails.

Reservations, fees: Reservations are not accepted; there is a $15 per vehicle park entrance fee. Open June–October, weather permitting.

Directions: From Tacoma on I-5, turn east on Highway 167 and drive nine miles to Highway 410. Continue 11 miles east on Highway 410 to the town of Buckley and Highway 165. Turn right (south) on Highway 165 and drive to a fork with Carbon River Park Road. Bear right and stay on Highway 165 for eight miles to the campground at the end of the road. Only high-clearance vehicles are recommended on this access road.

Contact: Mount Rainier National Park,

CAMPING

360/569-2211, fax 360/569-2170, www.nps.gov/mora.

28 IPSUT CREEK

Scenic rating: 8

near the Carbon River in
Mount Rainier National Park

This former drive-to trailhead camp now requires a five-mile hike in and a Wilderness Permit from Mount Rainier National Park. Located at the end of Carbon River Road, the camp road was gated by the National Park Service because of flooding. Still popular, this is a launch point for hikers heading into the backcountry of Mount Rainier National Park, past lakes, glaciers, waterfalls, and many other wonders. From the campground, the seven-mile (round-trip) Carbon Glacier Trail follows the Carbon River through the forest to the snout of the glacier; watch for falling rocks. In addition, the Carbon River Rain Forest Nature Trail begins at the Carbon River entrance to the park. This 0.3-mile loop trail explores the only inland rainforest at Mount Rainier National Park. Note that fishing is prohibited on Ipsut Creek above the campground at the water supply intake. The elevation is 2,300 feet.

Campsites, facilities: There are 20 sites for tents and two group camps for up to 25 and 30 people respectively. Picnic tables are provided. Pit toilets are available. There is no drinking water.

Reservations, fees: Reservations are not accepted. There is no fee for camping, but there is a national park entrance fee of $15. Open year-round, weather permitting.

Directions: From Puyallup, drive east on Highway 167 to Highway 410. Turn east on Highway 410 and drive 11 miles to the town of Buckley and Highway 165. Turn right (south) on Highway 165 and drive to a fork with Carbon River Park Road. Park and hike five miles to the campground (the trail/former road is subject to flooding after heavy rains).

Contact: Mount Rainier National Park, 360/569-2211, fax 360/569-2170, www.nps.gov/mora.

29 WHITE RIVER

Scenic rating: 7

on the White River in
Mount Rainier National Park

This campground is set on the White River at 4,400 feet elevation. The Glacier Basin Trail, a seven-mile round-trip, starts at the campground and leads along the Emmons Moraine for a short distance before ascending above it. A view of the Emmons Glacier, the largest glacier in the continental United States, is possible by hiking the spur trail, the Emmons Moraine Trail. It is sometimes possible to spot mountain goats, as well as mountain climbers, on the surrounding mountain slopes. Note that another trail near camp leads a short distance (but vertically, for a rise of 2,200 feet) to the Sunrise Visitor Center. Local rangers recommend that trailers be left at the White River Campground and the 11-mile road trip to Sunrise be made by car. From there, you can take several trails that lead to backcountry lakes and glaciers. Also note that this campground is located in what is considered a geohazard zone, where there is risk of a mudflow, although it hasn't happened in recent years.

Campsites, facilities: There are 112 sites for tents or RVs up to 27 feet long. Picnic tables and fire grills are provided. Flush toilets and drinking water are available. A small amphitheater is nearby. Some facilities are wheelchair accessible. Leashed pets are permitted in camp, but not on trails or in the wilderness.

Reservations, fees: Reservations are not accepted. Sites are $12 per night, plus $15 per vehicle park entrance fee. Some credit cards are accepted. Open July–mid-September.

Directions: From Enumclaw, drive southeast on Highway 410 to the entrance of Mount

CAMPING

Rainier National Park and White River Road. Turn right and drive seven miles to the campground on the left.

Contact: Mount Rainier National Park, 360/569-2211, fax 360/569-2170, www.nps.gov/mora.

30 SILVER SPRINGS

Scenic rating: 9

in Mount Baker–Snoqualmie National Forest

Silver Springs campground along the White River on the northeastern border of Mount Rainier National Park offers a good alternative to the more crowded camps in the park. It's located in a beautiful section of old-growth forest, primarily with Douglas fir, cedar, and hemlock. Recreational options are limited to hiking. A U.S. Forest Service information center is located one mile away from the campground entrance on Highway 410.

Campsites, facilities: There are 56 sites for tents or RVs up to 40 feet long and one group site for up to 50 people. Picnic tables and fire grills are provided. Flush toilets, drinking water, and downed firewood for gathering are available. The group site has a picnic shelter. Some facilities are wheelchair accessible. Leashed pets are permitted.

Reservations, fees: Reservations are accepted for all sites and are required for the group site at 877/444-6777 or www.recreation.gov ($10 reservation fee). Sites are $18–32 per night, $9 per night extra vehicle fee. The group site is $50 per night. Open mid-May–late September, weather permitting.

Directions: From Enumclaw, drive east on Highway 410 for 31 miles (one mile south of the turnoff for Corral Pass) to the campground entrance on the right.

Contact: Mount Baker–Snoqualmie National Forest, White River Ranger District, 360/825-6585, fax 360/825-0660, www.fs.fed.us.

31 LODGEPOLE

Scenic rating: 6

on the American River in Wenatchee National Forest

This campground is set at an elevation of 3,500 feet along the American River, just eight miles east of the boundary of Mount Rainier National Park. Winter activities in the park include cross-country skiing, snowshoeing, and inner-tube sledding down slopes. Fishing access is available nearby.

Campsites, facilities: There are 33 sites for tents or RVs up to 20 feet long. Picnic tables and fire grills are provided. Drinking water, vault toilets, garbage service, and firewood are available. A camp host is on-site. Some facilities are wheelchair accessible. Leashed pets are permitted.

Reservations, fees: Reservations are accepted at 877/444-6777 or www.recreation.gov ($10 reservation fee). Sites are $17–19 per night, $5 per night for each additional vehicle. Open mid-May–mid-September, weather permitting.

Directions: From Yakima, drive northwest on U.S. 12 for 18 miles to Highway 410. Bear northwest on Highway 410 and drive 40.5 miles (eight miles east of the national park boundary) to the campground on the right.

Contact: Okanogan and Wenatchee National Forests, Naches Ranger District, 509/653-1401, fax 509/653-2638, www.fs.fed.us.

32 PLEASANT VALLEY

Scenic rating: 7

on the American River in Wenatchee National Forest

It's always strange how campgrounds get their names. Pleasant Valley? More like Camp Thatcher, as in Thatcher ants, which have infested the campground and can inflict painful bites on you and your pet. Even the Forest Service advises, "Camp at your own risk. No refunds." If still set on camping here, plan to stay off the ground or bring an RV. That said, the campground (elevation of 3,300 feet) does provide a good base camp for a hiking or fishing trip. A trail from the camp follows Kettle Creek up to the American Ridge and Kettle Lake in the William O. Douglas Wilderness. It joins another trail that follows the ridge and then drops down to Bumping Lake (a U.S. Forest Service map is essential). You can fish here for whitefish, steelhead, trout, and salmon in season; check regulations. In the winter, the area is popular with cross-country skiers.

Campsites, facilities: There are 16 sites for tents or RVs up to 32 feet long. Picnic tables and fire grills are provided. Drinking water, garbage service, vault toilets, and a picnic shelter are available. Downed firewood may be gathered. A camp host is on-site. Some facilities are wheelchair accessible. Leashed pets are permitted.

Reservations, fees: Reservations are accepted at 877/444-6777 or www.recreation.gov ($10 reservation fee). Sites are $17–38 per night, $5 per night for each additional vehicle. Open mid-May–mid-September, weather permitting.

Directions: From Yakima, drive northwest on U.S. 12 for 18 miles to Highway 410. Bear northwest on Highway 410 and drive 37 miles to the campground on the left.

Contact: Okanogan and Wenatchee National Forests, Naches Ranger District, 509/653-1401, fax 509/653-2638, www.fs.fed.us.

33 HELLS CROSSING

Scenic rating: 7

on the American River in
Wenatchee National Forest

Hells Crossing campground lies along the American River at an elevation of 3,250 feet.

A steep trail from the camp leads up to Goat Peak and follows the American Ridge in the William O. Douglas Wilderness. Other trails join the ridgeline trail and connect with lakes and streams. Fishing here is for trout, steelhead, salmon, and whitefish in season; check regulations.

Campsites, facilities: There are 18 sites, including three multi-family sites, for tents or RVs up to 20 feet long. Picnic tables and fire grills are provided. Drinking water (at the west end of camp) and vault toilets are available. Downed firewood may be gathered. Leashed pets are permitted.

Reservations, fees: Reservations are accepted at 877/444-6777 or www.recreation.gov ($10 reservation fee). Sites are $17–19 per night for single sites, $34 per night for double sites, and $5 per night for each additional vehicle. Open mid-May–mid-September, weather permitting.

Directions: From Yakima, drive northwest on U.S. 12 for 18 miles to Highway 410. Bear northwest on Highway 410 and drive 33.5 miles to the campground on the right.

Contact: Okanogan and Wenatchee National Forests, Naches Ranger District, 509/653-1401, fax 509/653-2638, www.fs.fed.us.

34 PINE NEEDLE GROUP CAMP

Scenic rating: 7

on the American River in
Wenatchee National Forest

This reservations-only group campground sits on the edge of the William O. Douglas Wilderness along the American River at an elevation of 3,000 feet. There are trails leading south into the backcountry at nearby camps; consult a U.S. Forest Service map. The camp is easy to reach, rustic, and beautiful. Fishing is available for whitefish, trout, steelhead, and salmon in season. For a side trip, visit Bumping

Lake to the south, where recreation options include boating, fishing, and swimming.

Campsites, facilities: There is one group site for tents or RVs up to 30 feet long that can accommodate up to 60 people. Picnic tables and fire grills are provided. Vault toilets are available. There is no drinking water here, but it is available 2.5 miles west at Hells Crossing campground. Garbage must be packed out. Downed firewood may be gathered. Leashed pets are permitted.

Reservations, fees: Reservations are accepted at 877/444-6777 or www.recreation.gov ($10 reservation fee). The camp is $50 per night. Open mid-May–mid-November, weather permitting.

Directions: From Yakima, drive northwest on U.S. 12 for 18 miles to Highway 410. Bear northwest on Highway 410 and drive 30.5 miles to the campground on the left.

Contact: Okanogan and Wenatchee National Forests, Naches Ranger District, 509/653-1401, fax 509/653-2638, www.fs.fed.us.

35 COUGAR FLAT

Scenic rating: 5

on the Bumping River in
Wenatchee National Forest

One of several camps in the immediate vicinity, this spot along the Bumping River is close to good fishing; a trail from the camp follows the river and then heads up the tributaries. The elevation is 3,100 feet.

Campsites, facilities: There are 12 sites for tents or RVs up to 40 feet long. Picnic tables and fire grills are provided. Drinking water, vault toilets, and garbage bins are available. Some facilities are wheelchair accessible. Leashed pets are permitted.

Reservations, fees: Reservations are accepted at 877/444-6777 or www.recreation.gov ($10 reservation fee). Sites are $15–17 per night, $5 per night for each additional vehicle.

Open mid-May–mid-September, weather permitting.

Directions: From Yakima, drive northwest on U.S. 12 for 18 miles to Highway 410. Turn left (northwest) on Highway 410 and drive 28.5 miles to Forest Road 1800. Turn left (southwest) and drive six miles (along the Bumping River) to the campground on the left.

Contact: Okanogan and Wenatchee National Forests, Naches Ranger District, 509/653-1401, fax 509/653-2638, www.fs.fed.us.

36 SODA SPRINGS

Scenic rating: 6

on the Bumping River in
Wenatchee National Forest

Highlights at this camp along Bumping River include natural mineral springs and a nature trail. The mineral spring is located next to a trail across the river from the campground, where the water bubbles up out of the ground. This cold-water spring is popular with some campers for soaking and drinking. Many campers use this camp for access to nearby Bumping Lake. Fishing access is available. A sheltered picnic area is provided.

Campsites, facilities: There are 26 sites for tents or RVs up to 30 feet in length. Picnic tables and fire grills are provided. Drinking water, vault toilets, firewood, a picnic shelter with a fireplace, and garbage service are available. A camp host is on-site. Some facilities are wheelchair accessible. Leashed pets are permitted.

Reservations, fees: Reservations are accepted at 877/444-6777 or www.recreation.gov ($10 reservation fee). Sites are $17–19 per night, $5 per night for each additional vehicle. Open mid-May–mid-September, weather permitting.

Directions: From Yakima, drive northwest on U.S. 12 for 18 miles to Highway 410. Turn left (northwest) on Highway 410 and drive 28.5

miles to Forest Road 1800. Turn left (southwest) and drive five miles (along the Bumping River) to the campground on the left.

Contact: Okanogan and Wenatchee National Forests, Naches Ranger District, 509/653-1401, fax 509/653-2638, www.fs.fed.us.

37 CEDAR SPRINGS

Scenic rating: 6

on the Bumping River in
Wenatchee National Forest

The Bumping River runs alongside this camp, set at an elevation of 2,800 feet. Fishing here follows the seasons for trout, steelhead, and whitefish; check regulations. If you continue driving southwest for 11 miles on Forest Road 1800/Bumping River Road, you'll reach Bumping Lake, where recreation options abound.

Campsites, facilities: There are 15 sites for tents or RVs up to 22 feet long, including two double sites. Picnic tables and fire grills are provided. Drinking water and vault toilets are available. Leashed pets are permitted.

Reservations, fees: Reservations are accepted at 877/444-6777 or www.recreation.gov ($10 reservation fee). Single sites are $14–18 per night, $34 per night for double sites, and $5 per night for each additional vehicle. Open mid-May–mid-September, weather permitting.

Directions: From Yakima, drive northwest on U.S. 12 for 18 miles to Highway 410. Bear northwest on Highway 410 and drive 28.5 miles to the campground access road (Forest Road 1800/Bumping River Road). Turn left (southwest) and drive 0.5 mile to the campground on the left.

Contact: Okanogan and Wenatchee National Forests, Naches Ranger District, 509/653-1401, fax 509/653-2638, www.fs.fed.us.

38 INDIAN FLAT GROUP CAMP

Scenic rating: 7

on the American River in
Wenatchee National Forest

This reservations-only group campground is set along the American River at an elevation of 2,600 feet. Fishing access is available for trout, steelhead, and whitefish in season; check regulations. A trail starts just across the road from camp and leads into the backcountry, west along Fife's Ridge, and farther north to the West Quartz Creek drainage.

Campsites, facilities: There is one group site for tents or RVs up to 30 feet long, with a maximum capacity of 65 campers and 22 vehicles. Picnic tables and fire grills are provided. Drinking water, vault toilets, and firewood are available. Garbage must be packed out. Leashed pets are permitted.

Reservations, fees: Reservations are accepted at 877/444-6777 or www.recreation.gov ($10 reservation fee). The camp is $70 per night on weekdays and $100 per night on weekends. Open late May–mid-November, weather permitting.

Directions: From Yakima, drive northwest on U.S. 12 for 18 miles to Highway 410. Bear northwest on Highway 410 and drive 27 miles to the campground on the left.

Contact: Okanogan and Wenatchee National Forests, Naches Ranger District, 509/653-1401, fax 509/653-2638, www.fs.fed.us.

39 LITTLE NACHES

Scenic rating: 5

on the Little Naches River in
Wenatchee National Forest

This campground on the Little Naches River near the American River is just 0.1 mile off the road and 24 miles from Mount Rainier. The easy access is a major attraction for highway cruisers, but the location also means you can sometimes hear highway noise, and at four sites, you can see highway vehicles. Trees act as a buffer between the highway and the campground at other sites. Fishing access is available from camp. The elevation is 2,562 feet.

Campsites, facilities: There are 17 sites for tents or RVs up to 49 feet long and one double site. Picnic tables and fire grills are provided. Drinking water, vault toilets, firewood, and garbage service are available. A camp host is on-site. Leashed pets are permitted.

Reservations, fees: Reservations are accepted at 877/444-6777 or www.recreation.gov ($10 reservation fee). Sites are $17–34 per night, $5 per night for each additional vehicle. Open mid-May–mid-September, weather permitting.

Directions: From Yakima, drive northwest on U.S. 12 for 18 miles to Highway 410. Bear northwest on Highway 410 and drive 25 miles to the campground access road (Forest Road 1900). Turn left and drive 100 yards to the campground on the left.

Contact: Okanogan and Wenatchee National Forests, Naches Ranger District, 509/653-1401, fax 509/653-2638, www.fs.fed.us.

40 COTTONWOOD

Scenic rating: 7

on the Naches River in
Wenatchee National Forest

Pretty, shaded sites and river views are the main draw at this camp along the Naches River. The fishing is similar to that of the other camps in the area—primarily for trout in summer and whitefish in winter. The elevation here is 2,300 feet.

Campsites, facilities: There are 16 sites for tents or RVs up to 22 feet long. Picnic tables and fire grills are provided. Drinking water,

vault toilets, and garbage service are available. A store, café, and ice are available nearby. Leashed pets are permitted.

Reservations, fees: Reservations are not accepted. Sites are $17–19 per night, $5 per night for each additional vehicle. Open mid-May–mid-September, weather permitting.

Directions: From Yakima, drive northwest on U.S. 12 for 18 miles to Highway 410. Turn left (northwest) on Highway 410 and drive 17.5 miles to the campground on the left.

Contact: Okanogan and Wenatchee National Forests, Naches Ranger District, 509/653-1401, fax 509/653-2638, www.fs.fed.us.

41 SAWMILL FLAT

Scenic rating: 6

on the Naches River in
Wenatchee National Forest

This campground on the Naches River near Halfway Flat is used by motorcyclists more than any other types of campers. It offers fishing access and a hiking trail that leads west from Halfway Flat campground for several miles into the backcountry. Fishing is primarily for trout in summer, whitefish in winter—check regulations. Another trailhead is located at Boulder Cave to the south.

Campsites, facilities: There are 24 sites for tents or RVs up to 24 feet long. Picnic tables and fire grills are provided. Drinking water, vault toilets, garbage bins, firewood, and an Adirondack group shelter are available. A camp host is on-site in summer. Downed firewood may be gathered. Some facilities are wheelchair accessible. Leashed pets are permitted.

Reservations, fees: Reservations are accepted at 877/444-6777 or www.recreation.gov ($10 reservation fee). Sites are $15–21 per night, $5 per night for each additional vehicle. Open mid-May–mid-September, weather permitting.

Directions: From Yakima, drive northwest on

CAMPING

U.S. 12 for 18 miles to Highway 410. Bear northwest on Highway 410 and drive 23.5 miles to the campground on the left.

Contact: Okanogan and Wenatchee National Forests, Naches Ranger District, 509/653-1401, fax 509/653-2638, www.fs.fed.us.

42 HALFWAY FLAT
🚶 🚴 🛶 🏕 🐕 ♿ 🚐 ⛺

Scenic rating: 7

on the Naches River in
Wenatchee National Forest

Fishing, hiking, and off-road vehicle (OHV) opportunities abound at this campground along the Naches River. A motorcycle trail leads from the campground into the backcountry adjacent to the William O. Douglas Wilderness; no motorized vehicles are permitted in the wilderness itself, however. Do not expect peace and quiet. This campground is something of a chameleon—sometimes primarily a family campground, but at other times dominated by OHV users.

Campsites, facilities: There are nine sites for tents or RVs up to 27 feet long and an area for dispersed tent or RV camping. Picnic tables and fire grills are provided. Drinking water, vault toilets, and garbage service are available. Some facilities are wheelchair accessible. Leashed pets are permitted.

Reservations, fees: Reservations are not accepted. Sites are $10 per night, dispersed campsites are $8 per night, $5 per night per additional vehicle. Open mid-May–mid-September, weather permitting.

Directions: From Yakima, drive northwest on U.S. 12 for 18 miles to Highway 410. Turn left (northwest) on Highway 410 and drive 17 miles to Forest Road 1704. Turn left and drive one mile to the campground.

Contact: Okanogan and Wenatchee National Forests, Naches Ranger District, 509/653-1401, fax 509/653-2638, www.fs.fed.us.

43 LOWER BUMPING LAKE
🚶 🏊 🛶 🚐 🏕 🐕 ♿ 🚙 ⛺

Scenic rating: 7

on Bumping Lake in
Wenatchee National Forest

This popular campground is set at an elevation of 3,200 feet near Bumping Lake amid a forest of primarily lodgepole pine. Bumping Lake features a variety of water activities, including waterskiing, fishing for salmon and trout, and swimming. A boat ramp is available near the camp. There are also several hiking trails that go into the William O. Douglas Wilderness surrounding the lake.

Campsites, facilities: There are 17 sites for tents or RVs up to 40 feet long. Picnic tables and fire grills are provided. Drinking water, vault toilets, and a dump station are available. Boat-launching facilities are nearby at Upper Bumping Lake campground. Some facilities are wheelchair accessible. Leashed pets are permitted.

Reservations, fees: Reservations are accepted at 877/444-6777 or www.recreation.gov ($10 reservation fee). Note that the website combines Lower and Upper Bumping Lake campgrounds into one listing; use the facility map to confirm your site. Sites are $15–17 per night, $34 for a double site, and $5 per night for each additional vehicle. Open June–mid-September, weather permitting.

Directions: From Yakima, drive northwest on U.S. 12 for 18 miles to Highway 410. Turn left (northwest) on Highway 410 and drive 28.5 miles to Forest Road 1800. Turn left (southwest) and drive 11 miles (along the Bumping River); look for the campground entrance road on the right.

Contact: Wenatchee National Forest, Naches Ranger District, 509/653-1401, fax 509/653-2638, www.fs.fed.us.

44 UPPER BUMPING LAKE

Scenic rating: 7

on Bumping Lake in
Wenatchee National Forest

Woods and water—this spot has them both. The cold lake is stocked with trout, and the nearby boat launch makes it a winner for campers with boats. This popular camp fills up quickly on summer weekends. A variety of water activities are allowed at Bumping Lake, including waterskiing, fishing (for salmon and trout), and swimming. A picnic area is adjacent to the boat facilities. In addition, several hiking trails lead into the William O. Douglas Wilderness surrounding the lake. This is one of the more developed camps in the area.

Campsites, facilities: There are 48 sites for tents or RVs up to 30 feet long. Picnic tables and fire grills are provided. Drinking water, vault toilets, and firewood are available. A camp host is on-site. Boat docks, launching facilities, and a dump station are nearby. Some facilities are wheelchair accessible. Leashed pets are permitted.

Reservations, fees: Reservations are accepted at 877/444-6777 or www.recreation.gov ($10 reservation fee). Note that the website combines Lower and Upper Bumping Lake campgrounds into one listing. Sites are $15–17 per night, $5 per night for each additional vehicle. Open June–late September, weather permitting.

Directions: From Yakima, drive northwest on U.S. 12 for 18 miles to Highway 410. Turn left (northwest) on Highway 410 and drive 28.5 miles to Forest Road 1800. Turn left (southwest) and drive 11 miles (along the Bumping River); look for the campground entrance road on the right.

Contact: Okanogan and Wenatchee National Forests, Naches Ranger District, 509/653-1401, fax 509/653-2638, www.fs.fed.us.

45 MOUNTHAVEN RESORT

Scenic rating: 6

near Mount Rainier National Park

This campground is located within 0.5 mile of the Nisqually (southwestern) entrance to Mount Rainier National Park. In turn, it can provide a launching point for your vacation. One option: Enter the park at the Nisqually entrance, then drive on Nisqually Paradise Road for about five miles to Longmire Museum; general park information and exhibits about the plants and geology of the area are available. If you then continue into the park for 10 more miles, you'll arrive at the Jackson Visitor Center in Paradise, which has more exhibits and an observation deck. This road is the only one into the park that's open year-round. Winter activities in the park include cross-country skiing, snowshoeing, and inner-tube sledding down slopes. A creek runs through this wooded camp.

Campsites, facilities: There are 16 sites with full hookups (20 and 30 amps) for RVs of any length and eight furnished cabins. Picnic tables and fire grills are provided. A restroom with a toilet and shower, drinking water, coin laundry, firewood, and a playground are available. A restaurant and a store are within one mile. Leashed pets are permitted.

Reservations, fees: Reservations are accepted at 800/456-9380. Sites are $30 per night, $3 per pet per night. Some credit cards are accepted. Open year-round.

Directions: From Chehalis, drive south on I-5 for 10 miles to U.S. 12. Turn east and drive 31 miles to Morton and Highway 7. Turn left (north) on Highway 7 and drive 17 miles to Elbe and Highway 706. Turn right (east) on Highway 706 and drive to Ashford; continue for six miles to the resort on the right.

Contact: Mounthaven Resort, 360/569-2594, fax 360/569-2949, www.mounthaven.com.

CAMPING

46 BIG CREEK

Scenic rating: 8

on Big Creek in Gifford Pinchot National Forest

This camp is useful as an overflow spot for Mount Rainier Sound–area campers. It is set along a stream next to a rural residential area in a forest setting made up of Douglas fir, western hemlock, western red cedar, and big leaf and vine maple.

Campsites, facilities: There are 24 sites for tents or RVs up to 20 feet long. Picnic tables and fire rings are provided. Drinking water, firewood, and vault toilets are available. A camp host is on-site. Some facilities are wheelchair accessible. Leashed pets are permitted.

Reservations, fees: Reservations are accepted at 877/444-6777 or www.recreation.gov ($10 reservation fee). Sites are $17 per night, $34 for a double site per night, and $5 per night for each additional vehicle. Open May–mid-September.

Directions: On I-5, drive to Exit 68 (south of Chehalis) and U.S. 12. Turn east on U.S. 12 and drive 62 miles to Packwood and Forest Road 52/Skate Creek Road. Turn left (northwest) and drive 23 miles to the campground on the left.

Contact: Gifford Pinchot National Forest, Cowlitz Valley Ranger District, 360/497-1100, fax 360/497-1102, www.fs.fed.us.

47 COUGAR ROCK

Scenic rating: 9

in Mount Rainier National Park

Cougar Rock is a national park campground at 3,180 feet elevation at the foot of awesome Mount Rainier. To the east lies the Nisqually Vista Trail, a beautiful 1.2-mile loop trail. It begins at the visitors center at Paradise and provides stellar views of Mount Rainier and the Nisqually Glacier. Fishing tends to be marginal. As in all national parks, no trout are stocked, and lakes without natural fisheries provide zilch. Nearby Mounthaven Resort offers winter activities in Mount Rainier Park, such as cross-country skiing, snowshoeing, and inner-tube sledding down slopes.

Campsites, facilities: There are 173 sites for tents or RVs up to 35 feet long and five group sites for up to 24–40 people each. Picnic tables and fire rings are provided. Restrooms with flush toilets, drinking water, a dump station, and an amphitheater are available. A general store is located two miles away at Longmire. Some facilities are wheelchair accessible. Leashed pets are permitted.

Reservations, fees: Reservations are accepted at 877/444-6777 or www.recreation.gov ($10 reservation fee). Sites are $12–15 per night, plus a $15 per vehicle park entrance fee. Group sites are $40–64 per night. Open late May–mid-October.

Directions: From Tacoma, drive south on I-5 for five miles to Highway 512. Turn east on Highway 512 and drive two miles to Highway 7. Turn right (south) on Highway 7 and drive to Elbe and Highway 706. Continue east on Highway 706 and drive 12 miles to the park entrance. Continue 11 miles to the campground entrance on the left (about two miles past the Longmire developed area).

Contact: Mount Rainier National Park, 360/569-2211, fax 360/569-2170, www.nps.gov/mora.

48 OHANAPECOSH

Scenic rating: 8

on the Ohanapecosh River in Mount Rainier National Park

BEST (

This camp is set at an elevation of 1,914 feet at the foot of North America's most beautiful volcano, 14,410-foot Mount Rainier. It is also set along the Ohanapecosh River, adjacent to the Ohanapecosh Visitor Center, which features exhibits on the history of the forest, plus visitor information. A 0.5-mile loop trail leads from the campground, behind the visitors center, to Ohanapecosh Hot Springs. The Silver Falls Trail, a three-mile loop trail, follows the Ohanapecosh River to 75-foot Silver Falls. Warning: Do not climb on the wet rocks near the waterfall; they are wet and slippery. Note that Stevens Canyon Road heading west and Highway 123 heading north are closed by snowfall in winter.

Campsites, facilities: There are 195 sites for tents or RVs up to 32 feet long and two group sites for up to 25 people each. Picnic tables and fire rings are provided. Flush toilets, drinking water, and a dump station are available. An amphitheater is nearby. Some facilities are wheelchair accessible. Leashed pets are permitted in camp, but not on trails.

Reservations, fees: Reservations are accepted at 877/444-6777 or www.recreation.gov ($10 reservation fee). Sites are $15 per night, plus a $15 per vehicle park entrance fee. The group site is $40 per night. Some credit cards are accepted. Open mid-May–October.

Directions: On I-5, drive to Exit 68 (south of Chehalis) and U.S. 12. Turn east on U.S. 12 and drive 72 miles (seven miles past Packwood) to Highway 123. Turn left (north) and drive 6.5 miles to the Ohanapecosh entrance to the park. As you enter the park, the camp is on the left, next to the visitors center.

Contact: Mount Rainier National Park, 360/569-2211, fax 360/569-2170, www.nps.gov/mora.

49 PACKWOOD RV PARK

Scenic rating: 6

in Packwood

This is a pleasant campground, especially in the fall when the maples turn color. Groups are welcome. Mount Rainier National Park

is located just 25 miles north, and this camp provides a good alternative if the park is full. Nearby recreation options include a riding stable. Note that some sites are filled with monthly renters.

Campsites, facilities: There are 88 sites, most with full hookups (30 amps), for RVs of any length and 15 tent sites. Some sites are pull-through. Picnic tables are provided at some sites and portable fire pits are available on request. Restrooms with flush toilets and showers, a dump station, cable TV, and coin laundry are available. A café, store, and propane gas are within walking distance. Leashed pets are permitted.

Reservations, fees: Reservations are accepted. Sites are $16–21 per night, $3 per person per night for more than two people. Open year-round.

Directions: On I-5, drive to Exit 68 (south of Chehalis) and U.S. 12. Turn east on U.S. 12 and drive 65 miles to Packwood. The park is on the left (north) side of the highway in town at 12985 U.S. Highway 12.

Contact: Packwood RV Park, 360/494-5145.

50 LA WIS WIS

Scenic rating: 9

on the Cowlitz River in
Gifford Pinchot National Forest

This camp is ideally located for day trips to Mount Rainier and Mount St. Helens. It's set at an elevation of 1,400 feet along the Clear Fork of the Cowlitz River, near the confluence with the Ohanapecosh River. Trout fishing is an option. The landscape features an old-growth forest of Douglas fir, western hemlock, western red cedar, and Pacific yew, with undergrowth of big leaf maple. A 200-yard trail provides access to the Blue Hole on the Ohanapecosh River, a deep pool designated by an observation point and interpretive signs. Another trail leads less than 0.25

CAMPING

mile to Purcell Falls. The entrance to Mount Rainier National Park is about seven miles south of the camp.

Campsites, facilities: There are 122 sites for tents or RVs up to 60 feet long. Picnic tables and fire rings are provided. Flush and vault toilets, drinking water, garbage bins, and firewood are available. Some facilities are wheelchair accessible. Leashed pets are permitted.

Reservations, fees: Reservations are accepted at 877/444-6777 or www.recreation.gov ($10 reservation fee). RV sites are $18 per night, tent sites are $16 per night, $5 per extra vehicle per night. Open late May–early September, weather permitting.

Directions: On I-5, drive to Exit 68 (south of Chehalis) and U.S. 12. Turn east on U.S. 12 and drive 69 miles (about six miles past Packwood) to Forest Road 1272. Turn left and drive 0.5 mile to the campground on the left.

Contact: Gifford Pinchot National Forest, Cowlitz Valley Ranger District, 360/497-1100, fax 360/497-1102, www.fs.fed.us.

51 WHITE PASS

Scenic rating: 7

on Leech Lake in Wenatchee National Forest

This campground on the shore of Leech Lake sits at an elevation of 4,500 feet and boasts nearby trails leading into the Goat Rocks Wilderness to the south and the William O. Douglas Wilderness to the north. A trailhead for the Pacific Crest Trail is also nearby. Beautiful Leech Lake is popular for fly-fishing for rainbow trout. Note that this is the only type of fishing allowed here—check regulations. No gas motors are permitted on Leech Lake. White Pass Ski Area is located across the highway, 0.2 mile away.

Campsites, facilities: There are 16 sites for tents or RVs up to 20 feet long. Picnic tables and fire grills are provided. Vault toilets,

garbage bins, and firewood are available, but there is no drinking water. A store and ice are located within one mile. Boat-launching facilities are nearby. No gas motors on boats are allowed; electric motors are permitted. Leashed pets are permitted.

Reservations, fees: Reservations are not accepted. Sites are $8 per night, $5 per night per additional vehicle. Open mid-May–mid-September, weather permitting.

Directions: On I-5, drive to Exit 68 (south of Chehalis) and U.S. 12. Turn east on U.S. 12 and drive 81 miles (one mile past the White Pass Ski Area) to the campground entrance road on the left side. Turn left (north) and drive 200 yards to Leech Lake and the campground.

Contact: Okanogan and Wenatchee National Forests, Naches Ranger District, 509/653-1401, fax 509/653-2638, www.fs.fed.us.

52 DOG LAKE

Scenic rating: 5

on Dog Lake in Wenatchee National Forest

Set on the shore of Dog Lake at 3,400 feet elevation is little Dog Lake campground. Fishing can be good for native rainbow trout, and the lake is good for hand-launched boats, such as canoes and prams. Nearby trails lead into the William O. Douglas Wilderness.

Campsites, facilities: There are 11 sites for tents or RVs up to 24 feet long. Picnic tables and fire grills are provided. Vault toilets and garbage bins are available, but there is no drinking water. No horses are allowed in the campground. Leashed pets are permitted.

Reservations, fees: Reservations are not accepted. Sites are $8 per night, $5 per extra vehicle per night. Open mid-May–early September, weather permitting.

Directions: On I-5, drive to Exit 68 (south of Chehalis) and U.S. 12. Turn east on U.S. 12 and drive 84 miles (three miles past the White

Pass Ski Area) to the campground entrance road on the left side.

Contact: Okanogan and Wenatchee National Forests, Naches Ranger District, 509/653-1401, fax 509/653-2638, www.fs.fed.us.

53 CLEAR LAKE NORTH

Scenic rating: 7

on Clear Lake in Wenatchee National Forest

This primitive campground is set along the shore of Clear Lake at an elevation of 3,100 feet; it gets relatively little use. A 5-mph speed limit keeps the lake quiet and ideal for fishing, which is often good for rainbow trout. It is stocked regularly in the summer. Clear Lake is the forebay for Rimrock Lake. Swimming is allowed.

Campsites, facilities: There are 33 sites for tents or RVs up to 22 feet long. Picnic tables and fire grills are provided. Vault toilets and garbage service are available. There is no drinking water at Clear Lake North, but there is drinking water at Clear Lake South campground. Boat docks and launching facilities are nearby. Some facilities are wheelchair accessible. Leashed pets are permitted.

Reservations, fees: Reservations are not accepted. Sites are $10 per night, $5 per extra vehicle per night. Open mid-May–mid-November, weather permitting.

Directions: From Yakima, drive northwest on U.S. 12 for 17 miles to the junction with Highway 410. Turn west on U.S. 12 and drive 31 miles to Forest Road 1200. Turn left (south) and drive 0.25 mile to Forest Road 1200-740. Continue south for 0.5 mile to the campground.

Contact: Okanogan and Wenatchee National Forests, Naches Ranger District, 509/653-1401, fax 509/653-2638, www.fs.fed.us.

54 CLEAR LAKE SOUTH

Scenic rating: 7

in Wenatchee National Forest

This campground (elevation 3,100 feet) is located near the east shore of Clear Lake, which is the forebay for Rimrock Lake. Fishing and swimming are recreation options. For winter travelers, several Sno-Parks in the area offer snowmobiling and cross-country skiing. Many hiking trails lie to the north.

Campsites, facilities: There are 22 sites for tents or RVs up to 22 feet long. Picnic tables and fire grills are provided. Drinking water, vault toilets, and garbage bins are available. Downed firewood may be gathered. Boat-launching facilities are nearby. Some facilities are wheelchair accessible. Leashed pets are permitted.

Reservations, fees: Reservations are not accepted. Sites are $10 per night, $5 per extra vehicle per night. Open mid-May–mid-November, weather permitting.

Directions: From Yakima, drive northwest on I-82 for 17 miles to the junction with Highway 410. Turn west on U.S. 12 and drive 31 miles to Forest Road 1200. Turn left (south) and drive one mile to Forest Road 1200-740. Continue south and drive 0.25 mile to the campground.

Contact: Okanogan and Wenatchee National Forests, Naches Ranger District, 509/653-1401, fax 509/653-2638, www.fs.fed.us.

55 SILVER BEACH RESORT

Scenic rating: 8

on Rimrock Lake

This resort along the shore of Rimrock Lake is one of several camps in the immediate area. It's very scenic, with beautiful lakefront sites. Hiking trails, marked bike trails, a full-service marina, a sandy swimming beach, and a riding stable are close by.

CAMPING

Campsites, facilities: There are 46 sites with full or partial hookups for tents or RVs up to 40 feet long, 46 sites for tents or RVs up to 40 feet long (no hookups), three cabins with kitchens, and 16 motel rooms. Some sites are pull-through. Picnic tables and fire pits are provided. Restrooms with flush toilets and coin showers, a café, convenience store, dump station, bait and tackle, bottled gas, ice, a playground, boat docks, launching facilities, and boat and personal watercraft rentals are available. Leashed pets are permitted.

Reservations, fees: Reservations are accepted. Sites are $17–23 per night, $5 per extra vehicle per night. Some credit cards are accepted. Open year-round, with limited winter facilities.

Directions: From Yakima, drive northwest on U.S. 12 for 40 miles to the resort on the left.

Contact: Silver Beach Resort, 509/672-2500, www.campingatsilverbeach.com.

56 INDIAN CREEK

Scenic rating: 7

on Rimrock Lake in Wenatchee National Forest

Fishing, swimming, and waterskiing are among the activities at this shorefront campground on Rimrock Lake (elevation 3,000 feet). The camp is adjacent to Rimrock Lake Marina and Silver Beach Resort. This is a developed lake and an extremely popular campground, often filling on summer weekends. Fishing is often good for rainbow trout. The treasured Indian Creek Trail and many other excellent hiking trails about 5–10 miles north of the campground lead into the William O. Douglas Wilderness.

Campsites, facilities: There are 39 sites for tents or RVs up to 45 feet long. Picnic tables and fire grills are provided. Drinking water, vault toilets, and garbage bins are available. Downed firewood may be gathered. A camp host is on-site. A café, store, ice, boat docks, launching facilities, and rentals are nearby. Leashed pets are permitted.

Reservations, fees: Reservations are accepted at 877/444-6777 or www.recreation.gov ($10 reservation fee). Sites are $15–19 per night, $5 per extra vehicle per night. Open mid-May–mid-September, weather permitting.

Directions: From Yakima, drive northwest on I-82 for 17 miles to the junction with Highway 410. Turn west on U.S. 12 and drive 20 miles to Rimrock Lake and the campground entrance at the lake.

Contact: Okanogan and Wenatchee National Forests, Naches Ranger District, 509/653-1401, fax 509/653-2638, www.fs.fed.us.

57 PENINSULA

Scenic rating: 7

on Rimrock Lake in Wenatchee National Forest

Fishing for silvers and rainbow trout, swimming, and waterskiing are all allowed at Rimrock Lake (elevation 3,000 feet), where this shorefront recreation area and camp are located. The lake is stocked regularly in summer and is popular, in part because of the nearby boat ramp. This camp is one of several on the lake. A point of interest, the nearby emergency airstrip here features a grass runway. A nearby Sno-Park offers wintertime fun, including cross-country skiing and snowmobiling.

Campsites, facilities: There is a dispersed camping area for tents or RVs up to 20 feet long. Picnic tables are provided. Vault toilets and garbage bins are available. There is no drinking water. Boat docks and launching facilities are nearby. Some facilities are wheelchair accessible. Leashed pets are permitted.

Reservations, fees: Reservations are not accepted. Sites are $8 per night, $5 per night per additional vehicle. Open May–mid-November, weather permitting.

Directions: From Yakima, drive northwest on I-82 for 17 miles to the junction with Highway 410. Turn west on U.S. 12 and drive 22 miles to Forest Road 1200. Turn left (south) and

drive three miles (across the cattle guard) to Forest Road 711. Turn right (west) and drive a short distance to the campground.

Contact: Okanogan and Wenatchee National Forests, Naches Ranger District, 509/653-1401, fax 509/653-2638, www.fs.fed.us.

58 SOUTH FORK GROUP CAMP

Scenic rating: 8

on the South Fork of the Tieton River in Wenatchee National Forest

South Fork Group Camp is set at 3,000 feet elevation along the South Fork of the Tieton River, less than one mile from where it empties into Rimrock Lake. Note that fishing is prohibited to protect the bull trout. By traveling a bit farther south on Tieton River Road, you can see huge Blue Slide, an enormous prehistoric rock and earth slide that has a curious blue tinge to it. Note: In 2009, a fire burned south of this area.

Campsites, facilities: There is one group site for up to 80 people for tents or RVs up to 40 feet long. Picnic tables and fire grills are provided. Vault toilets are available. There is no drinking water, and garbage must be packed out. Some facilities are wheelchair accessible. Leashed pets are permitted.

Reservations, fees: Reservations are accepted at 877/444-6777 or www.recreation.gov ($25 reservation fee). The site is $60 per night. Open May–mid-November, weather permitting.

Directions: From Yakima, drive northwest on I-82 for 17 miles to the junction with Highway 410. Turn west on U.S. 12 and drive 22 miles to Forest Road 1200. Turn left (south) and drive four miles to Forest Road 1203. Bear left and drive 0.75 mile to Forest Road 1203-517. Turn right and drive 200 feet to the campground.

Contact: Okanogan and Wenatchee National Forests, Naches Ranger District, 509/653-1401, fax 509/653-2638, www.fs.fed.us.

59 IRON CREEK

Scenic rating: 7

on the Cispus River in Gifford Pinchot National Forest

This popular U.S. Forest Service campground is set along the Cispus River near its confluence with Iron Creek. Trout fishing is available. The landscape features primarily Douglas fir, western red cedar, and old-growth forest on fairly flat terrain. The camp is also located along the access route that leads to the best viewing areas on the eastern flank for Mount St. Helens. Take a 25-mile drive to Windy Ridge Vista Point for a breathtaking view of Spirit Lake and the blast zone of the volcano.

Campsites, facilities: There are 99 sites for tents or RVs up to 40 feet long. Picnic tables and fire rings are provided. Drinking water, vault toilets, firewood, and an amphitheater are available. A camp host is on-site. Some facilities are wheelchair accessible. Leashed pets are permitted.

Reservations, fees: Reservations are accepted at 877/444-6777 or www.recreation.gov ($10 reservation fee). Sites are $18–36 per night, $32 per night for a double site, $5 per extra vehicle per night. Open mid-May–early September, weather permitting.

Directions: From Chehalis, drive south on I-5 for six miles to Exit 68 and U.S. 12. Turn east on U.S. 12 and drive 48 miles to Randle and Highway 131. Turn south on Highway 131 and drive one mile (becomes Forest Road 25). Continue south on Forest Road 25 and drive nine miles to a fork. Bear left at the fork, continue across the bridge, turn left, and drive two miles to the campground entrance on the left (along the south shore of the Cispus River).

Contact: Gifford Pinchot National Forest, Cowlitz Valley Ranger District, 360/497-1100, fax 360/497-1102, www.fs.fed.us.

60 TOWER ROCK

Scenic rating: 5

on the Cispus River in
Gifford Pinchot National Forest

Tower Rock campground along the Cispus River is an alternative to nearby Iron Creek and North Fork. It has shaded and sunny sites, with lots of trees and plenty of room. The camp is set fairly close to the river; some sites feature river frontage. It is also fairly flat and forested with Douglas fir, western hemlock, red cedar, and big leaf maple. Fishing for trout is popular here.

Campsites, facilities: There are 22 sites for tents or RVs up to 40 feet long. Picnic tables and fire grills are provided. Drinking water, vault toilets, and firewood are available. Leashed pets are permitted.

Reservations, fees: Reservations are accepted at 877/444-6777 or www.recreation.gov ($10 reservation fee). Sites are $18–20 per night, $5 per extra vehicle per night. Open mid-May–mid-September, weather permitting.

Directions: From Chehalis, drive south on I-5 for six miles to Exit 68 and U.S. 12. Turn east on U.S. 12 and drive 48 miles to Randle and Highway 131. Turn right (south) on Highway 131 and drive one mile to Forest Road 23. Turn left on Forest Road 23 and drive eight miles to Forest Road 28. Turn right and drive two miles to Forest Road 76. Turn right and drive two miles to the campground entrance road on the right.

Contact: Gifford Pinchot National Forest, Cowlitz Valley Ranger District, 360/497-1100, fax 360/497-1102, www.fs.fed.us.

61 NORTH FORK & NORTH FORK GROUP

Scenic rating: 6

on the Cispus River in
Gifford Pinchot National Forest

This campground offers single sites, double sites, and group camps, with the North Cispus River flowing between the sites for individual and group use. The elevation is 1,500 feet. The campsites are set back from the river in a well-forested area. A national forest map details the backcountry access to the Valley Trail, which is routed up the Cispus River Valley for 16.7 miles. This trailhead provides access for hikers, bikers, all-terrain vehicles, and horses. Note that if you explore Road 2300-083 15 miles west you will find Layser Cave, a Native American archeological site that is open to the public.

Campsites, facilities: There are 33 sites for tents or RVs up to 31 feet long and three group camps for up to 35 people each. Picnic tables and fire grills are provided. Drinking water, vault toilets, garbage bins, and firewood are available. Leashed pets are permitted.

Reservations, fees: Reservations are accepted at 877/444-6777 or www.recreation.gov ($10 reservation fee). Sites are $18–20 per night, $36 per night for double sites, $5 per extra vehicle per night, and $70–90 per night for group sites. Open mid-May–mid-September, weather permitting.

Directions: From Chehalis, drive south on I-5 for six miles to Exit 68 and U.S. 12. Turn east on U.S. 12 and drive 48 miles to Randle and Highway 131. Turn right (south) on Highway 131 and drive one mile to Forest Road 23. Bear left and drive 11 miles to the campground on the left.

Contact: Gifford Pinchot National Forest, Cowlitz Ranger District, 360/497-1100, fax 360/497-1102, www.fs.fed.us.

62 BLUE LAKE CREEK

🚶 🚲 🏊 🏠 ♿ �off-road 🏕

Scenic rating: 7

near Blue Lake in
Gifford Pinchot National Forest

This camp is set at an elevation of 1,900 feet along Blue Lake Creek. With access to a network of all-terrain vehicle (ATV) trails, it is a significant camp for ATV owners. There is nearby access to 16.7-mile Valley Trail. This camp is also near the launch point for the 3.5-mile hike to Blue Lake; the trailhead lies about a half mile from camp.

Campsites, facilities: There are 11 sites for tents or RVs up to 22 feet long. Picnic tables and fire rings are provided. Drinking water, vault toilets, and garbage bins are available. Firewood can be gathered outside of the campground area. A camp host is on-site. Some facilities are wheelchair accessible. Leashed pets are permitted.

Reservations, fees: Reservations are accepted at 877/444-6777 or www.recreation.gov ($10 reservation fee). Sites are $15–16 per night, $5 per extra vehicle per night. Open mid-May–mid-September, weather permitting.

Directions: From Chehalis, drive south on I-5 for six miles to Exit 68 and U.S. 12. Turn east on U.S. 12 and drive 48 miles to Randle and Highway 131. Turn right (south) on Highway 131 and drive one mile to Forest Road 23. Turn south and drive about 10 miles to the campground on the left.

Contact: Gifford Pinchot National Forest, Cowlitz Ranger District, 360/497-1100, fax 360/497-1102, www.fs.fed.us.

63 ADAMS FORK

🚶 🚲 🏊 🏠 🚐 🏕

Scenic rating: 7

on the Cispus River in
Gifford Pinchot National Forest

Adams Fork campground is set at 2,600 feet elevation along the Upper Cispus River near Adams Creek and is popular with off-road vehicle (ORV) enthusiasts. There are many miles of trails designed for use by ORVs. A trail just 0.5 mile away leads north to Blue Lake, which is about a five-mile hike (one-way) from the camp. Most of the campsites are small, but a few are large enough for comfortable RV use. The area has many towering trees. The Cispus River provides trout fishing.

Campsites, facilities: There are 24 sites for tents or RVs up to 22 feet long and three group camps for up to 20 people each. Picnic tables and fire grills are provided. Drinking water and vault toilets are available. Firewood may be gathered outside the campground area. Leashed pets are permitted.

Reservations, fees: Reservations are accepted at 877/444-6777 or www.recreation.gov ($10 reservation fee). Sites are $18 per night, group sites are $25–35 per night, $5 per extra vehicle per night. Open May–mid-September, weather permitting.

Directions: On I-5, drive to Exit 68 (south of Chehalis) and U.S. 12. Turn east on U.S. 12 and drive 48 miles to Randle and U.S. 131. Turn right (south) and drive one mile to Forest Road 23. Turn left (southeast) and drive 18 miles to Forest Road 21. Turn left (southeast) on Forest Road 21 and drive five miles to Forest Road 56. Turn right on Forest Road 56 and drive 200 yards to the campground on the left.

Contact: Gifford Pinchot National Forest, Cowlitz Valley Ranger District, 360/497-1100, fax 360/497-1102, www.fs.fed.us.

CAMPING

64 OLALLIE LAKE

Scenic rating: 9

on Olallie Lake in
Gifford Pinchot National Forest

Located at an elevation of 4,200 feet, this campground lies on the shore of Olallie Lake, one of several small alpine lakes in the area fed by streams coming off the glaciers on nearby Mount Adams (elevation 12,276 feet). Trout fishing is good here in early summer. The campsites are situated close to the lake and feature gorgeous views of Mount Adams across the lake. Several of the campsites are small, and there is one larger area with room for RVs. A word to the wise: Mosquitoes can be a problem in the spring and early summer.

Campsites, facilities: There are five sites for tents or RVs up to 22 feet long. Picnic tables and fire rings are provided. Vault toilets are available, but there is no drinking water. Firewood may be gathered outside the campground area. Boat-launching facilities are nearby, but gasoline motors are prohibited on the lake. Some facilities are wheelchair accessible. Leashed pets are permitted.

Reservations, fees: Reservations are not accepted. Sites are $14 per night, $5 per night per additional vehicle. Open June–September, weather permitting.

Directions: From Chehalis, drive south on I-5 for 10 miles to Exit 68 and U.S. 12. Turn east on U.S. 12 and drive 48 miles to Randle and U.S. 131. Turn right (south) and drive one mile to Forest Road 23. Turn left (southeast) and drive 29 miles to Forest Road 2329. Turn left (northeast) and drive one mile to a junction with Forest Road 5601. Bear left and drive 0.5 mile to the campground on the right.

Contact: Gifford Pinchot National Forest, Cowlitz Valley Ranger District, 360/497-1100, fax 360/497-1102, www.fs.fed.us.

65 TAKHLAKH LAKE

Scenic rating: 9

on Takhlakh Lake in
Gifford Pinchot National Forest

This campground is situated along the shore of Takhlakh Lake, one of five lakes in the area, all accessible by car. It's a beautiful place, set at 4,500 feet elevation, but, alas, mosquitoes abound until late July. A viewing area (Mount Adams is visible across the lake) is available for visitors, while the more ambitious can go berry picking, fishing, and hiking. This lake is much better than nearby Horseshoe Lake, and the fishing is much better, especially for trout early in the season. The Takhlakh Meadow Loop Trail, a barrier-free trail, provides a 1.5-mile hike.

Campsites, facilities: There are 54 sites for tents or RVs up to 40 feet long. Picnic tables are provided. Vault toilets and garbage bins are available. There is no drinking water. Firewood may be gathered outside the campground area. A camp host is on-site. Boat-launching facilities are available in the day-use area, but gasoline motors are prohibited on the lake. Some facilities are wheelchair accessible. Leashed pets are permitted.

Reservations, fees: Reservations are accepted at 877/444-6777 or www.recreation.gov ($10 reservation fee). Single sites are $15–16 per night, double sites are $32 per night, $5 per night for each additional vehicle. Open mid-June–late September, weather permitting.

Directions: From Chehalis, drive south on I-5 for 10 miles to Exit 68 and U.S. 12. Turn east on U.S. 12 and drive 48 miles to Randle and U.S. 131. Turn right (south) and drive one mile to Forest Road 23. Turn left (southeast) and drive 29 miles to Forest Road 2329. Turn left (northeast) and drive 1.5 miles to the campground entrance road on the right.

Contact: Gifford Pinchot National Forest, Cowlitz Valley Ranger District, 360/497-1100, fax 360/497-1102, www.fs.fed.us.

66 CAT CREEK

Scenic rating: 5

on Cat Creek and the Cispus River in
Gifford Pinchot National Forest

This small, rustic camp is set along Cat Creek
at its confluence with the Cispus River, about
10 miles from the summit of Mount Adams.
The camp, which features a forested setting,
gets a lot of all-terrain vehicle (ATV) use. A
trail starts less than one mile from camp and
leads up along Blue Lake Ridge to Blue Lake.
The area has many towering trees and the Cispus River provides trout fishing.

Campsites, facilities: There are five sites for
tents or RVs up to 15 feet long. Picnic tables
and fire grills are provided. Vault toilets and
firewood are available. There is no drinking water, and garbage must be packed out.
Firewood may be gathered outside the campground area. Some facilities are wheelchair
accessible. Leashed pets are permitted.

Reservations, fees: Reservations are not
accepted. There is no fee. Open June–mid-
September, weather permitting.

Directions: On I-5, drive to Exit 68 (south of
Chehalis) and U.S. 12. Turn east on U.S. 12
and drive 48 miles to Randle and U.S. 131.
Turn right (south) and drive one mile to Forest
Road 23. Turn left (southeast) and drive 18
miles to Forest Road 21. Turn left (southeast)
on Forest Road 21 and drive six miles to the
campground on the right.

Contact: Gifford Pinchot National Forest,
Cowlitz Valley Ranger District, 360/497-1100,
fax 360/497-1102, www.fs.fed.us.

67 HORSESHOE LAKE

Scenic rating: 9

on Horseshoe Lake in
Gifford Pinchot National Forest

This camp is set on the shore of picturesque, 10-
acre Horseshoe Lake. The campsites are poorly
defined, more like camping areas, though some
are close to the lake. A trail runs partway around
the lake and is open to mountain bikers and
horseback riders (who occasionally come from
a nearby camp). Fishing for trout is just fair in
the lake, which is stocked infrequently. The
water is too cold for swimming. A trail from the
camp, about a three-mile round-trip, goes up to
nearby Green Mountain (elevation 5,000 feet).
This is a multi-use trail that ties into the High
Lakes Trail system. Another trail heads up the
north flank of Mount Adams. Berry picking is
an option in the late summer months.

Campsites, facilities: There are 10 sites for
tents or RVs up to 16 feet long. Picnic tables
and fire rings are provided. Vault toilets are
available. There is no drinking water, and
garbage must be packed out. Firewood may
be gathered outside the campground area.
Primitive launching facilities are located on
the lake, but gasoline motors are prohibited on
the water. Leashed pets are permitted.

Reservations, fees: Reservations are not accepted. There is no fee. Open mid-June–late
September, weather permitting.

Directions: From Chehalis, drive south on I-5
for 10 miles to Exit 68 and U.S. 12. Turn east on
U.S. 12 and drive 48 miles to Randle and U.S.
131. Turn right (south) and drive one mile to
Forest Road 23. Turn left (southeast) and drive
29 miles to Forest Road 2329. Turn left (northeast) and drive seven miles (bearing right at the
junction with Forest Road 5601) to Forest Road
078. Turn left on Forest Road 078 and drive 1.5
miles to the campground on the left.

Contact: Gifford Pinchot National Forest,
Cowlitz Valley Ranger District, 360/497-1100,
fax 360/497-1102, www.fs.fed.us.

CAMPING

68 KEENE'S HORSE CAMP
👫🚣🛶♿🚐⛺

Scenic rating: 7

on the South Fork of Spring Creek in
Gifford Pinchot National Forest

This equestrians-only camp is set at 4,200 feet elevation along the South Fork of Spring Creek on the northwest flank of Mount Adams (elevation 12,276 feet). The Pacific Crest Trail passes within a couple miles of the camp. Several trails lead from here into the backcountry and to several alpine meadows. The meadows are fragile, so walk along their outer edges. Nearby Goat Rocks Wilderness has 50 miles of trails open to horses; other trails meander outside of the wilderness boundary.

Campsites, facilities: There are 16 sites in two areas for tents or RVs up to 22 feet long. Picnic tables and fire grills are provided. Vault toilets, water troughs, a mounting ramp, manure bins, and hitching facilities (high lines) are available, but there is no drinking water. Firewood may be gathered outside the campground area. Some facilities are wheelchair accessible. Leashed pets are permitted.

Reservations, fees: Reservations are not accepted. There is no fee. Open mid-June–late September.

Directions: On I-5, drive to Exit 68 (south of Chehalis) and U.S. 12. Turn east on U.S. 12 and drive 48 miles to Randle and U.S. 131. Turn right (south) and drive one mile to Forest Road 23. Turn left (southeast) and drive 18 miles to Forest Road 21. Turn left (southeast) on Forest Road 21 and drive five miles to Forest Road 56. Turn right on Forest Road 56 and drive five miles to Forest Road 5603. Turn right and drive five miles to Forest Road 2329. Turn right and drive two miles to the camp on the right.

Contact: Gifford Pinchot National Forest, Cowlitz Valley Ranger District, 360/497-1100, fax 360/497-1102, www.fs.fed.us.

69 KILLEN CREEK
👫🚣🛶🚐⛺

Scenic rating: 7

near Mount Adams in
Gifford Pinchot National Forest

This wilderness trailhead camp is ideal as a launch point for backpackers. The campground, set along Killen Creek at the foot of 12,276-foot Mount Adams, marks the start of a three-mile trail that leads up the mountain and connects with the Pacific Crest Trail. It's worth the effort. The Killen Trail goes up to secondary ridges and shoulders of Mount Adams for stunning views. Berry picking is a summertime option.

Campsites, facilities: There are nine sites for tents or RVs up to 22 feet long. Picnic tables and fire grills are provided. Vault toilets are available, but there is no drinking water. Garbage must be packed out. Firewood may be gathered outside the campground area. Leashed pets are permitted.

Reservations, fees: Reservations are not accepted. There is no fee. Open June–mid-September, weather permitting.

Directions: On I-5, drive to Exit 68 (south of Chehalis) and U.S. 12. Turn east on U.S. 12 and drive 48 miles to Randle and U.S. 131. Turn right (south) and drive one mile to Forest Road 23. Turn left (southeast) and drive 29 miles to Forest Road 2329. Turn left (northeast) and drive six miles to Forest Road 073. Turn left (west) and drive 200 yards to the campground.

Contact: Gifford Pinchot National Forest, Cowlitz Valley Ranger District, 360/497-1100, fax 360/497-1102, www.fs.fed.us.

70 WALUPT LAKE

🏃 🏊 ⛵ 🛶 🐎 🚙 ⛰️

Scenic rating: 8

on Walupt Lake in
Gifford Pinchot National Forest

This popular spot, set at 3,900 feet elevation along the shore of Walupt Lake, is a good base camp for a multi-day vacation. The trout fishing is often good here; check regulations. But note that only small boats are advisable here because the launch area at the lake is shallow and it can take a four-wheel-drive vehicle to get a boat in and out. A small swimming beach is nearby. In addition, several nearby trails lead into the backcountry and to other smaller alpine lakes. One trail out of the campground leads to the upper end of the lake, then launches off to the Goat Rocks Wilderness; it's an outstanding hike, and the trail is also excellent for horseback rides.

Campsites, facilities: There are 34 sites for tents or RVs up to 22 feet long and 10 walk-in sites. Picnic tables are provided. Drinking water and vault toilets are available. Fire rings are located next to the campground. There is primitive boat access with a 10-mph speed limit; no waterskiing is allowed. Leashed pets are permitted.

Reservations, fees: Reservations are accepted at 877/444-6777 or www.recreation.gov ($10 reservation fee). Sites are $18–36 per night, $5 per night for each additional vehicle. Open mid-June–mid-September.

Directions: On I-5, drive to Exit 68 (south of Chehalis) and U.S. 12. Turn east on U.S. 12 and drive 62 miles to Forest Road 21 (2.5 miles southwest of Packwood). Turn right (southeast) and drive 20 miles to Forest Road 2160. Turn left (east) and drive 4.5 miles to the campground.

Contact: Gifford Pinchot National Forest, Cowlitz Valley Ranger District, 360/497-1100, fax 360/497-1102, www.fs.fed.us.

71 WALUPT HORSE CAMP

🏃 🚵 🛶 🐎 🚙 ⛰️

Scenic rating: 7

near the Goat Rocks Wilderness in
Gifford Pinchot National Forest

This camp is for horse campers only and is set about one mile from Walupt Lake, which is good for trout fishing. Several trails lead from the lake into the backcountry of the southern Goat Rocks Wilderness, which has 50 miles of trails that can be used by horses; other trails meander outside of the wilderness boundary. If you have planned a multi-day horse-packing trip, you should bring in your own feed for the horses. Feed must be pellets or processed grain only. Hay is not permitted in the wilderness. The lake has a 10-mph speed limit for boats.

Campsites, facilities: There are nine sites for equestrians in tents or RVs up to 22 feet long. Picnic tables and fire grills are provided. Drinking water, vault toilets, and firewood are available. Garbage must be packed out. A horse ramp and high lines are available. Leashed pets are permitted.

Reservations, fees: Reservations are not accepted. There is no fee. Open June–late September, weather permitting.

Directions: On I-5, drive to Exit 68 (south of Chehalis) and U.S. 12. Turn east on U.S. 12 and drive 62 miles to Forest Road 21 (2.5 miles southwest of Packwood). Turn right (southeast) and drive 20 miles to Forest Road 2160. Turn left (east) and drive 3.5 miles to the campground on the right.

Contact: Gifford Pinchot National Forest, Cowlitz Valley Ranger District, 360/497-1100, fax 360/497-1102, www.fs.fed.us.

CAMPING

72 CLOVER FLATS

Scenic rating: 8

near the Goat Rocks Wilderness

Clover Flats campground is located in the sub-alpine zone on the slope of Darland Mountain, which peaks at 6,982 feet. Trails connect the area with the Goat Rocks Wilderness, six miles to the west. This is a popular area for winter sports.

Campsites, facilities: There are eight campsites for tents or RVs up to 16 feet long. Picnic tables and fire grills are provided. Vault toilets, drinking water, and garbage bins are available. Leashed pets are permitted.

Reservations, fees: Reservations are not accepted. There is no fee for camping. Open June–September, weather permitting.

Directions: From Yakima, drive south on I-82 for two miles to the Union Gap exit. Take that exit and turn right on East Valley Mall Road. Drive one mile to 3rd Avenue. Turn left and drive 0.25 mile to Ahtaman Road. Turn right (west) and drive 20 miles to Tampico and Road A-3000 (North Fork Road). Turn right (west) and drive 9.5 miles to the Ahtaman Camp. Continue to a junction with A-2000 (Middle Fork Road). Bear left and drive nine miles to the camp on the left. Note: The last few miles of Road A-2000 are very steep and unpaved, with a 12 percent grade. Only high-clearance vehicles are recommended.

Contact: Department of Natural Resources, Southeast Region, 509/925-8510, fax 509/925-8522, www.dnr.wa.gov.

73 TREE PHONES

Scenic rating: 7

on the Middle Fork of Ahtanum Creek

Forested Tree Phones campground is set along the Middle Fork of Ahtanum Creek at an elevation of 4,800 feet. It is close to hiking, motorbiking, and horseback-riding trails. A shelter with a wood stove is available year-round for picnics. During summer, there are beautiful wildflower displays.

Campsites, facilities: There are nine sites for tents or RVs up to 40 feet long. Picnic tables, fire grills, and tent pads are provided. Vault toilets are available. A 20- by 40-foot snow shelter and hitching rails are also available. There is no drinking water. Stock are permitted to drink from the creek. Some facilities are wheelchair accessible. Leashed pets are permitted.

Reservations, fees: Reservations are not accepted. There is no fee for camping. Open year-round, weather permitting (heavy snows are expected late November–March).

Directions: From Yakima, drive south on I-82 for two miles to the Union Gap exit. Take that exit and turn right on East Valley Mall Road. Drive one mile to 3rd Avenue. Turn left and drive 0.25 mile to Ahtaman Road. Turn right (west) and drive 20 miles to Tampico and Road A-3000 (North Fork Road). Turn right (west) and drive 9.5 miles to the Ahtaman Camp. Continue to a junction with A-2000 (Middle Fork Road). Bear left and drive six miles to the camp. Note: Only high-clearance vehicles are recommended.

Contact: Department of Natural Resources, Southeast Region, 509/925-8510, fax 509/925-8522, www.dnr.wa.gov.

74 GREEN RIVER HORSE CAMP

Scenic rating: 8

near Green River in
Gifford Pinchot National Forest

This premier equestrians-only horse camp is set on the Green River near an area of beautiful, old-growth timber, but the campsites themselves are in a reforested clear-cut area with trees about 25–40 feet tall. The camp features access to great trails into the Mount

St. Helens blast area. The lookout from Windy Ridge is one of the most drop-dead awesome views in North America, spanning Spirit Lake, the blast zone, and the open crater of Mount St. Helens. The campground features high lines at each site, and the access is designed for easy turning and parking with horse trailers.

Campsites, facilities: There are eight sites for up to two trailer rigs or three vehicles each. Picnic tables, fire grills, and high lines are provided. Vault toilets are available. No drinking water is provided, but it is available five miles north at Norway Pass Trailhead. In the past, stock water had to be hand-carried from the river, but new facilities are expected to solve this in 2010. Garbage must be packed out. Some facilities are wheelchair accessible. Leashed pets are permitted.

Reservations, fees: Reservations are not accepted. There is no fee. Open mid-May–November, weather permitting.

Directions: From Chehalis, drive south on I-5 for six miles to Exit 68 and U.S. 12. Turn east on U.S. 12 and drive 48 miles to Randle and Highway 131. Turn right (south) and drive one mile (becomes Forest Road 25). Continue south and drive 19 miles to Forest Road 99. Turn right (west, toward Windy Ridge) and drive 8.5 miles to Forest Road 26. Turn right (north) and drive five miles to Forest Road 2612 (gravel). Turn left (west) and drive about two miles to the campground entrance on the left.

Contact: Gifford Pinchot National Forest, Mount St. Helens National Volcanic Monument, 360/449-7800, fax 360/449-7801.

75 LEWIS RIVER HORSE CAMP

Scenic rating: 7

near the Lewis River and Quartz Creek in
Gifford Pinchot National Forest

During summer, this camp caters to equestrians only. The camp is not particularly

scenic, but the area around it is: There are six waterfalls nearby on the Lewis River. There are also many trails, all of which are open to mountain bikers and some to motorcycles. The spectacular Lewis River Trail is available for hiking, mountain biking, or horseback riding, and there is a wheelchair-accessible loop. Several other hiking trails in the area branch off along backcountry streams.

Campsites, facilities: There are nine sites for tents or RVs up to 35 feet long. Picnic tables and fire rings are provided. A composting toilet is available. No drinking water is provided. Garbage must be packed out. Horse facilities include high lines, mounting ramp, stock water, and three corrals. Some facilities are wheelchair accessible. Leashed pets are permitted.

Reservations, fees: Reservations are not accepted. There is no fee. Open May–November, weather permitting.

Directions: From Woodland on I-5, take Exit 21 for Highway 503. Drive east on Highway 503 and drive 23 miles to the Highway 503 spur. Drive northeast on the Highway 503 spur road for seven miles (becomes Forest Road 90). Continue east on Forest Road 90 for 33 miles to Forest Road 93. Turn left and drive a short distance to the campground (along the Lewis River) on the right.

Contact: Gifford Pinchot National Forest, Mount St. Helens National Volcanic Monument, 360/449-7800, fax 360/449-7801.

76 LOWER FALLS

Scenic rating: 10

on the Lewis River in
Gifford Pinchot National Forest

BEST (

This camp is set at 1,400 feet elevation in the primary viewing area for six major waterfalls on the Lewis River. The spectacular Lewis River Trail is available for hiking or horseback riding, and it features a wheelchair-

CAMPING

accessible loop. Several other hiking trails in the area branch off along backcountry streams. The sites are paved and set among large fir trees on gently sloping ground; access roads were designed for easy RV parking. Note that above the falls, the calm water in the river looks safe, but it is not! Stay out. In addition, the Lewis River Trail goes along cliffs, providing beautiful views but potentially dangerous hiking.

Campsites, facilities: There are 42 sites for tents or RVs up to 60 feet long and two group sites for up to 20 people each. Picnic tables and fire grills are provided. Drinking water and composting toilets are available. Some facilities are wheelchair accessible. Leashed pets are permitted.

Reservations, fees: Reservations are not accepted. Single sites are $15 per night for single sites, $30 per night for double sites, and $5 per extra vehicle per night. Group sites are $35 per night. Open May–November, weather permitting.

Directions: From Woodland on I-5, take Exit 21 for Highway 503. Drive east on Highway 503 for 23 miles to the Highway 503 spur. Drive northeast on the Highway 503 spur for seven miles (becomes Forest Road 90). Continue east on Forest Road 90 for 30 miles to the campground (along the Lewis River) on the right.

Contact: Gifford Pinchot National Forest, Mount St. Helens National Volcanic Monument, 360/449-7800, fax 360/449-7801.

77 TILLICUM AND SADDLE
🥾 🚴 🏊 ⛵ 🎣 🐕 ♿ 🚐 ⛺

Scenic rating: 8

near Meadow Lake in
Gifford Pinchot National Forest

Remote Tillicum and Saddle campgrounds are grouped together because of their location close to one another. These two pretty camps are primitive but well forested and within walking distance of several recreation options. Tillicum has a wheelchair-accessible vault toilet, but Saddle, a tiny and primitive camp, has no toilet facilities at all. A 4.5-mile trail from the Tillicum camp leads southwest past little Meadow Lake to Squaw Butte, then over to Big Creek. It's a nice hike, as well as an excellent ride for mountain bikers. This is a premium area for picking huckleberries in August and early September. The Lone Butte area about five miles to the south provides a side trip. Nearby Saddle camp, located one mile to the east, receives little use. There are two lakes nearby, Big and Little Mosquito Lakes, which are fed by Mosquito Creek. So, while we're on the subject, mosquito attacks in late spring and early summer can be like squadrons of World War II bombers moving in. The Pacific Crest Trail passes right by camp.

Campsites, facilities: Tillicum has 24 sites for tents or RVs up to 18 feet long. Saddle has three primitive sites for tents only. Picnic tables and fire grills are provided. Tillicum has a wheelchair-accessible vault toilet. There is no drinking water, and garbage must be packed out. Leashed pets are permitted.

Reservations, fees: Reservations are not accepted. Sites are $5 per night. Open June–late September, weather permitting.

Directions: From Vancouver, Washington on I-205, take Highway 14 and drive east for 66 miles to Highway 141. Turn left (north) on Highway 141 and drive 25 miles to Trout Lake and County Road 141 (Forest Road 24). Turn left (west) and drive two miles to a fork. Bear left at the fork and drive 20 miles (becomes Forest Road 24) to the campground on the left.

Contact: Gifford Pinchot National Forest, Mount St. Helens National Volcanic Monument, 360/449-7800, fax 360/449-7801.

78 MORRISON CREEK
🏃 🛖 ♿ ⛺

Scenic rating: 7

on Morrison Creek in
Gifford Pinchot National Forest

Here's a prime yet little-known spot. This camp is located along Morrison Creek at an elevation of 4,600 feet, near the southern slopes of 12,276-foot Mount Adams. Nearby trails will take you to the snowfields and alpine meadows of the Mount Adams Wilderness. In particular, the Shorthorn Trail is accessible from this campground.

Campsites, facilities: There are 12 tent sites. Picnic tables and fire rings are provided in some sites. Vault toilets are available, but there is no drinking water. Garbage must be packed out. Some facilities are wheelchair accessible. Leashed pets are permitted.

Reservations, fees: Reservations are not accepted. There is no fee. Open late June–late September, weather permitting.

Directions: From White Salmon, take Grangeview Loop Road to W. Jewett Boulevard/WA-141. Turn right on WA-141 and drive 21.4 miles to the campground.

Alternately, from Hood River, Oregon, drive north on Highway 35 (over the Columbia River) to Highway 14. Turn left and drive two miles to Highway 141-A. Turn right (north) on Highway 141-A and drive 20 miles to County Road 17 (just 200 yards east of the town of Trout Lake). Turn right (north) and drive two miles to Forest Road 80. Turn right (north) and drive 3.5 miles to Forest Road 8040. Bear left (north) and drive six miles to the campground on the left. The access road is rough and not recommended for RVs.

Contact: Gifford Pinchot National Forest, Mount Adams Ranger District, 509/395-3400, fax 509/395-3424, www.fs.fed.us.

79 ISLAND CAMP
🏃 🚣 ❄ 🛖 🚐 ⛺

Scenic rating: 8

on Bird Creek

Island campground sits in a forested area along Bird Creek and is close to lava tubes and blowholes. A strange one-foot-wide slit in the ground (too small to climb into and explore) can be reached by walking about 0.75 mile. Bird Creek provides a chance to fish for brook trout in late spring. In the winter, the roads are used for snowmobiling. A snowmobile shelter with a wood stove is available year-round for picnics.

Campsites, facilities: There are six campsites for tents or RVs up to 16 feet long. Picnic tables, fire grills, and tent pads are provided. Vault toilets are available, but there is no drinking water. Garbage must be packed out. Leashed pets are permitted.

Reservations, fees: Reservations are not accepted. There is no fee for camping. Open May–October, with limited winter access.

Directions: From Yakima, drive south on I-82 for 15 miles to U.S. 97. Turn south and drive 49 miles to Goldendale and Highway 142. Turn right (west) and drive 10 miles to Counts Road. Turn right (northwest) and drive 26 miles to Glenwood; continue for 0.25 mile to Bird Creek Road. Turn right and drive 0.9 mile to K-3000 Road (still Bird Creek Road). Turn left, drive over the cattle guard, and drive 1.2 miles to Road S-4000. Turn right and drive 1.3 miles to Road K-4000. Turn left and drive 3.4 miles to Road K-4200. Turn left and drive 1.1 miles to the campground entrance on the left. Turn left and drive 0.25 mile to the campground.

Contact: Department of Natural Resources, Southeast Region, 509/925-8510, fax 509/925-8522, www.dnr.wa.gov.

CAMPING

80 BIRD CREEK

Scenic rating: 7

near the Mount Adams Wilderness

Bird Creek campground is set in a forested area of old-growth Douglas fir and ponderosa pine along Bird Creek. This spot lies just east of the Mount Adams Wilderness and is one of two camps in the immediate area. (The other, Island Camp, is within three miles. It is also a primitive site, but it features snowmobile trails.)

Campsites, facilities: There are 10 sites for tents or RVs up to 22 feet long and one group camp for tents or RVs up to 35 feet long that can accommodate up to 25 people. Picnic tables, fire grills, and tent pads are provided. Pit and vault toilets are available, but there is no drinking water. Garbage must be packed out. Some facilities are wheelchair accessible. Leashed pets are permitted.

Reservations, fees: Reservations are not accepted. There is no fee for camping. Open May –mid-October, weather permitting.

Directions: From Yakima, drive south on I-82 for 15 miles to U.S. 97. Turn south and drive 49 miles to Goldendale and Highway 142. Turn right (west) and drive 10 miles to Counts Road. Turn right (northwest) and drive 26 miles to Glenwood. From the post office in Glenwood, continue 0.25 mile to Bird Creek Road. Turn right and drive 0.9 mile. Turn left (still Bird Creek Road), cross the cattle guard to Road K-3000, and drive 1.2 miles to Road S-4000 (gravel). Turn right and drive 1.3 miles to Road K-4000. Turn left and drive two miles to the campground on the left.

Contact: Department of Natural Resources, Southeast Region, 509/925-8510, fax 509/925-8522, www.dnr.wa.gov.

81 CAMP KALAMA RV PARK AND CAMPGROUND

Scenic rating: 6

on the Kalama River

This campground has a rustic setting, with open and wooded areas and some accommodations for tent campers. It's set along the Kalama River, where salmon and steelhead fishing is popular. A full-service marina is nearby. Note that some sites are filled with monthly renters.

Campsites, facilities: There are 113 sites with full or partial hookups (30 and 50 amps) for RVs of any length and 50 tent sites. Some sites are pull-through. Picnic tables and fire pits are provided. Restrooms with flush toilets and coin showers, drinking water, cable TV, propane gas, a dump station, general store, café, banquet room, firewood, coin laundry, ice, boat-launching facilities, a beach area, and a playground are available. Some facilities are wheelchair accessible. Leashed pets are permitted.

Reservations, fees: Reservations are accepted. RV sites are $29–32 per night, tent sites are $19–21, $1.50 per person per night for more than two adults, $1.50 per night per extra vehicle, and $1 per pet per night. Weekly and monthly rates are available. Some credit cards are accepted. Open year-round.

Directions: From the north end of Kalama (between Kelso and Woodland) on I-5, take Exit 32 and drive south on the frontage road for one block to the campground.

Contact: Camp Kalama RV Park and Campground, 360/673-2456 or 800/750-2456, fax 360/673-2324, www.kalama.com/campkalama.

82 PARADISE POINT STATE PARK

🏃 🏊 🛶 �... 🏕 ♿ 🚐 ⛺

Scenic rating: 8

on the East Fork of the Lewis River

Paradise Point is named for the serenity that once blessed this area. Alas, it has lost much of that peacefulness since the freeway went in next to the park. To reduce traffic noise, stay at one of the wooded sites in the small apple orchard. The sites in the grassy areas have little noise buffer. This park covers 88 acres and features 1,680 feet of river frontage. The two-mile hiking trail is good for families and children. Note that the dirt boat ramp is primitive and nonfunctional when the water level drops; it is recommended for car-top boats only. Fishing on the East Fork of the Lewis River is a bonus.

Campsites, facilities: There 58 sites for tents or RVs up to 50 feet long (no hookups), 18 sites with partial hookups (30 and 50 amps) for tents or RVs up to 40 feet long, nine hike-in/bike-in sites, and two yurts. Picnic tables and fire grills are provided. Restrooms with flush toilets and coin showers, drinking water, a dump station, firewood, an amphitheater, and summer interpretive programs are available. A primitive, dirt boat-launching area is located nearby on East Fork Lewis River. Some facilities are wheelchair accessible. Leashed pets are permitted.

Reservations, fees: Reservations are accepted at 888/CAMP-OUT (888/226-7688) or www.parks.wa.gov/reservations ($6.50–8.50 reservation fee). Sites are $21–28 per night, $12 per night for hike-in/bike-in sites, $10 per extra vehicle per night, and yurts are $55 per night. Some credit cards are accepted. Open year-round, with some sites closed October–April.

Directions: From Vancouver, Washington, drive north on I-5 for 15 miles to Exit 16 (La Center/Paradise Point State Park exit). Take that exit and turn right, then almost immediately at Paradise Park Road, turn left and drive one mile to the park.

Contact: Paradise Point State Park, tel./fax 360/263-2350; state park information, 360/902-8844, www.parks.wa.gov.

83 BIG FIR CAMPGROUND AND RV PARK

🏃 🛶 🚐 🏕 🚐 ⛺

Scenic rating: 6

near Paradise Point State Park

Big Fir campground is set in a heavily wooded, rural area not far from Paradise Point State Park. It's nestled among hills and features shaded gravel sites and wild berries. Recreation opportunities include hiking and fishing on the East Fork of the Lewis River.

Campsites, facilities: There are 37 sites with full hookups (30 and 50 amps) for RVs of any length and 33 tent sites. Some sites are pull-through. Picnic tables and barbecues are provided; no wood fires are allowed. Restrooms with flush toilets and coin showers, drinking water, volleyball, croquet, a horseshoe pit, board games, limited groceries, and ice are available. Boat-launching facilities are located within 1.5 miles. Leashed pets are permitted.

Reservations, fees: Reservations are accepted. Sites are $18–24 per night, $2 per night per extra vehicle, $4 per person per night for more than four people. Some credit cards are accepted. Open year-round, except for the tent area, which is open Memorial Day weekend–Labor Day weekend.

Directions: From Vancouver, Washington, drive north on I-5 to Exit 14 (Ridgefield exit). Take that exit to Highway 269. Drive east on Highway 269 (the road's name changes several times) for two miles to 10th Avenue. Turn right and drive to the first intersection at 259th Street. Turn left and drive two miles to the park on the right (route is well marked).

Contact: Big Fir Campground and RV Park, 360/887-8970 or 800/532-4397.

CAMPING

84 COLUMBIA RIVERFRONT RV PARK

Scenic rating: 8

near Portland

Columbia Riverfront RV Park is located directly on the Columbia River, north of Portland. That means it is away from freeway noise, airports, and train tracks. Quiet? Oh yeah. The park encompasses 10 acres and boasts 900 feet of sandy beach, perfect for fishing for steelhead or salmon and beachcombing.

Campsites, facilities: There are 76 sites with for RVs up to 78 feet (full hookups); some sites are pull-through. Picnic tables are provided, but only beach sites have fire rings. Drinking water, restrooms with flush toilets and coin showers, a park store (with groceries, propane, and ice), horseshoe pits, Wi-Fi, cable TV, coin laundry, and a playground are available. Some facilities are wheelchair accessible. Leashed pets are permitted.

Reservations, fees: Reservations are accepted. Sites are $32–38 per night.

Directions: From I-5 in Woodland, take Exit 22 and turn south onto Dike Access Road. Drive two miles on Dike Access Road to the T intersection and turn left onto Dike Road. Drive one mile on Dike Road to the campground on the right.

Contact: Columbia Riverfront RV Park, 360/225-2327 or 800/845-9842, www.columbiariverfrontrvpark.com.

85 BATTLE GROUND LAKE STATE PARK

Scenic rating: 8

on Battle Ground Lake

The centerpiece of this state park is Battle Ground Lake, a spring-fed lake that is stocked with trout but popular for bass and catfish fishing as well. Underground lava tubes feed water into the lake, which is similar to Crater Lake in Oregon, though smaller. The park covers 280 acres, primarily forested with conifers, in the foothills of the Cascade Mountains. There are 10 miles of trails for hiking and biking, including a trail around the lake, and an additional five miles of trails open to horses; a primitive equestrian camp is also available. The lake is good for swimming and fishing, and it has a nice beach area; boats with gas motors are not allowed. If you're traveling on I-5 and looking for a layover, this camp, just 15 minutes from the highway, is ideal. In July and August, the area hosts several fairs and celebrations. Like many of the easy-access state parks on I-5, this one fills up quickly on weekends. The average annual rainfall is 35 inches.

Campsites, facilities: There are 25 sites for tents or RVs up to 35 feet long (no hookups), six sites with partial hookups (50 amps) for RVs, 15 hike-in/bike-in sites, one group site for 25–32 people, a horse camp for 10–16 people, and four cabins. Picnic tables and fire grills are provided. Restrooms with flush toilets and coin showers, drinking water, a dump station, a store, firewood, a seasonal snack bar, sheltered picnic area, amphitheater, summer interpretive programs, a playground, horseshoe pits, and an athletic field are available. Boat-launching facilities and rentals are nearby. Some facilities are wheelchair accessible. Leashed pets are permitted.

Reservations, fees: Reservations are accepted at 888/CAMP-OUT (888/226-7688) or www.parks.wa.gov/reservations ($6.50–8.50 reservation fee). Sites are $21–28 per night, $12 per night for hike-in/bike-in sites, $10 per night per extra vehicle, $55–60 per night for cabins. Some credit cards are accepted. Open year-round.

Directions: From I-5 southbound, take Exit 11; from I-5 northbound, take Exit 9. Drive to the city of Battle Ground (well marked); continue to the east end of town to Grace Avenue. Turn left on NE Grace Avenue and drive three miles (a marked route) to the park.

Contact: Battle Ground Lake State Park, tel./ fax 360/687-4621; state park information, 360/902-8844, www.parks.wa.gov.

86 SUNSET FALLS
🏃 🚵 🛶 🐴 ♿ 🚐 ⛺

Scenic rating: 9

on the East Fork of the Lewis River in Gifford Pinchot National Forest

This campground is located at an elevation of 1,000 feet along the East Fork of the Lewis River. Fishing, hiking, and huckleberry and mushroom picking are some of the favored pursuits of visitors. Scenic Sunset Falls is located just upstream of the campground. A barrier-free viewing trail leads to an overlook.

Campsites, facilities: There are 16 sites for tents or RVs up to 22 feet long. Picnic tables and fire grills are provided. Vault toilets are available. There is no drinking water, and garbage must be packed out. Some facilities are wheelchair accessible. Leashed pets are permitted.

Reservations, fees: Reservations are not accepted. Sites are $12 per night, $5 per extra vehicle per night. Open year-round.

Directions: From Vancouver, Washington, drive north on I-5 about seven miles to County Road 502. Turn east on Highway 502 and drive six miles to Highway 503. Turn left and drive north for five miles to Lucia Falls Road. Turn right and drive eight miles to Moulton Falls and Old County Road 12. Turn right on Old County Road 12 and drive seven miles to the Forest Boundary and the campground entrance on the right.

Contact: Gifford Pinchot National Forest, Mount St. Helens National Volcanic Monument, 360/449-7800, fax 360/449-7801.

87 COLD CREEK CAMP
🏃 🚵 🐴 ♿ 🚐 ⛺

Scenic rating: 6

on Cedar Creek

The late Waylon Jennings once told me that few things worth remembering come easy, right? Well, sometimes. First, don't expect to find a "cold creek" here. There just is no such thing. And second, the directions are complicated. This campground is set in a forested area with plenty of trails nearby for hiking and horseback riding. The camp gets minimal use. A large shelter is available at the day-use area. There is a seven-day stay limit.

Campsites, facilities: There are seven sites for tents or RVs up to 20 feet long. Picnic tables, fire grills, and tent pads are provided. Vault toilets are available. There is no drinking water, and garbage must be packed out. A camp host is on-site. Some facilities are wheelchair accessible. Leashed pets are permitted.

Reservations, fees: Reservations are not accepted. There is no fee for camping. Open year-round, weather permitting.

Directions: From Vancouver, Washington, drive north on I-5 to Exit 9 and NE 179th Street. Turn east and drive 5.5 miles to Highway 503. Turn right and drive 1.5 miles to NE 159th Street. Turn left on NE 159th Street and drive three miles to 182nd Avenue. Turn right and drive one mile to NE 139th. Turn left and drive eight miles (becomes Rawson, then Road L-1400) to Road L-1000. Turn left and drive four miles to the campground entrance road. Turn left, past the yellow gate, and drive one mile to the camp.

Contact: Department of Natural Resources, Pacific Cascade Region South, 360/577-2025, fax 360/274-4196, www.dnr.wa.gov.

CAMPING

CAMPING

88 ROCK CREEK CAMPGROUND AND HORSE CAMP

Scenic rating: 6

on Rock Creek

This camp is located in a wooded area along Rock Creek. It is popular among equestrians and mountain bikers, especially on weekends, because of the Tarbell Trail, a 25-mile loop trail that is accessible from the campground and goes to the top of Larch Mountain (this road becomes Rawson, then L-1400). Camping is limited to seven days.

Campsites, facilities: There are 19 sites for tents or RVs up to 20 feet long. Picnic tables, fire grills, and tent pads are provided. Vault toilets, a horse-loading ramp, and corrals are available. There is no drinking water, and garbage must be packed out. There is a campground host on-site. Some facilities are wheelchair accessible. Leashed pets are permitted.

Reservations, fees: Reservations are not accepted. There is no fee for camping. Open year-round, weather permitting.

Directions: From Vancouver, Washington, drive north on I-5 to Exit 9 and NE 179th Street. Turn east and drive 5.5 miles to Highway 503. Turn right and drive 1.5 miles to NE 159th Street. Turn left on NE 159th Street and drive three miles to 182nd Avenue. Turn right and drive one mile to NE 139th (Road L-1400). Turn left and drive eight miles (road becomes Rawson, then L-1400) to Road L-1000. Turn left and drive 4.5 miles (passing Cold Creek Campground after three miles) to Road L-1200/Dole Valley Road. Turn left and drive 200 yards to the campground on your right.

Contact: Department of Natural Resources, Pacific Cascade Region South, 360/577-2025, fax 360/274-4196, www.dnr.wa.gov.

89 REED ISLAND BOAT-IN

Scenic rating: 10

east of Washougal on Reed Island

Where else can you have your own personal island? Only in Washington, that's where. Reachable only by boat, this 510-acre marine park is part of the Columbia River Water Trail. Activities include boating, bird-watching, and picnicking, and there is a heron rookery on the southwest side of the island.

Campsites, facilities: There are 10 primitive sites. Picnic tables and pedestal stoves are provided. A vault toilet and dump station are available. There is no drinking water. Garbage must be packed out. Leashed pets are permitted.

Reservations, fees: Reservations are not accepted. Sites are $12 per night, $10 per each additional vehicle. Open year-round.

Directions: From the Port of Camas, head east on the Columbia River for approximately three miles. Signs on the southwest end of the island indicate where the campsites are located.

Contact: Reed Island State Park, 360/902-8844, www.parks.wa.gov.

90 DOUGAN CREEK

Scenic rating: 7

near the Washougal River

Insider's note: Dougan Creek campground is available only when a camp host is on-site. Located on Dougan Creek where it empties into the Washougal River, this campground is small and remote. Heavily forested with second-growth Douglas fir, it features pretty sites with river views.

Campsites, facilities: There are seven sites for tents or RVs up to 20 feet long. Picnic tables, fire grills, and tent pads are provided. Vault toilets are available. There is no drinking water, and garbage must be packed out. Some facilities are wheelchair accessible. Leashed pets are permitted.

Reservations, fees: Reservations are not accepted. There is no fee for camping. Open mid-May–mid-October, weather permitting.

Directions: From Vancouver, Washington, on I-205, take Highway 14 and drive east for 20 miles to Highway 140. Turn north on Highway 140 and drive five miles to Washougal River Road. Turn right on Washougal River Road and drive about seven miles until you come to the end of the pavement and pass the picnic area on the left. The campground is 0.25 mile beyond the picnic area.

Contact: Department of Natural Resources, Pacific Cascade Region South, 360/577-2025, fax 360/274-4196, www.dnr.wa.gov.

91 BEACON ROCK STATE PARK

Scenic rating: 8

in Columbia River Gorge National Scenic Area

BEST (

This state park features Beacon Rock, the second-largest monolith in the world, which overlooks the Columbia River Gorge. Lewis and Clark gave Beacon Rock its name on their expedition to the Pacific Ocean in 1805. The Beacon Rock Summit Trail, a 1.8-mile round-trip hike, provides excellent views of the gorge. The park is excellent for rock climbing, with the climbing season running mid-July–January. The park covers nearly 5,000 acres and includes 9,500 feet of shoreline along the Columbia River and more than 22 miles of nearby trails open for hiking, mountain biking, and horseback riding. An eight-mile loop trail to Hamilton Mountain (2,300 feet elevation) is one of the best hikes, featuring even better views than from Beacon Rock. Fishing for sturgeon, salmon, steelhead, smallmouth bass (often excellent), and walleye is available in season on the Lower Columbia River below Bonneville Dam; check regulations.

Campsites, facilities: There are 28 sites for tents or small RVs (no hookups), five sites with full hookups (30 amps) for RVs, one hike-in/bike-in site, and one group site for up to 200 people. Picnic tables and fire grills are provided. Restrooms with flush toilets and coin showers, drinking water, picnic areas, and a playground are available. Boat docks and launching facilities, moorage, and boat pumpout are available. Some facilities are wheelchair accessible. Leashed pets are permitted.

Reservations, fees: Reservations are not accepted for family sites but are required for the group camp at 888/CAMP-OUT (888/226-7688) or www.parks.wa.gov/reservations ($6.50–8.50 reservation fee). Sites are $16–22 per night, $10 per night for hike-in/bike-in sites, $10 per night per extra vehicle. The group site is $2.45 per person per night with a 20-person minimum. Boat launch fee is $7, and daily mooring fee is $0.50 per foot with a $10 minimum. Open April–October, with two sites available year-round.

Directions: From Vancouver, Washington, take Highway 14 and drive east for 35 miles. The park straddles the highway; follow the signs to the campground.

Contact: Beacon Rock State Park, 509/427-8265, fax 509/427-4471; state park information, 360/902-8844, www.parks.wa.gov.

92 CULTUS CREEK

Scenic rating: 7

near the Indian Heaven Wilderness in Gifford Pinchot National Forest

This camp is set at an elevation of 4,000 feet along Cultus Creek on the edge of the Indian Heaven Wilderness. It offers nearby access to trails that will take you into the backcountry, which has numerous small meadows and lakes among old-growth stands of fir and pine. Horse trails are available as well. Access to the Pacific Crest Trail requires a two-mile climb. This camp is popular during the fall huckleberry season, when picking is good, but gets light use the rest of the year. Situated amid gentle terrain, the sites are graveled and level.

Campsites, facilities: There are 51 sites for tents or RVs up to 32 feet long. Picnic tables and fire grills are provided. Vault toilets and firewood are available. There is no drinking water, and garbage must be packed out. Some facilities are wheelchair accessible. Leashed pets are permitted.

Reservations, fees: Reservations are not accepted. Sites are $10 per night, $5 per night per additional vehicle. Open late June–late September, weather permitting.

Directions: From Vancouver, Washington, on I-205, take Highway 14 east and drive 66 miles to State Route 141-A. Turn left (north) on State Route 141-A and drive 28 miles (becomes Forest Road 24); continue two miles to a junction. Turn right (staying on Forest Road 24) and drive 13.5 miles to the campground.

Contact: Gifford Pinchot National Forest, Mount Adams Ranger District, 509/395-3400, fax 509/395-3424, www.fs.fed.us.

93 SMOKEY CREEK

Scenic rating: 7

near the Indian Heaven Wilderness in
Gifford Pinchot National Forest

This primitive, little-used campground is set in an area of old-growth Douglas fir along Smokey Creek. A trail leading into the Indian Heaven Wilderness passes near the camp. Berry picking can be good here in summer and early fall. The elevation is 3,700 feet.

Campsites, facilities: There are three sites for tents only. Picnic tables and fire rings are

provided. Pit toilets are available. There is no drinking water, and garbage must be packed out. Leashed pets are permitted.

Reservations, fees: Reservations are not accepted. There is no fee. Open July–late September, weather permitting.

Directions: From Vancouver, Washington, on I-205, take Highway 14 east and drive 66 miles to State Route 141-A. Turn left (north) on State Route 141-A and drive 28 miles (becomes Forest Road 24); continue two miles to a junction. Turn right (staying on Forest Road 24) and drive seven miles to the campground.

Contact: Gifford Pinchot National Forest, Mount Adams Ranger District, 509/395-3400, fax 509/395-3424, www.fs.fed.us.

94 LITTLE GOOSE AND HORSE CAMP

Scenic rating: 5

on Little Goose Creek in
Gifford Pinchot National Forest

This campground is near Little Goose Creek (located between Smokey and Cultus campgrounds). Huckleberry picking is quite good in August and early September. The camp sits close to the road and is sometimes dusty. Note that the access road is paved but rough and not recommended for RVs or trailers. Campers with horse trailers must drive slowly. This camp has sites ranging from good to poor and is lightly used in fall. Several trails are available leading out from the campground. The elevation is 4,000 feet.

Campsites, facilities: There are eight sites for tents or RVs up to 32 feet long and three sites for campers with stock animals. Picnic tables and fire grills are provided. Vault toilets are available. There is no drinking water, and garbage must be packed out. Leashed pets are permitted.

Reservations, fees: Reservations are not

accepted. There is no fee. Open late June–late September, weather permitting.

Directions: From Vancouver, Washington, on I-205, take Highway 14 east and drive 66 miles to State Route 141-A. Turn left (north) on State Route 141-A and drive 28 miles (becomes Forest Road 24); continue two miles to a junction. Turn right (staying on Forest Road 24) and drive eight miles (one mile past Smokey Creek) to the campground.

Contact: Gifford Pinchot National Forest, Mount Adams Ranger District, 509/395-3400, fax 509/395-3424, www.fs.fed.us.

95 PETERSON PRAIRIE AND GROUP

Scenic rating: 8

near the town of Trout Lake in Gifford Pinchot National Forest

Here's a good base camp if you want a short ride to town as well as access to the nearby wilderness areas. Peterson Prairie is a prime spot for huckleberry picking in the fall. A trail from the camp leads about one mile to nearby ice caves; a stairway into the caves provides access to a variety of ice formations. An area Sno-Park with snowmobiling and cross-country skiing trails is open for winter recreation. The elevation is 2,800 feet.

Campsites, facilities: There are 30 sites for tents or RVs up to 40 feet long, and one group site for up to 50 people. Picnic tables and fire grills are provided. Drinking water, vault toilets, and firewood are available. A camp host is available in summer. Leashed pets are permitted.

Reservations, fees: Reservations are accepted and are required for the group site at 877/444-6777 or www.recreation.gov ($10 reservation fee). Single sites are $15 per night, $34 per night for double sites, $5 per extra vehicle per night. The group site is $70 per night. Open May–mid-September, weather permitting.

Directions: From White Salmon, take Grangeview Loop Road to W. Jewett Boulevard/WA-141. Turn right on WA-141 and drive 26 miles to Carson Guler Road/NF Development Road 24. Follow Carson Guler Road/NF Development Road 24 two miles to the campground.

Alternately, from Hood River, Oregon, drive north on Highway 35 (over the Columbia River) to Highway 14. Turn left and drive two miles to Highway 141-A. Turn right (north) on Highway 141-A and drive 25.5 miles to Forest Road 24 (5.5 miles beyond and southwest of the town of Trout Lake). Bear right (west) and drive 2.5 miles to the campground on the left.

Contact: Gifford Pinchot National Forest, Mount Adams Ranger District, 509/395-3400, fax 509/395-3424, www.fs.fed.us.

96 TROUT LAKE CREEK

Scenic rating: 7

on Trout Lake Creek in Gifford Pinchot National Forest

This spot makes a popular base camp for folks fishing at Trout Lake (five miles away). Many anglers will spend the day at the lake, where fishing is good for stocked rainbow trout, then return to this camp for the night. Some bonus brook trout are occasionally caught at Trout Lake. The camp is set along a creek in a forest of Douglas fir. In season, berry picking can be good here.

Campsites, facilities: There are 16 sites for tents or RVs up to 28 feet long. Picnic tables and fire rings are provided. Vault toilets are available. There is no drinking water, and garbage must be packed out. Leashed pets are permitted.

Reservations, fees: Reservations are not accepted. Sites are $10 per night, $5 per night per additional vehicle. Open mid-May–mid-September, weather permitting.

CAMPING

Directions: From White Salmon, take Grangeview Loop Road to W. Jewett Boulevard/WA-141. Turn right on WA-141 and drive 22 miles to Trout Creek Road/Trout Lake Creek Road. Turn right on Trout Creek Road/Trout Lake Creek Road and drive four miles to National Forest Development Road 010. Take a slight right and drive about 0.5 mile to the campground on the left.

Alternately, from Hood River, Oregon, drive north on Highway 35 (over the Columbia River) to Highway 14. Turn left and drive two miles to Highway 141-A. Turn right (north) on Highway 141-A and drive 25 miles north to Forest Road 88. Turn right and drive four miles to Forest Road 8810. Turn right and drive 1.5 miles to Forest Road 8810-010. Turn right and drive 0.25 mile to the campground on the right. Note that the access road is rough.

Contact: Gifford Pinchot National Forest, Mount Adams Ranger District, 509/395-3400, fax 509/395-3424, www.fs.fed.us.

97 PARADISE CREEK
🏃 🐕 ♿ 🚐 ⛺

Scenic rating: 9

on Paradise Creek and the Wind River in Gifford Pinchot National Forest

This camp is located deep in Gifford Pinchot National Forest at the confluence of Paradise Creek and the Wind River. It gets light use despite easy access and easy RV parking. The well-shaded campsites are set among old-growth woods, primarily Douglas fir, cedar, and western hemlock. Lava Butte, located a short distance from the camp, is accessible by trail; the 1.2-mile round-trip hike from the campground provides a good view of the valley. Fishing is closed here. The elevation is 1,500 feet.

Campsites, facilities: There are 42 sites for tents or RVs up to 40 feet long. Picnic tables and fire grills are provided. Drinking water, vault toilets and firewood are available. A camp host is on-site. Some facilities are wheelchair accessible. Leashed pets are permitted.

Reservations, fees: Reservations are accepted at 877/444-6777 or www.recreation.gov ($10 reservation fee). Sites are $15 per night, double sites are $34 per night, $5 per extra vehicle per night. Open mid-May–mid-September, weather permitting.

Directions: From Vancouver, Washington, take Highway 14 east and drive 50 miles to Carson and the Wind River Highway (County Road 30). Turn left (north) on the Wind River Highway and drive 20 miles to the camp on the right.

Contact: Gifford Pinchot National Forest, Mount Adams Ranger District, 509/395-3400, fax 509/395-3424, www.fs.fed.us.

98 FALLS CREEK HORSE CAMP
🏃 🚲 🛶 🏠 ♿ 🚐 ⛺

Scenic rating: 5

near the Pacific Crest Trail in Gifford Pinchot National Forest

This camp sits at the threshold of a great launch point for hiking, horseback riding, and mountain biking. There are 90 miles of trail for horses and hiking and 40 miles for mountain bikes. The camp is set along Race Track Trail, adjacent to the western border of Indian Heaven Wilderness. A wilderness trailhead is available right at the camp. Although this is a multiple-use campground, note that the sites are small and the turnaround is tight for RVs.

Campsites, facilities: There are six sites for tents or RVs up to 15 feet long. Picnic tables and fire grills are provided. Pit toilets are available. A loading ramp for horses is available. There is no drinking water, and garbage must be packed out. Some facilities are wheelchair accessible. Leashed pets are permitted.

Reservations, fees: Reservations are not accepted. There is no fee. Open mid-June–November.

Directions: From Vancouver, Washington, on I-205, take Highway 14 and drive east for 50 miles to Carson and the Wind River Highway (County Road 30). Turn left (north) on the Wind River Highway and drive 9.5 miles to Forest Road 6517. Continue 1.5 miles to Forest Road 65. Turn left and drive 15 miles to the campground on the left.

Contact: Gifford Pinchot National Forest, Mount Adams Ranger District, 509/395-3400, fax 509/395-3424, www.fs.fed.us.

99 CREST HORSE CAMP

Scenic rating: 6

bordering Big Lava Bed in
Gifford Pinchot National Forest

Crest Horse Camp is a small, primitive, multiple-use camp set near the Pacific Crest Trail, adjacent to the eastern boundary of the Indian Heaven Wilderness. It is an excellent jumping-off spot for wilderness treks with horses or other stock animals. The camp features a forested setting, primarily second-growth Douglas fir. Adjacent to the camp is the Big Lava Bed, a volcanic flow known for its lava tubes and lava tube caves.

Campsites, facilities: There are three sites for tents or RVs up to 16 feet long. Picnic tables and fire pits are provided. A vault toilet is available. A loading ramp and high lines for horses are available. There is no drinking water, and garbage must be packed out. Some facilities are wheelchair accessible. Leashed pets are permitted.

Reservations, fees: Reservations are not accepted. There is no fee. Open mid-May–mid-October, weather permitting.

Directions: From Vancouver, Washington, take Highway 14 east and drive 50 miles to Carson and the Wind River Highway (County Road 30). Turn left (north) and drive nine miles to Forest Road 6517. Turn right (east) on Forest Road 6517 and drive 1.5 miles to

Forest Road 65. Turn left (north) on Forest Road 65 and drive about 10 miles to Forest Road 60. Turn right and drive two miles to the camp on the right.

Contact: Gifford Pinchot National Forest, Mount Adams Ranger District, 509/395-3400, fax 509/395-3424, www.fs.fed.us.

100 GOOSE LAKE

Scenic rating: 8

on Goose Lake in
Gifford Pinchot National Forest

This campground is set along the shore of beautiful Goose Lake at an elevation of 3,200 feet. It can be crowded in summer. Trout fishing and berry picking are available. Adjacent to the camp is the northern edge of Big Lava Bed, a volcanic flow known for its lava tubes and lava tube caves. Though the lake is quite pretty, the camp itself is set well above the lake and is not as nice as the lake. A 5-mph speed limit is enforced on the lake.

Campsites, facilities: There are 18 tent sites and one site for RVs up to 18 feet long. Picnic tables and fire rings are provided. Vault toilets and firewood are available, but there is no drinking water. A camp host is on-site. A boat ramp is nearby. Leashed pets are permitted.

Reservations, fees: Reservations are accepted at 877/444-6777 or www.recreation.gov ($10 reservation fee). Sites are $17 per night, $5 per extra vehicle per night. Open mid-May–mid-September, weather permitting.

Directions: From Vancouver, Washington, on I-205, take Highway 14 east and drive 46 miles to County Road 30/Wind River Road. Turn left and drive six miles to Panther Creek Road and Forest Road 6517. Turn right on Forest Road 6517 and drive 10 miles to a four-way intersection called Four Corners. Turn right on Forest Road 60 and drive 10 miles to the campground on the left.

Contact: Gifford Pinchot National Forest,

CAMPING

Mount Adams Ranger District, 509/395-3400, fax 509/395-3424, www.fs.fed.us.

101 BEAVER

Scenic rating: 7

on the Wind River in
Gifford Pinchot National Forest

This is the closest campground north of Stevenson in the Columbia Gorge. Set along the Wind River at an elevation of 1,100 feet, it features pretty, shaded sites. No fishing is permitted. The campsites are paved, and a large grassy day-use area is nearby. Hiking highlights include two nearby trailheads. Two miles north lies the trailhead for the Trapper Creek Wilderness, with 30 miles of trails, including a loop possibility. Three miles north is the Falls Creek Trail.

Campsites, facilities: There are 24 sites for tents or RVs up to 25 feet long and one group site for up to 40 people. Picnic tables and fire grills are provided. Drinking water, firewood, and flush and vault toilets are available. A camp host is on-site. Some facilities are wheelchair accessible. Leashed pets are permitted.

Reservations, fees: Reservations are accepted and are required for the group site at 877/444-6777 or www.recreation.gov ($10 reservation fee). Sites are $15.60–31.20 per night, $30 per night for double sites, $5 per extra vehicle per night. The group site is $91.75 per night. Open early May–late September.

Directions: From Vancouver, Washington, take Highway 14 east and drive 50 miles to Carson and the Wind River Highway (County Road 30). Turn left (north) and drive 12 miles to the campground entrance (five miles past Stabler) on the left.

Contact: Gifford Pinchot National Forest, Mount Adams Ranger District, 509/395-3400, fax 509/395-3424, www.fs.fed.us.

102 PANTHER CREEK AND HORSE CAMP

Scenic rating: 8

on Panther Creek in
Gifford Pinchot National Forest

This campground is set along Panther Creek in a second-growth forest of Douglas fir and western hemlock, adjacent to an old-growth forest. The sites are well defined, but despite a paved road to the campground and easy parking and access, it gets light use. The camp lies 3.5 miles from the Wind River, an option for those who enjoy fishing, hiking, and horseback riding. The Pacific Crest Trail is accessible from the adjacent Panther Creek Horse Camp. The elevation is 1,000 feet.

Campsites, facilities: There are 33 sites for tents or RVs up to 25 feet long and one equestrian site with a stock loading ramp at the adjacent horse camp. Picnic tables and fire rings are provided. Drinking water, pit toilets, garbage bins, and firewood are available. A camp host is on-site. Some facilities are wheelchair accessible. Leashed pets are permitted.

Reservations, fees: Reserve at 877/444-6777 or www.recreation.gov ($10 reservation fee). Sites are $15–34 per night, $5 per extra vehicle per night. Open mid-May–mid-September.

Directions: From Vancouver, Washington, take Highway 14 east and drive 50 miles to Carson and the Wind River Highway (County Road 30). Turn north and drive nine miles to Forest Road 6517 (just past Stabler). Turn right (east) on Forest Road 6517 and drive 1.5 miles to the campground entrance road on the right.

Contact: Gifford Pinchot National Forest, Mount Adams Ranger District, 509/395-3400, fax 509/395-3424, www.fs.fed.us.

103 OKLAHOMA
🛶 🏕 ♿ 🚐 ⛺

Scenic rating: 7

on the Little White Salmon River in
Gifford Pinchot National Forest

Pretty Oklahoma campground is set along
the Little White Salmon River at an elevation
of 1,700 feet. Fishing can be excellent in this
area and the river is stocked in the spring with
rainbow trout. The camp gets light use. It features some open meadow but is generally flat.
Close to the Columbia River Gorge, it features
paved road all the way into the campground
and easy RV parking. As to why they named
the camp Oklahoma, who knows? If you do,
drop me a line.
Campsites, facilities: There are 23 sites for
tents or RVs up to 40 feet long. Drinking
water, fire rings, and picnic tables are provided. Vault toilets are available. Some facilities are wheelchair accessible. Leashed pets
are permitted.
Reservations, fees: Reservations are accepted
at 877/444-6777 or www.recreation.gov ($10
reservation fee). Sites are $15–17 per night,
$5 per night for each additional vehicle.
Open mid-May–mid-September, weather
permitting.
Directions: From White Salmon, take N. Main
Avenue to E. Jewett Boulevard. Turn left on E.
Jewett Boulevard and drive 0.5 mile to SE 6th
Avenue/Dock Grade Road. Turn right on SE
6th Avenue/Dock Grade Road and drive 0.8
mile to Lewis and Clark Highway/WA-14W.
Turn right on Lewis and Clark Highway/WA-
14W and drive 1.5 miles to Cook Underwood
Road. Turn right on Cook Underwood Road
and drive 8.3 miles to Willard Road. Turn
right on Willard Road and drive two miles
to Oklahoma Road. Turn right on Oklahoma
Road and drive five miles to National Forest
Development Road 18/Oklahoma Road. Turn
right on National Forest Development Road
18/Oklahoma Road and drive three miles to
the campground on the left.

Alternately, From Hood River, Oregon,
drive north on Highway 35 for one mile over
the Columbia River to Highway 14. Turn left
on Highway 14 and drive about five miles to
Cook and County Road 1800. Turn right
(north) and drive 14 miles (becomes Cook-
Underwood Road, then Willard Road, then
Oklahoma Road) to the campground entrance
at the end of the paved road.
Contact: Gifford Pinchot National Forest,
Mount Adams Ranger District, 509/395-
3400, fax 509/395-3424, www.fs.fed.us.

104 MOSS CREEK
🛶 🏕 ♿ 🚐 ⛺

Scenic rating: 7

on the Little White Salmon River in
Gifford Pinchot National Forest

This campground is set at 1,400 feet elevation,
about one mile from the Little White Salmon
River. Although it's a short distance from Willard and Big Cedars County Park, the camp
gets light use. The river provides good fishing
prospects for trout in the spring, usually with
few other people around. The sites are generally small but are shaded and still functional
for most RVs. The road is paved all the way
to the campground.
Campsites, facilities: There are 18 sites for
tents or RVs up to 32 feet long. Picnic tables
and fire grills are provided. Drinking water,
vault toilets, and firewood are available. A
camp host is available in the summer. Some
facilities are wheelchair accessible. Leashed
pets are permitted.
Reservations, fees: Reservations are accepted at 877/444-6777 or www.recreation.gov
($10 reservation fee). Sites are $17 per night,
and $5 per night for each additional vehicle.
Open mid-May–mid-September, weather
permitting.
Directions: From White Salmon, take N. Main
Avenue to E. Jewett Boulevard. Turn left on E.
Jewett Boulevard and drive 0.5 mile to SE 6th

Avenue/Dock Grade Road. Turn right on SE 6th Avenue/Dock Grade Road and drive 0.8 mile to Lewis and Clark Highway/WA-14W. Turn right on Lewis and Clark Highway/WA-14W and drive 1.5 miles to Cook Underwood Road. Turn right on Cook Underwood Road and drive 8.3 miles to Willard Road. Turn right on Willard Road and drive two miles to Oklahoma Road. Turn right on Oklahoma Road and drive 1.3 miles to the campground on the left.

Alternately, from Hood River, Oregon, drive north on Highway 35 for one mile over the Columbia River to Highway 14. Turn left on Highway 14 and drive about five miles to Cook and County Road 1800. Turn right (north) and drive 10 miles (becomes Cook-Underwood Road, then Willard road, then Oklahoma Road) to the campground entrance on the right.

Contact: Gifford Pinchot National Forest, Mount Adams Ranger District, 509/395-3400, fax 509/395-3424, www.fs.fed.us.

105 COLUMBIA HILLS STATE PARK

🏃 🛶 🚌 🐕 🚐 ⛺

Scenic rating: 10

near the Dalles Dam

You may remember this park by its former name: Horsethief Lake State Park. The 338-acre park boasts 7,500 feet of Columbia River shoreline. It also adjoins the 3,000-acre Dalles Mountain Ranch State Park. Horsethief Lake, created by the Dalles Dam, covers approximately 100 acres and is part of the Columbia River. Horsethief Butte, adjacent to the lake, dominates the skyline. The bloom of lupine and balsamroot in mid-April create stunning views. Rock climbing in the park is popular,

but the river canyon is often windy, especially in late spring and early summer. Most people find the place as a spot to camp while driving along the Columbia River Highway. There are hiking trails and access to both the lake and the Columbia River. The boat speed limit is 5 mph, and anglers can try for trout and bass. Guided tours on weekends feature pictographs and petroglyphs; reservations are required at 509/767-1159.

Campsites, facilities: There are eight sites with partial hookups (15 amps, converters available) for tents or RVs up to 30 feet long, four sites for tents or RVs up to 30 feet long (no hookups), six primitive tent sites, and one hike-in/bike-in site. Picnic tables and fire grills are provided. Drinking water, restrooms with flush toilets and coin showers, firewood, a dump station, a horseshoe pit, and a picnic area are available. A store is within three miles. Boat-launching facilities are located on both the lake and the river. Leashed pets are permitted.

Reservations, fees: Reservations are not accepted. Sites are $19–25 per night, $12 per night for primitive sites and the hike-in/bike-in site, $10 per extra vehicle per night. Open April–late October.

Directions: From Dallesport, drive east on 6th Avenue to Dallesport Road. Turn left on Dallesport Road and drive 2.3 miles to Lewis and Clark Highway/WA-14E. Turn right at Lewis and Clark Highway/WA-14E and drive four miles to the campground on the left.

Alternately, from The Dalles in Oregon, turn north on Highway 197, cross over the Columbia River, and drive four miles to Highway 14. Turn right (east) and drive two miles to Milepost 85 and the park entrance on the right.

Contact: Columbia Hills State Park, 509/767-1159, fax 509/767-4304; state park information, 360/902-8844, www.parks.wa.gov.

WASHINGTON'S COLUMBIA RIVER GORGE HIKING

© SCOTT LEONARD

BEST HIKES

By far the Northwest's tallest point, Mount Rainier

never seems to be far from view. At 14,411 feet, the towering mass of The Mountain looms over life in Puget Sound, southern Washington, and a good chunk of the east side as well. Perhaps because Mount Rainier is such familiar sight, many of the forests and mountains to her south go unnoticed. That's a shame, for the South Cascades of Washington are home to some excellent adventures in waiting. This area not only contains the living outdoor laboratory that is Mount St. Helens, it also has the glaciers and meadows of Mount Adams and Goat Rocks.

First and foremost on the agenda of most visitors to the region is Mount Rainier, since it is, to say the least, the embodiment of hiking in the Evergreen State. From old-growth forest to alpine meadows, from icy glaciers to milky white rivers, Mount Rainier has it all. A total of 26 glaciers grace the slopes of Takhoma (which, in the Puyallup language, means "breast of the milk-white waters"). These glistening masses of ice give birth to opalescent rivers flowing in every direction.

There are several points of access: Route 410 and 123 transect the eastern side of the park, accessing Sunrise (6,400 feet), where great day hikes and longer trips exploring the north and east sides of Mount Rainier begin. Along the south side of the park, Nisqually and Stevens Canyon Roads meet at the glorious high country of Paradise. Again, numerous trails branch out from the visitors center and historic Park Lodge, exploring the meadows and glaciers of the area. Skyline Trail is a mecca for wildflowers. Although the west side of the park is inaccessible by car, Mowich Lake and Carbon River in the northwest corner can still be reached by road, the easiest park access from Seattle.

To the south is the Cascades' most restless sister, Mount St. Helens. Once one of the nation's most majestic mountains, it erupted in a mighty explosion in 1980, drastically altering its figure. Cubic miles of rock and mud slid off the mountain, and many square miles of forest were completely leveled. Today, life around the mountain is making a comeback. Shrubs and wildflowers are taking hold, and trees are even popping up here and there. But the devastation of the eruption is still readily evident. Johnston Ridge Visitor Center is a great stop, with trails leading into the blast zone. Or you can drive right into the blast zone at Windy Ridge Viewpoint, on the east side. Hikes along Plains of Abraham or Meta Lake make for great day trips.

Not to be outdone, the Gifford Pinchot National Forest boasts two beautiful wildernesses. Near White Pass are the snowcapped and rocky peaks of Goat Rocks. Numerous trails access this complex of obsolete volcanoes. Snowgrass Flats and Goat Ridge are the most scenic – and popular – routes into the area. Farther south is Indian Heaven, another group of high peaks and ridges left over from old volcanoes. Thomas Lake and Indian Heaven Trails are great routes to explore the meadows and get good views of Mounts Hood, Adams, St. Helens, and even Rainier.

The rest of the Gifford Pinchot National Forest is crisscrossed by a large network of paved and unpaved roads. Mount Adams stands as Washington's second-tallest peak and enjoys a wealth of trails and campgrounds. Although Round-the-Mountain doesn't actually make it all the way around, it's a great through-hike amongst meadows and waterfalls. Mount Adams is another fun one to climb. Many ridge trails are perfect for those on wheels (check out Langille Ridge, Boundary Trail, or Badger Ridge). Thanks to all the volcanic soil of the South Cascades, huckleberries are a plentiful backcountry harvest; Juniper Ridge, Dark Meadows, and Hidden Lakes are great berry-picking trails. Rounding out the hiking selection is every kid's favorite school field trip: Ape Cave, a long underground lava tube. For water lovers, there's the White Salmon River, a very popular white-water rafting river, and while driving along the Columbia River Gorge, perhaps on your way to hike Beacon Rock, you're sure to notice hundreds of windsurfers on the river near Hood River.

HIKING

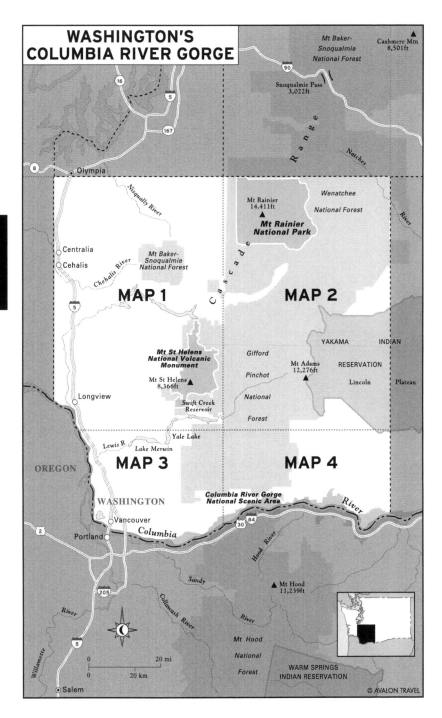

Map 1

Hikes 1-17

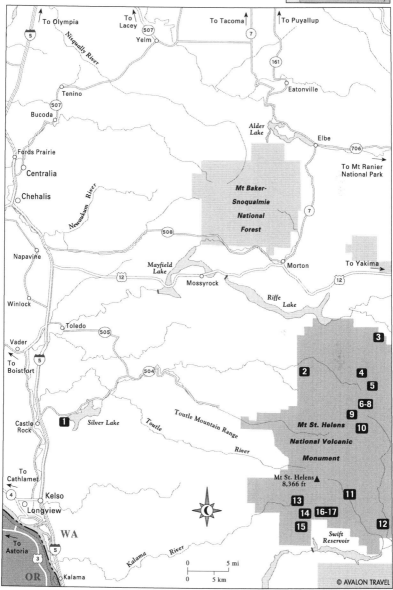

To Olympia
To Lacey
To Tacoma
To Puyallup
Yelm
5
507
7
161
Nisqually River

Tenino
507
Bucoda
Eatonville

Alder Lake
Elbe
706
To Mt Ranier National Park

Fords Prairie
Centralia
Chehalis

Mt Baker-Snoqualmie National Forest

Newaukum River
508
7

Napavine
Mayfield Lake
12
Mossyrock
Morton
To Yakima
12

Winlock
Riffe Lake

Toledo
505
Vader
To Boistfort
5

504

Castle Rock
Silver Lake
Toutle
Toutle Mountain Range
River

Mt St. Helens National Volcanic Monument

Mt St. Helens 8,366 ft

To Cathlamet
4
Kelso
Longview

WA

To Astoria
3
5
Kalama River
Kalama

OR

Swift Reservoir

0   5 mi
0   5 km

© AVALON TRAVEL

1 **2** **3** **4** **5** **6-8** **9** **10** **11** **12** **13** **14** **15** **16-17** **1**

HIKING

Map 2

Hikes 18-110

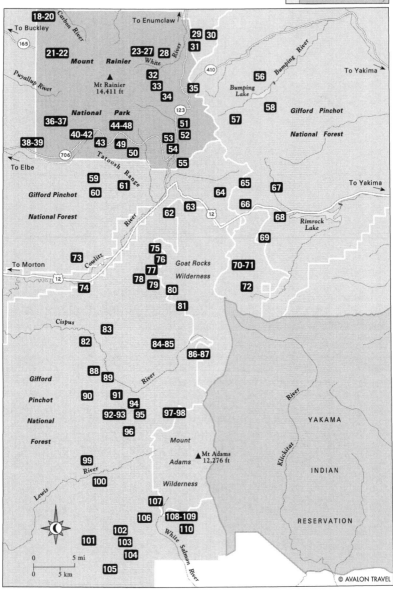

Map 3

Hikes 111–112

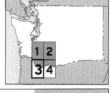

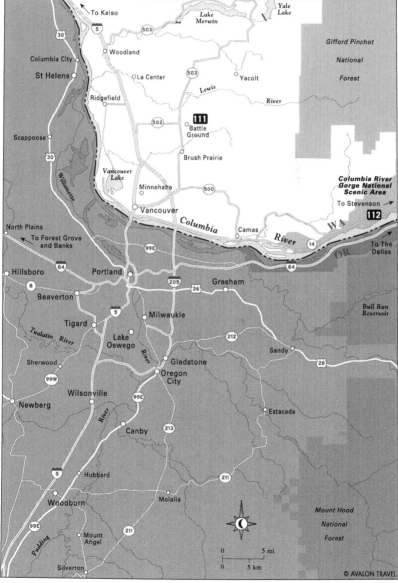

Map 4

Hikes 113-119

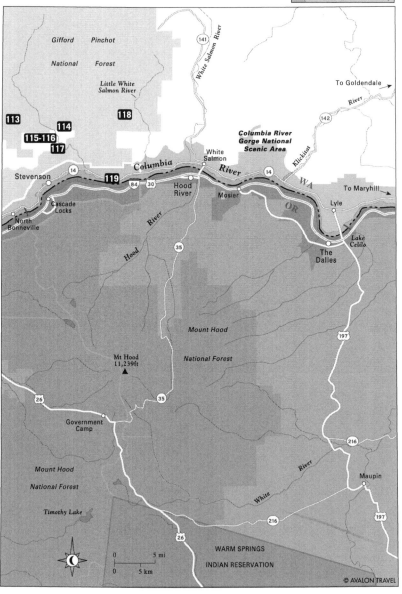

1 SILVER LAKE
1.0 mi/0.5 hr

east of Castle Rock in Silver Lake State Park

The quick, one-mile loop of Silver Lake Trail is a great leg stretcher for folks hitting up the Silver Lake Visitor Center. The trail delves into the growing wetlands that in turn are slowly shrinking Silver Lake. The lake itself was formed by lava flows more than 2,000 years ago and is now on its last legs. Although the outlook may not be good for the lake, wildlife is abundant around the lake. This is a favorite winter haunt for deer and elk, while spring and fall bring loads of migrating waterfowl. On clear days, Mount St. Helens is visible across Silver Lake. The trail is barrier free and accessible to wheelchairs.

User Groups: Hikers and leashed dogs. No horses or mountain bikes are allowed. The trail is wheelchair accessible.

Permits: This trail is accessible year-round. A federal Northwest Forest Pass is not required to park here.

Maps: For a topographic map, ask the USGS for Silver Lake.

Directions: From Castle Rock, drive east 5 miles on Highway 504 to Silver Lake Mount St. Helens Visitor Center. The trailhead is on the south side of the visitors center.

Contact: Gifford Pinchot National Forest, Mount St. Helens National Volcanic Monument, 42218 Yale Bridge Rd., Amboy, WA 98601, 360/449-7871.

2 COLDWATER LAKE
5.5 mi/3.0 hr

east of Castle Rock in Mount St. Helens National Volcanic Monument of Gifford Pinchot National Forest

Hikers along the shores of Coldwater Lake can thank the 1980 eruption of Mount St. Helens for the trail they're enjoying. That's because before the blast, there was no Coldwater Lake. Massive amounts of mud and debris rushed down from the erupting volcano and created a large natural dam on Coldwater Creek, slowly filling up to become Coldwater Lake.

Coldwater Lake Trail follows the shores of this lake before climbing abruptly to the ridge above. The trail is easy to reach, beginning at the Coldwater Ridge Visitor Center. The trail follows the shores, now regenerating with small shrubs and plants. Although the gray, ashen hillsides look unfit for survival, many species of wildlife are spotted here, including deer, elk, squirrels, and frogs, and trout have been stocked in the lake. The trail hugs the shoreline for nearly 3 miles before climbing steeply. It's best to turn around and enjoy the walk back before the steep ascent.

User Groups: Hikers only. No dogs, horses, or mountain bikes are allowed. No wheelchair access.

Permits: This trail is accessible April–November. A federal Northwest Forest Pass, or an $8.00 day-use pass, is required to park here.

Maps: For a map of Gifford Pinchot National Forest, contact the Outdoor Recreation Information Center at the downtown Seattle REI. For a topographic map, ask Green Trails for No. 364, Mount St. Helens, or ask the USGS for Elk Rock and Spirit Lake West.

Directions: From Castle Rock, drive east 35 miles to the Coldwater Visitor Center in Mount St. Helens National Monument. The signed trailhead appears immediately following the visitors center on the left.

Contact: Gifford Pinchot National Forest, Mount St. Helens National Volcanic Monument, 42218 Yale Bridge Rd., Amboy, WA 98601, 360/449-7871.

HIKING

3 STRAWBERRY MOUNTAIN
12.0 mi/6.0 hr   🏃2 ⛰9

south of Randle in Mount St. Helens National
Volcanic Monument of Gifford Pinchot National Forest

Running south to north along the edge of
Mount St. Helens' blast zone, Strawberry
Mountain tells a great story of the effects of
the 1980 eruption. Strawberry Mountain Trail
rides the crest of the long mountain (which
is more a ridge than a mountain). Along the
western side, entire forests were leveled by a
wave of searing gas and ash. The blast leveled
the trees like blades of grass, leaving them arranged in neat rows. On the eastern side, it's
business as usual. Subalpine meadows filled
with wildflowers now dominate the southern
part of the route, which climbs to a pair of
open peaks.

Strawberry Mountain Trail runs the length
of the ridge, 11 miles in all. The southern trailhead saves a lot of elevation gain and is more
open and scenic. Thus it's the preferred route.
Start at Bear Meadows and hike Boundary
Trail to Strawberry Mountain Trail (0.4 mile).
Turn left and follow Strawberry Mountain
Trail north. Old-growth forest is mixed with
open meadows. A short side trail (2.7 miles)
cuts off to the west and quickly finds an expansive viewpoint. Views of the alpine Mount
Margaret backcountry and the crater within
Mount St. Helens are terrific. The trail continues into open meadows of heather and lupine
(5 miles). It's a good time to turn around and
retrace your steps to the car when you've had
your fill of views. Don't expect to find any
water along this high route.

User Groups: Hikers, leashed dogs, horses, and
mountain bikes. No wheelchair access.

Permits: This trail is accessible June–October.
A federal Northwest Forest Pass is not required
to park here.

Maps: For a map of Gifford Pinchot National
Forest, contact the Outdoor Recreation Information Center at the downtown Seattle REI.

For a topographic map, ask Green Trails for
No. 332, Spirit Lake, or ask the USGS for
Cowlitz Falls and Vanson Peak.

Directions: From Randle, drive south 1 mile
on Highway 131 to Forest Service Road 25.
Stay to the right and drive 19 miles to Forest
Service Road 99. Turn right and drive 6 miles
to Bear Meadow Trailhead. The trail starts on
the north side of Road 99.

Contact: Gifford Pinchot National Forest,
Mount St. Helens National Volcanic Monument, 42218 NE Yale Bridge Rd., Amboy, WA
98601, 360/449-7871.

4 QUARTZ CREEK BIG TREES
0.5 mi/0.5 hr   🏃1 ⛰9

southwest of Randle in Gifford Pinchot National Forest

So close to such devastated landscape, it's
amazing to see what much of the forest near
Mount St. Helens previously looked like.
Not far from the blast zone, Quartz Creek
Big Trees Trail is a short loop into an ancient
forest of Douglas fir, western hemlock, and
western red cedar. Mosses and ferns blanket
every branch and inch of ground, a moist
contrast to the barren landscapes just a few
miles away over the ridge. Quartz Creek Big
Trees Trail is flat, level, and barrier free, perfect for hikers of all ages and abilities. The
trail makes a short 0.5-mile loop within this
old-growth forest.

User Groups: Hikers and leashed dogs. No
horses or mountain bikes are allowed. The
trail is wheelchair accessible.

Permits: This trail is accessible year-round.
A federal Northwest Forest Pass is required
to park here.

Maps: For a map of Gifford Pinchot National
Forest, contact the Outdoor Recreation Information Center at the downtown Seattle REI.
For a topographic map, ask Green Trails for
No. 332, Spirit Lake, or ask the USGS for
Cowlitz Falls.

HIKING

Directions: From Randle, drive south 1 mile on Highway 131 to Forest Service Road 25. Stay to the right and drive 8 miles to Forest Service Road 26. Turn right and drive 8 miles to Forest Service Road 2608. Turn left and drive 1.5 miles to the signed trailhead on the right.

Contact: Gifford Pinchot National Forest, Cowlitz Valley Ranger Station, 10024 U.S. 12, Randle, WA 98377, 360/497-1100.

5 GOAT MOUNTAIN
8.0 mi/5.0 hr

north of Mount St. Helens in Gifford Pinchot National Forest

Situated 12 miles north of Mount St. Helens (as the crow flies), Goat Mountain managed to escape much of the eruption's devastating impact. Thank goodness, because Goat Mountain is a subalpine wonderland. Covered in open meadows, this rocky ridge provides great views of the eruption's impact to the south. Goat Mountain is an excellent way to see the altered landscape yet still enjoy a hike among lush meadows.

Goat Mountain Trail climbs from Ryan Lake, zigzaging in and out of affected forest, now a graveyard of standing dead trees. The trail reaches the ridge (1.5 miles) and navigates a mix of meadows and rocky bluffs, each awash in wildflowers (bear grass, lupine, spirea, and stonecrop, to name a few). The towering slopes of Mount Margaret loom from the south.

Goat Mountain Trail traverses the ridge for three spectacular miles, eventually dropping to Deadman Lake (4.8 miles) and on to Vanson Lake (8.1 miles). Unless you're looking for a long hike or tough climb back, the best turnaround is before the trail drops to Deadman Lake. You'll see that Goat Mountain is an appropriate name. Fluffy white goats are a common sight, scrambling along the rocky cliffs.

User Groups: Hikers, leashed dogs, horses, and mountain bikes. No wheelchair access.

Permits: This trail is accessible June–September. A federal Northwest Forest Pass is not required to park here.

Maps: For a map of Gifford Pinchot National Forest, contact the Outdoor Recreation Information Center at the downtown Seattle REI. For a topographic map, ask Green Trails for No. 332, Spirit Lake, or ask the USGS for Cowlitz Falls and Vanson Peak.

Directions: From Randle, drive south 1 mile on Highway 131 to Forest Service Road 25. Stay to the right and drive 8 miles to Forest Service Road 26. Turn right and drive 14 miles to Forest Service Road 2612. Turn right and drive 0.5 mile to the trailhead on the right.

Contact: Gifford Pinchot National Forest, Mount St. Helens National Volcanic Monument, 42218 NE Yale Bridge Rd., Amboy, WA 98601, 360/449-7871.

6 BOUNDARY, WEST END
12.0 mi/5.0-6.0 hr

in Mount St. Helens National Volcanic Monument

This western end of Boundary Trail is the most glorious stretch of trail in Mount St. Helens National Monument. Every step is better than the one before it, as you experience beautiful meadows of wildflowers with expansive views of the eruption's impact. This section of Boundary Trail runs 13.8 miles (one-way) between Johnston Ridge Observatory and Norway Pass, near Winder Ridge Viewpoint. A car-drop between these two points involves hundreds of miles of driving and is hardly worthwhile. No worries, because each trailhead offers access to a great peak in about 12 miles.

Visitors to Johnston Ridge Observatory can hike to Coldwater Peak (12.2 miles round-trip), an up-close look at the crater. From the observatory, hike east on Boundary Trail above sprawling plains of ash and mud. The

HIKING

trail heads north and climbs above St. Helens Lake, a site of total devastation. A side trail leads to the summit (elevation 5,727 feet).

From Forest Service Road 99, a hike to Mount Margaret (11.6 miles round-trip) makes for an incredible trip through alpine meadows and views of sparkling lakes. From Norway Pass Trailhead, hike west on Boundary Trail to Norway Pass (2.2 miles). The trail travels through the heart of the blast zone, but lush meadows survived to the north. A side trail leads to Margaret's summit.

Both hikes are exposed and dry, with no water to be found. They also have rocky sections along steep slopes; care is necessary at times.

User Groups: Hikers only. No dogs, horses, or mountain bikes are allowed. No wheelchair access.

Permits: This trail is accessible June–mid-October. A federal Northwest Forest Pass is required to park here.

Maps: For a map of Gifford Pinchot National Forest, contact the Outdoor Recreation Information Center at the downtown Seattle REI. For a topographic map, ask Green Trails for No. 332, Spirit Lake, or ask the USGS for Spirit Lake West and Spirit Lake East.

Directions: From Randle, drive south 1 mile on Highway 131 to Forest Service Road 25. Stay to the right and drive 19 miles to Forest Service Road 99. Turn right and drive 11 miles to Forest Service Road 26. Turn right and drive 1.5 miles to Norway Pass Trailhead.

Contact: Gifford Pinchot National Forest, Mount St. Helens National Volcanic Monument, 42218 NE Yale Bridge Rd., Amboy, WA 98601, 360/449-7871.

❼ BOUNDARY TRAIL
27.8 mi one-way/3.0 days

across Gifford Pinchot National Forest

Boundary Trail is a long through-hike traversing Gifford Pinchot National Forest west

to east. The trail previously began near the Mount Margaret backcountry, but the 1980 eruption destroyed the western trailhead and made the western 6 miles an adventuresome and entirely new out-and-back hike (see previous listing). The eastern contiguous section of Boundary Trail gets in miles of meadow rambling and even some old-growth shade. Views of surrounding valleys and peaks are nonstop in the middle segment.

The best place to start is Elk Pass, an easy access on Forest Service Road 25. From here, Boundary Trail travels alternating patches of old-growth and clear-cuts for about 7 miles. The trail gets interesting as it skirts Badger and Craggy Peaks, where meadows and views reign supreme. The trail leads to the southern ends of Langille and Juniper Ridges, an exposed and beautiful 11-mile segment. The remainder of the trail (9 miles) sticks mostly to forest, ending at Council Lake.

Many so-called feeder trails offer access to Boundary Trail, making numerous segments of the route accessible for day hikes. Water is often scarce along the route, so plan well and bring your full capacity. Campsites are rarely designated; low-impact cross-country camping is necessary. Although few hikers complete the whole trip in one go, occasional crowds are likely because of the many access points. Also, be ready for noisy motorcycles on summer weekends.

User Groups: Hikers, leashed dogs, horses, mountain bikes, and motorcycles. No wheelchair access.

Permits: This trail is accessible July–mid-October. A federal Northwest Forest Pass is required to park at the trailheads.

Maps: For a map of Gifford Pinchot National Forest, contact the Outdoor Recreation Information Center at the downtown Seattle REI. For a topographic map, ask Green Trails for No. 332, Spirit Lake, No. 333, McCoy Peak, and No. 334, Blue Lake, or ask the USGS for French Butte, McCoy, Spirit Lake East, and Spirit Lake West.

Directions: From Randle, drive south 1 mile

on Highway 131 to Forest Service Road 25. Stay to the right and drive 23 miles to the well-signed trailhead.

Contact: Gifford Pinchot National Forest, Cowlitz Valley Ranger Station, 10024 U.S. 12, Randle, WA 98377, 360/497-1100.

8 META LAKE
0.5 mi/0.5 hr

northeast of Mount St. Helens in Mount St. Helens National Volcanic Monument in Gifford Pinchot National Forest

Lying behind a small ridge, Meta Lake received less than a death blow from Mount St. Helens' eruption despite being squarely in the blast zone. It helped that a snowpack lingered around the still-frozen lake, providing plants and trees a modest insulation from the searing heat and gas. With such protection in place, Meta Lake survived the blast and today provides a great example of the regeneration of life after the 1980 eruption.

Meta Lake Trail makes a quick trip to the lake (just 0.25 mile one-way). Several interpretive signs line the route, filling visitors in on the ability of life to survive and thrive here. Firs and hemlocks are once again creating a forest among blown-down logs, with lots of huckleberry bushes filling in the holes. Brook trout are still found in the lake, as are salamanders and frogs. The path is paved and is one of the best in the area for wheelchair access.

User Groups: Hikers only. No dogs, horses, or mountain bikes are allowed. The trail is wheelchair accessible.

Permits: This trail is accessible June–September. A federal Northwest Forest Pass is required to park here.

Maps: For a map of Gifford Pinchot National Forest, contact the Outdoor Recreation Information Center at the downtown Seattle REI. For a topographic map, ask Green Trails for No. 332, Spirit Lake, or ask the USGS for Spirit Lake East.

Directions: From Randle, drive south 1 mile on Highway 131 to Forest Service Road 25. Stay to the right and drive 19 miles to Forest Service Road 99. Turn right and drive 11.5 miles to the signed trailhead on the right.

Contact: Gifford Pinchot National Forest, Mount St. Helens National Volcanic Monument, 42218 NE Yale Bridge Rd., Amboy, WA 98601, 360/449-7871.

9 HARMONY FALLS
2.0 mi/1.5 hr

northeast of Mount St. Helens in Mount St. Helens National Volcanic Monument in Gifford Pinchot National Forest

Before the 1980 eruption of Mount St. Helens, Spirit Lake was home to houses and lodges, campgrounds, and an old, lush forest. All of that was quickly destroyed by the eruption, which left behind a surreal landscape. Harmony Trail passes right through this devastated area down to Spirit Lake, surveying the enormously changed scene.

Harmony Trail provides the only access to Spirit Lake, reaching the lakeshore where Harmony Falls drops in. The trail drops 600 feet to the lake, a considerable climb out. Bare trees lie scattered on the hillsides in neat rows, leveled by the searing gases of the eruption. Part of Spirit Lake is covered by dead trees, neatly arranged in the northern arm. On the hillsides, now covered in fine ash, small plants and shrubs work hard to revegetate the land. With a significant chunk of the mountain now lying at the bottom of the lake, the shores of Spirit Lake were raised 200 feet. This significantly enlarged the lake and cut off much of the height of Harmony Falls. Harmony Trail is a great way to experience one of the most affected areas of the blast zone.

User Groups: Hikers only, horses, and mountain bikes are allowed. No wheelchair access.

HIKING

© SCOTT LEONARD

Mount Rainier stands in the distance, with Spirit Lake in the foreground.

Permits: This trail is accessible June–September. A federal Northwest Forest Pass is required to park here.

Maps: For a map of Gifford Pinchot National Forest, contact the Outdoor Recreation Information Center at the downtown Seattle REI. For a topographic map, ask Green Trails for No. 332, Spirit Lake, or ask the USGS for Spirit Lake West and Spirit Lake East.

Directions: From Randle, drive south 1 mile on Highway 131 to Forest Service Road 25. Stay to the right and drive 19 miles to Forest Service Road 99. Turn right and drive 16 miles to the signed trailhead on the right.

Contact: Gifford Pinchot National Forest, Mount St. Helens National Volcanic Monument, 42218 NE Yale Bridge Rd., Amboy, WA 98601, 360/449-7871.

🔟 PLAINS OF ABRAHAM
9.0 mi/5.0 hr   🏃2 ⛰10

south of Randle in Mount St. Helens National Volcanic Monument in Gifford National Forest

Other than Loowit Trail, a round-the-mountain trek, no route gets closer to Mount St. Helens than Abraham Trail. Even better, Plains of Abraham makes a loop, with only 2 miles of trail hiked twice. The route, shaped like a lasso, spends its entirety within the blast zone, a barren landscape leveled by the 1980 eruption. During summer, when wildflowers speckle the slopes with color, this is undoubtedly the best option for a longer day hike near Mount St. Helens.

The route begins at popular Windy Ridge Viewpoint and follows the ridge on Truman Trail. Turn left on Abraham Trail (1.7 miles) as the path rounds five narrow draws (3 miles) to Loowit Trail (4 miles), within the Plains of Abraham. The plains are a wide, barren landscape repeatedly pounded by mud and landslides. Other than the smallest of plants and mosses, life is absent. It's an eerie but impressive scene.

Turn right on Loowit Trail to climb to Windy Pass (5 miles), an appropriate name on most days. The loop returns to the car via Truman Trail (6 miles) and Windy Ridge. July and August are great months to hike Abraham Trail, when wildflowers are at their peak. Water and shade are not found at any time along the trail, so consider packing extra water and sunscreen.

User Groups: Hikers only. No dogs, horses, or mountain bikes are allowed. No wheelchair access.

Permits: This trail is accessible June–October. A federal Northwest Forest Pass is required to park here.

Maps: For a map of Gifford Pinchot National Forest, contact the Outdoor Recreation Information Center at the downtown Seattle REI. For a topographic map, ask Green Trails for No. 364S, Mount St. Helens NW, or ask the USGS for Spirit Lake East.

Directions: From Randle, drive south 1 mile on Highway 131 to Forest Service Road 25. Stay to the right and drive 19 miles to Forest Service Road 99. Turn right and drive to Windy Ridge Trailhead at road's end.

Contact: Gifford Pinchot National Forest, Mount St. Helens National Volcanic Monument, 42218 NE Yale Bridge Rd., Amboy, WA 98601, 360/449-7871.

11 LAVA CANYON
2.0 mi/1.5 hr

northeast of Cougar in Mount St. Helens National Volcanic Monument in Gifford Pinchot National Forest

Spared from the blast zone of the 1980 eruption, Sheep Canyon nonetheless felt a few effects. The eruption created a raging torrent of mud and debris that gushed through the narrow gorge. The violent flow scoured the canyon bottom clean, leaving only barren bedrock for the Muddy River. That was a good thing, as it created a colorful river canyon with numerous pools and cascades. The trail through the gorge is one of the coolest places in Mount St. Helens National Volcanic Monument.

The first section of Lava Canyon Trail descends a steep series of switchbacks to several views of the canyon (0.5 mile). Platforms are in place with interpretive signs. This section is paved and accessible to wheelchairs, although it's very steep and assistance is usually needed. From here, a signed loop crosses the river via a bridge and follows the river down. This section of river has many pools and channels carved

into the bedrock. The loop crosses back over the river via a high suspension bridge (1 mile). Although Lava Canyon Trail continues to a lower trailhead (2.5 miles), the lower suspension bridge marks a good place to turn around.

User Groups: Hikers and leashed dogs. No horses or mountain bikes are allowed. Part of the trail is wheelchair accessible (for the first 0.5 mile, down to a viewpoint of the canyon, although very steep).

Permits: This trail is accessible June –November. A federal Northwest Forest Pass is required to park here.

Maps: For a map of Gifford Pinchot National Forest, contact the Outdoor Recreation Information Center at the downtown Seattle REI. For a topographic map, ask Green Trails for No. 364, Mount St. Helens, or ask the USGS for Smith Creek Butte.

Directions: From Vancouver, drive north on I-5 to Highway 503 (Woodland, exit 21). Drive east 35 miles to Forest Service Road 83. Turn left and drive 10 miles to the signed trailhead at road's end.

Contact: Gifford Pinchot National Forest, Mount St. Helens National Volcanic Monument, 42218 NE Yale Bridge Rd., Amboy, WA 98601, 360/449-7871.

12 CEDAR FLATS
1.0 mi/0.5 hr

north of Cougar in Gifford Pinchot National Forest

BEST (

Quick and easy, Cedar Flats Trail ventures through Southern Washington's most impressive old-growth forest. It's easy to imagine you've been transported to the Olympic Peninsula when wandering among these giants. Douglas fir, western hemlock, and western red cedar create a forest of immense proportions. The area is preserved as part of Cedar Flats Natural Area, which was set aside in the 1940s. This area serves as important, undisturbed habitat for a variety of animals. Herds of elk winter in this area and deer are year-round inhabitants. Cedar Flats Trail makes a short and flat loop, arranged like a lasso, making this a great walk for families and hikers who prefer to avoid difficult hikes. Part of the trail nears the steep cliffs overlooking the Muddy River (inaccessible from the trail). The trail can be easily walked in a half hour, but it's well worth spending an afternoon in this peaceful setting.

User Groups: Hikers and leashed dogs. No horses or mountain bikes are allowed. No wheelchair access.

Permits: This trail is accessible year-round. A federal Northwest Forest Pass is required to park here.

Maps: For a map of Gifford Pinchot National Forest, contact the Outdoor Recreation Information Center at the downtown Seattle REI. For a topographic map, ask Green Trails for No. 364, Mount St. Helens, or ask the USGS for Cedar Flat.

Directions: From Cougar, drive east on Highway 503 (Forest Service Road 90) to Forest Service Road 25, at Pine Creek Information Station. Turn left and drive 6 miles to the trailhead on the right.

Contact: Gifford Pinchot National Forest, Mount St. Helens National Volcanic Monument, 42218 NE Yale Bridge Rd., Amboy, WA 98601, 360/449-7871.

13 SHEEP CANYON
4.4 mi/3.0 hr

north of Cougar in Mount St. Helens National Volcanic Monument of Gifford Pinchot National Forest

Not all of Mount St. Helens' destruction in May 1980 was the result of searing gas and ash. Areas not directly in the line of fire were instead affected by torrents of mud, water, and debris. That's what happened along Sheep Creek, a muddy, ashen stream running

through a steep canyon. The trail provides access to Loowit Trail, the route running around the mountain, home to impressive views of the flattened volcano.

Sheep Canyon Trail quickly leaves a patch of clear-cut land to enter an old-growth forest of noble fir. The route climbs much of its length, gaining more than 1,400 feet, rendering the shady, old forest a welcome friend. The highlight of the trail is Sheep Canyon, where Sheep Creek flows between vertical rock walls. Raging mudflows scoured the bottom of the canyon, leaving debris scattered over bare bedrock. Finally, the trail climbs harshly to Loowit Trail, where hikers can add extra miles by exploring to the north or south.

User Groups: Hikers and leashed dogs. No horses or mountain bikes are allowed. No wheelchair access.

Permits: This trail is accessible June–October. A federal Northwest Forest Pass is required to park here.

Maps: For a map of Gifford Pinchot National Forest, contact the Outdoor Recreation Information Center at the downtown Seattle REI. For a topographic map, ask the USGS for Mount St. Helens and Goat Mountain.

Directions: From Vancouver, drive north on I-5 to Highway 503 (Woodland, exit 21). Drive east 35 miles to Forest Service Road 83. Turn left and drive 3.5 miles to Forest Service Road 81. Turn left and drive to Forest Service Road 8123. Turn right and drive to the signed trailhead at road's end.

Contact: Gifford Pinchot National Forest, Mount St. Helens National Volcanic Monument, 42218 NE Yale Bridge Rd., Amboy, WA 98601, 360/449-7871.

14 APE CAVE

2.5 mi/3.0 hr

north of Cougar in Mount St. Helens National
Volcanic Monument in Gifford Pinchot
National Forest

BEST (

The name Ape Cave conjures images of Sasquatch huddled in a narrow underground passage, hiding from people and their cameras. Sorry to disappoint. The caves were first explored by members of a local outdoors club, "The Apes," hence the name. Ape Cave is a long, large cave (known as a lava tube) naturally carved into the basalt by lava and water through thousands of years. Explored by thousands of visitors each year (including busloads of schoolchildren), these deep, pitch-black tunnels make for an eerie and memorable experience.

From the main entrance, the cave heads in two directions. The Lower Passage is easier and shorter. It delves about 0.7 mile past a number of formations, including a Lava Ball and mudflow floor. The Upper Passage is 1.3 miles long underground with a 1.3-mile trail aboveground that returns to the trailhead. Upper Passage is more challenging, with segments that climb over rock piles and a small lava ledge. Near the upper exit, a large hole in the ceiling of the cave creates a natural skylight.

Be prepared for a chilly hike. Year-round temperature is a steady 42°F. Imagine that, 85 outside but 42 inside! Two sources of light are recommended, and headlamps don't count. The deep darkness of the caves requires very strong flashlights or, preferably, large gas lanterns. Parts of the upper passage are rocky, so sturdy shoes and pants are also recommended.

User Groups: Hikers only. No dogs, horses, or mountain bikes are allowed. Wheelchair accessible.

Permits: This trail is accessible year-round. A federal Northwest Forest Pass is required to park here.

Maps: For a map of Gifford Pinchot National Forest, contact the Outdoor Recreation Information Center at the downtown Seattle REI. For a topographic map, ask Green Trails for No. 364, Mount St. Helens, or ask the USGS for Mount Mitchell.

Directions: From Vancouver, drive north on I-5 to Highway 503 (Woodland, exit 21). Drive east 35 miles to Forest Service Road 83. Turn left and drive 2 miles to Forest Service Road 8303. Turn left and drive 1.5 miles to the signed trailhead on the right.

Contact: Gifford Pinchot National Forest, Mount St. Helens National Volcanic Monument, 42218 NE Yale Bridge Rd., Amboy, WA 98601, 360/449-7871.

15 TRAIL OF TWO FORESTS

0.3 mi/0.5 hr

northeast of Cougar in Mount St. Helens
National Volcanic Monument in Gifford
Pinchot National Forest

Trail of Two Forests is a quick nature loop into one of the most unlikely natural phenomena in the Northwest. Nearly two millennia ago, Mount St. Helens sent a wave of molten lava down her south flank. This wave of lava consumed everything in its path before eventually cooling and stopping. Trail of Two Forests is perfectly situated near the bottom of the flow, where the lava still moved but was not hot enough to immediately destroy trees. Here, lava cooled around the trees, which eventually decomposed and left small tunnels, caves, and pits as a testament to the old forest. The second of the two forests is the one that stands today. Interpretive signs do a great job of explaining the story in depth. Conveniently, boardwalk lines the entire route, making Trail of Two Forests accessible to wheelchairs. The boardwalk also protects the fragile forest ground, so please stay on the trail. The one chance visitors have to get off-trail is a chance to crawl

HIKING

through a tunnel, or lava tube, nearly 30 feet long. It's a trip!

User Groups: Hikers and leashed dogs. No horses or mountain bikes are allowed. Wheelchair accessible.

Permits: This trail is accessible March–November. A federal Northwest Forest Pass is required to park here.

Maps: For a map of Gifford Pinchot National Forest, contact the Outdoor Recreation Information Center at the downtown Seattle REI. For a topographic map, ask Green Trails for No. 364, Mount St. Helens, or ask the USGS for Mount Mitchell.

Directions: From Vancouver, drive north on I-5 to Highway 503 (Woodland, exit 21). Drive east 35 miles to Forest Service Road 83. Turn left and drive 2 miles to Forest Service Road 8303. Turn left and drive 0.1 mile to the signed trailhead on the left.

Contact: Gifford Pinchot National Forest, Mount St. Helens National Volcanic Monument, 42218 NE Yale Bridge Rd., Amboy, WA 98601, 360/449-7871.

16 JUNE LAKE
2.8 mi/2.0 hr   👫 2 ⛰ 9

northeast of Cougar in Mount St. Helens National Volcanic Monument in Gifford Pinchot National Forest

June Lake achieves recognition by being the only subalpine lake on the slopes of Mount St. Helens. As the volcano forms a nice, neat cone, few basins are created to host a beautiful lake. Well, that's what Mount St. Helens has done here, nestling a great lake below a cliff of basalt, complete with waterfall. Subalpine forest and meadow ring the lake, which has a sandy beach perfect for summer afternoon lounging.

June Lake Trail gains just 500 feet in 1.4 miles and is ideal for families. It courses its way through young forest with views of a gorge before emerging upon a large field of basalt boulders (1 mile). The trail sticks to

the forest and soon finds June Lake. For a view of Mount St. Helens, hike past the lake a few hundred yards on Loowit Trail. Several campsites are scattered around the lake, and campers are expected to follow strict Leave-No-Trace principles.

User Groups: Hikers, leashed dogs, and mountain bikes are allowed. No horses are allowed. No wheelchair access.

Permits: This trail is accessible May–November. A federal Northwest Forest Pass is required to park here.

Maps: For a map of Gifford Pinchot National Forest, contact the Outdoor Recreation Information Center at the downtown Seattle REI. For a topographic map, ask Green Trails for No. 364S, Mount St. Helens NW, or ask the USGS for Mount St. Helens.

Directions: From Vancouver, drive north on I-5 to Highway 503 (Woodland, exit 21). Drive east 35 miles to Forest Service Road 83. Turn left and drive 6 miles to the signed trailhead on the left.

Contact: Gifford Pinchot National Forest, Mount St. Helens National Volcanic Monument, 42218 NE Yale Bridge Rd., Amboy, WA 98601, 360/449-7871.

17 LOOWIT TRAIL
30.5 mi/3-4 days   👫 3 ⛰ 10

around the mountain in Mount St. Helens National Volcanic Monument in Gifford Pinchot National Forest

Loowit Trail is the grand loop encircling Mount St. Helens. It was an interesting trip before 1980, and the eruption of the volcano turned this trek into an unforgettable outing. Loowit experiences everything imaginable— old-growth forest, alpine meadows, and barren, ravaged landscapes. Compared to Wonderland Trail, elevation changes along the route are modest. Still, many sections of the trail are difficult and rocky.

Loowit Trail has no definite trailhead.

Instead, several feeder trails lead to the 27.7-mile loop. Among these trails are June Lake in the south (1.7 miles one-way), Truman Trail at Windy Ridge (3 miles), and Sheep Canyon on the west side (2.2 miles). Diligent planning is a must before setting out on Loowit Trail. Water sources and campsites are limited throughout the route and often change year to year. The Forest Service suggests that you call ahead to get the current scoop. Finally, be ready for ash, lots and lots of ash. The fine, gray particles will invade everything you own. Bring a coffee filter to tie around your water filter and protect it. Also, take special care with cameras, binoculars, or eyeglasses, all easily damaged by ash.

Loowit Trail is often hiked counterclockwise. From June Lake, the trail climbs beneath the rocky toe of the Worm Flows to Shoestring Glacier, from the barren Plains of Abraham to Loowit Falls and impressive views of the crater. Loowit Trail traverses the blast zone, a real lesson in the magnitude of the destructive blast, before crossing the mud-ravaged Toutle River. Meadow and old-growth forest line the route as it returns to June Lake.

User Groups: Hikers and mountain bikes (not in the blast zone) only. No dogs or horses are allowed. No wheelchair access.

Permits: This trail is accessible June–October. A federal Northwest Forest Pass is required to park here.

Maps: For a map of Gifford Pinchot National Forest, contact the Outdoor Recreation Information Center at the downtown Seattle REI. For a topographic map, ask Green Trails for No. 364S, Mount St. Helens NW, or ask the USGS for Mount St. Helens, Smith Creek Butte, and Goat Mountain.

Directions: From Vancouver, drive north on I-5 to Highway 503 (Woodland, exit 21). Drive east 35 miles to Forest Service Road 83. Turn left and drive 6 miles to the signed trailhead on the left for June Lake (the shortest access on the south side).

Contact: Gifford Pinchot National Forest, Mount St. Helens National Volcanic Monument, 42218 NE Yale Bridge Rd., Amboy, WA 98601, 360/449-7871.

18 GREEN LAKE
9.6 mi/5.0 hr   🥾2 △8

in northwest Mount Rainier National Park

You don't need amnesia to forget about Mount Rainier when hiking the trail to Green Lake. Grabbing your attention from the start are granddaddy Douglas firs and western hemlocks as the hike gets better each step of the way. This hike has been considerably lengthened (by 6 miles) due to the closure of Carbon River Road. The extra 3 miles from the park entrance to the trailhead are easy hiking. The Park Service also allows mountain bikes along the road, making this an outstanding bike-and-hike option on the weekend.

From the old trailhead, the hike wanders beneath giant trees towering over the trail that are estimated to be more than 800 years of age. The trail then climbs alongside Ranger Creek, within earshot but mostly out of sight. A must-see stop is a small side trail to Ranger Falls (4 miles). During the spring snowmelt, this large series of cascades creates a thunderous roar heard throughout the forest. The trail switchbacks 0.5 mile before leveling and crossing the creek. Green Lake sits among pristine forest and a little meadow. Anglers can try their luck here for trout. South of the lake and peeking through a large valley stands Tolmie Peak. Green Lake is a great day hike during the summer but also makes a good snowshoe trek during the winter. Old-growth forest, big waterfalls, and a serene mountain lake—now what was the name of that mountain everyone keeps talking about?

User Groups: Hikers only. No dogs or horses are allowed. Mountain bikes are permitted on the Carbon River Road, the first 3 miles of the hike. No wheelchair access.

Permits: This area is usually accessible April–November. A National Parks Pass is required to enter the park.

Maps: For a map of Mount Rainier National Park, contact the Outdoor Recreation Information Center at the downtown Seattle REI. For a topographic map, ask Green Trails for No. 269, Mount Rainier West, or ask the USGS for Mowich Lake.

Directions: From Tacoma, drive east on Highway 410 to Buckley. Turn south on Highway 165 and drive 14 miles to Carbon River Road. Turn left and drive 8 miles to Carbon River Entrance Station, where Carbon River Road is closed to motor vehicles.

Contact: Mount Rainier National Park, Longmire Wilderness Information Center, Tahoma Woods, Star Route, Ashford, WA 98304, 360/569-4453.

19 WINDY GAP

23.0-27.0 mi/2-3 days

in northern Mount Rainier National Park

Mount Rainier grabs the most attention (it stands more than 14,000 feet tall, after all). But the park holds miles of amazing terrain, tucked away from the mountain's view. Windy Gap is a perfect example. The enjoyable trail climbs into a high-country playground of meadows and rocky peaks, with plenty to see and do. Hikes to Lake James and the Natural Bridge (a large rock arch) start here. Unfortunately, flooding closed a section of the access road, adding a total of 10 extra road miles, which is easy hiking and is also open to mountain bikes. Fortunately, Windy Gap features two great backcountry camps for overnight visits.

First, hike or bike 5 miles along the closed Carbon River Road to Ipsut Creek Campground. Here, the trail begins and joins Wonderland Trail (5.5 miles), eventually leaving to cross the Carbon River (7.4 miles). Turn left and do the switchback shuffle up Northern Loop Trail to Windy Gap. The sighting of colorful Yellowstone Cliffs (10.1 miles) signals the arrival of parkland meadows, reflective tarns, and craggy horizons. Boulder-strewn Windy Gap (11.4 miles), a good place to turn around, is truly a blustery experience, and mountain goats roam the surrounding ridges.

Beyond Windy Gap, Northern Loop Trail drops 1.5 miles to lightly visited Lake James, clad in subalpine meadows. Beyond Windy Gap 0.25 mile, a signed trail leads to Natural Bridge. Rising out of the forest, the large rock formation seems lost from the sea. After crossing the Carbon, the trail is dry; bring plenty of water. Beautiful backcountry camps are situated at Yellowstone Cliffs and Lake James and require camping permits.

User Groups: Hikers only. No dogs, horses, or mountain bikes are allowed. No wheelchair access.

Permits: This area is usually accessible mid-July–September. A National Parks Pass is required to enter the park. Overnight stays within the national park require backcountry camping permits, which are available at Carbon River Ranger Station.

Maps: For a map of Mount Rainier National Park, contact the Outdoor Recreation Information Center at the downtown Seattle REI. For a topographic map, ask Green Trails for No. 269, Mount Rainier West, and No. 270, Mount Rainier East, or ask the USGS for Mowich Lake and Sunrise.

Directions: From Tacoma, drive east on Highway 410 to Buckley. Turn south on Highway 165 and drive 14 miles to Carbon River Road. Turn left and drive 8 miles to Carbon River Entrance Station, where Carbon River Road is closed to motor vehicles.

Contact: Mount Rainier National Park, Longmire Wilderness Information Center, Tahoma Woods, Star Route, Ashford, WA 98304, 360/569-4453.

20 CARBON GLACIER/ MYSTIC LAKE

25.5 mi/2 days   👣4 ⛰10

north of The Mountain in Mount Rainier National Park

Situated on the famed Wonderland Trail, there isn't a lake closer to Mount Rainier than Mystic Lake. This hike visits a 7-mile stretch of Washington's most esteemed trail is incredibly diverse. It travels through old-growth forest on the Carbon River, past Rainier's lowest and longest glacier, and upward to rocky alpine meadows and a majestic lake. This is one of the park's premier hikes.

The first 5 miles are spent hiking or biking along the now-closed Carbon River Road to Ipsut Campground, the former trailhead. From here, the length of the route follows the Wonderland Trail. The trail starts mildly, cruising through ancient forests. After crossing Carbon River on an impressive suspension bridge (8 miles), however, the trail climbs unrelentingly to Mystic Lake. Somehow, the trail finds a path between Carbon Glacier and the valley wall. Those cracking noises you hear are the glacier giving way to the hot summer sun; walking on the glacier is ill advised without an ice ax and proper training.

Wonderland Trail parts ways with the glacier as it enters Moraine Park (10.5 miles), featuring acres of wildflower meadows. A welcome sight on hot days, Mystic Lake lies just below Mineral Mountain. Although it stands 800 feet above the lake, Mineral Mountain can do little to block Mount Rainier and its ragged Willis Wall. Backcountry camps are situated at Dick Creek (9 miles) and Mystic Lake (12.7 miles); they require permits and are frequented by Wonderland trekkers.

User Groups: Hikers only. No dogs, horses, or mountain bikes are allowed. No wheelchair access.

Permits: This area is usually accessible mid-July–September. A National Parks Pass is required to enter the park. Overnight stays within the national park require backcountry camping permits, which are available at Carbon River Ranger Station.

Maps: For a map of Mount Rainier National Park, contact the Outdoor Recreation Information Center at the downtown Seattle REI. For a topographic map, ask Green Trails for No. 269, Mount Rainier West, or ask the USGS for Mowich Lake.

Directions: From Tacoma, drive east on Highway 410 to Buckley. Turn south on Highway 165 and drive 14 miles to Carbon River Road. Turn left and drive 8 miles to Carbon River Entrance Station, where Carbon River Road is closed to motor vehicles.

Contact: Mount Rainier National Park, Longmire Wilderness Information Center, Tahoma Woods, Star Route, Ashford, WA 98304, 360/569-4453.

21 TOLMIE PEAK LOOKOUT

6.5 mi/3.5 hr   👣2 ⛰10

northwest of Tahoma in Mount Rainier National Park

BEST (

The best job in the United States is a summer spent staffing the Tolmie Peak Lookout. The job description includes: a 3-mile commute through pristine subalpine forest, picturesque Eunice Lake surrounded in parkland meadows, and panoramic views from the office, encompassing The Mountain and miles of national forest. Ready to sign up?

Tolmie Peak Trail begins at Mowich Lake, a spectacular setting itself. The trail leaves the large, forested lake and rises gently to Ipsut Pass (1.5 miles), a junction with Carbon River Trail. Stay to the left and continue climbing to Eunice Lake (2.3 miles), where meadows reach to the lake's edges. The trail then climbs steeply 1 more mile to Tolmie Lookout (elevation 5,939 feet) atop the windswept peak. Mount Rainier is the obvious attraction, but Mount St. Helens and the North Cascades make appearances as well. Talk about your prime picnic spots. If the final steep climb to the lookout sounds unappealing, stopping short at Eunice Lake is a good hike as well. In late July, wildflowers fill the meadows bordering Eunice, and views of Mount Rainier are still to be had.

User Groups: Hikers only. No dogs, horses, or mountain bikes are allowed. No wheelchair access.

Permits: This area is accessible June–October. A National Parks Pass is required to enter the park.

Maps: For a map of Mount Rainier National Park, contact the Outdoor Recreation Information Center at the downtown Seattle REI. For a topographic map, ask Green Trails for No. 269, Mount Rainier West, or ask the USGS for Mowich Lake and Golden Lakes.

Directions: From Tacoma, drive east on Highway 410 to Buckley. Turn south on Highway 165 and drive 14 miles to Carbon River Road junction. Stay to the right on Mowich Lake Road and drive 17 miles to Mowich Lake Campground at road's end. The trailhead is well marked.

Contact: Mount Rainier National Park, Longmire Wilderness Information Center, Tahoma Woods, Star Route, Ashford, WA 98304, 360/569-4453.

22 SPRAY PARK
8.8 mi/4.5 hr 🏃2 ⛺10

northwest of The Mountain in Mount Rainier National Park

BEST (

Spray Park is without a doubt one of the most beautiful places on Mount Rainier. Meadows measured by the square mile cover the upper reaches of this trail, dominated by the imposing stature of The Mountain. Wildflowers erupt and blanket the high country in late July, while black bears in search of huckleberries roam in late August. The trail is one of the greats in the national park and receives heavy use.

Spray Park Trail leaves from Mowich Lake,

Spray Falls cascades near the trail to Spray Park

© SCOTT LEONARD

an inviting dip after a hot summer day on the trail. The trail meanders through the forest to Eagle Cliff (1.5 miles), where the trail follows the precipitous slope. A side trail wanders over to Spray Falls (1.9 miles) before making a steep ascent on switchbacks. The reward for the effort is a breakout from forest into open meadow. Spray Park Trail wanders through this open country, past tarns and rock fields to a saddle (elevation 6,400 feet) with views of even more meadows. The saddle is a good turnaround point, as the trail drops beyond it to Carbon River. Be sure to bring ample water, a rarity beyond Spray Falls. And remember, the meadows here are very fragile; please stay on established trails.

User Groups: Hikers only. No dogs, horses, or mountain bikes are allowed. No wheelchair access.

Permits: This area is usually accessible July–September. A National Parks Pass is required to enter the park. Overnight stays within the national park require backcountry camping permits, which are available at Longmire Wilderness Information Center.

Maps: For a map of Mount Rainier National Park, contact the Outdoor Recreation Information Center at the downtown Seattle REI. For a topographic map, ask Green Trails for No. 269, Mount Rainier West, or ask the USGS for Mowich Lake.

Directions: From Tacoma, drive east on Highway 410 to Buckley. Turn south on Highway 165 and drive 14 miles to Carbon River Road junction. Stay to the right on Mowich Lake Road and drive 17 miles to Mowich Lake Campground at road's end. The trailhead is well marked.

Contact: Mount Rainier National Park, Longmire Wilderness Information Center, Tahoma Woods, Star Route, Ashford, WA 98304, 360/569-4453.

23 SUNRISE NATURE TRAILS
1.5-3.2 mi/0.5-1.5 hr 🏃1 ⛰10

near Sunrise in Mount Rainier National Park

The beauty of Sunrise's high placement means that hikers don't have to venture far for an incredible hike. Although the views start at the parking lot, pavement is usually something we're trying to avoid. Several great options are well suited to hikers of all abilities. Options vary from trips to Shadow Lake or Frozen Lake to a nature trail and a walk through a silver forest. These are perfect trails for families with little ones or for folks conducting an auto tour around the park.

Although the network of trails surrounding Sunrise seems like a jumbled cobweb, every junction is well signed and easy to navigate. Trails to the two lakes are easy walks. Shadow Lake is a level 3-mile round-trip, with meadows and views of Rainier all the way. Frozen Lake gains a little more elevation and peers out over the colorful meadows of Berkeley Park (3.2 miles round-trip).

The west end of Sourdough Ridge Trail features a self-guided nature trail, a 1.5-mile loop with some elevation gain. Lupine and bistort are on full display in July. On the south side of the visitors center is Silver Forest Trail (2.4 miles), a unique path through a forest of bare snags, long ago killed but not toppled by fire.

User Groups: Hikers only. No dogs, horses, or mountain bikes are allowed. No wheelchair access.

Permits: This area is usually accessible July–September. A National Parks Pass is required to enter the park.

Maps: For a map of Mount Rainier National Park, contact the Outdoor Recreation Information Center at the downtown Seattle REI. For a topographic map, ask Green Trails for No. 270, Mount Rainier East, or ask the USGS for Sunrise.

DBirections: From Puyallup, drive east 52 miles on Highway 410 to Sunrise Road in Mount Rainier National Park. Turn right and drive 15 miles to the trailhead at Sunrise Visitor Center.

Contact: Mount Rainier National Park, White River Wilderness Information Center, 70004 Hwy. 410 E., Enumclaw, WA 98022, 360/569-221 x6030.

24 BERKELEY AND GRAND PARKS
7.6-15.2 mi/4.0-8.0 hr 🏃1 ⛰10

out of Sunrise in Mount Rainier National Park

BEST (

A grand destination indeed—wide, flat Grand Park stretches for more than a mile with incredible views of Mount Rainier. On the way, Berkeley Park dazzles with its own wildflower displays and beautiful stream. In a land of many high-country meadows, this is a dandy of a choice.

The route leaves the high country of Sunrise and gently wanders through meadows to Frozen Lake (1.5 miles), tucked beneath Mount Fremont and Burroughs Mountain. Follow the Wonderland Trail for 1 mile to Northern Loop Trail and drop into Berkeley Park (2.5 miles), where streams crisscross the lush meadows. This is a good turnaround spot for hikers uninterested in making the longer trip to Grand Park.

Northern Loop Trail leaves Berkeley Park and travels through open subalpine forest to Grand Park (7.6 miles). Grand Park and its meadows stretch more than a mile to the north. Deer and elk are frequent visitors to the meadows, where they find an abundance of summer grazing. Although Grand Park is preferably accomplished in a day, hikers hoping to spend the night can pitch camp at Berkeley Camp (3.8 miles) or hike 3.3 miles beyond Grand Park to Lake Eleanor (11.4 miles one-way). Access to Lake Eleanor via an unofficial trail from national forest land is frowned upon by the Park Service; besides, it misses out on the best sections of the route.

User Groups: Hikers only. No dogs, horses, or mountain bikes are allowed. No wheelchair access.

Permits: This area is usually accessible mid-July–September. A National Parks Pass is required to enter the park.

Maps: For a map of Mount Rainier National Park, contact the Outdoor Recreation Information Center at the downtown Seattle REI. For a topographic map, ask Green Trails for No. 270, Mount Rainier East, or ask the USGS for Sunrise.

Directions: From Puyallup, drive east 52 miles on Highway 410 to Sunrise Road in Mount Rainier National Park. Turn right and drive 15 miles to the trailhead at Sunrise Visitor Center.

Contact: Mount Rainier National Park, White River Wilderness Information Center, 70004 Hwy. 410 E., Enumclaw, WA 98022, 360/569-2211 x6030.

25 MOUNT FREMONT LOOKOUT

6.0 mi/3.0 hr   🏃2 ⛰9

out of Sunrise in Mount Rainier National Park

 BEST (

Where there's a lookout, there are views. And there's no lookout closer to Mount Rainier

than the one atop Mount Fremont. Never mind that the lookout doesn't sit on Fremont's summit. There still plenty of views along this great trail. Hiking in Rainier high country is all about meadows, and this trail is no different. It travels exclusively through open meadows, and as long as the weather is clear (never a guarantee around The Mountain), you can expect knock-your-boots-off views. Best of all, Mount Fremont is an easy trail to navigate for hikers, gaining just 1,200 feet in about 3 miles.

Mount Fremont Trail leaves the popular Sunrise Visitor Center and quickly climbs to Sourdough Ridge. Mount Rainier is almost too close, crowding much of the southern horizon. Pass picturesque Frozen Lake at 1.5 miles as the trail encounters a large but well-signed junction. Mount Fremont Trail heads north along the rocky ridge, tops out in elevation, and drops to the lookout, built in the 1930s. Although it's hard to take your eyes off Tahoma and its glaciers, the Cascades and Olympics will call from distant horizons. The vast meadows of Grand Park below the lookout are a painter's palette of color in July. Be sure to carry enough water for the trip; there's none to be found along the way.

User Groups: Hikers only. No dogs, horses, or mountain bikes are allowed. No wheelchair access.

Permits: This trail is accessible mid-July–September. A National Parks Pass is required to enter the park.

Maps: For a map of Mount Rainier National Park, contact the Outdoor Recreation Information Center at the downtown Seattle REI. For a topographic map, ask Green Trails for No. 270, Mount Rainier East, or ask USGS for Sunrise.

Directions: From Puyallup, drive east 52 miles on Highway 410 to Sunrise Road in Mount Rainier National Park. Turn right and drive 15 miles to the trailhead at Sunrise Visitor Center.

Contact: Mount Rainier National Park, White River Wilderness Information Center, 70004

Hwy. 410 E., Enumclaw, WA 98022, 360/569-2211 x6030.

26 SOURDOUGH RIDGE/ DEGE PEAK

2.5 mi/1.5 hr   🏃2   ⛰9

near Sunrise in Mount Rainier National Park

Sourdough Ridge Trail covers more than 4 miles of immaculate subalpine meadows immersed in grand views of Mount Rainier and much more. The trail follows Sourdough Ridge from Sunrise Visitor Center out to Dege Peak and Sunrise Point on the east end. A visit here in July will yield acre upon acre of blooming wildflowers, with swaths of paintbrush, lupine, and daisies on the mountainside. This is a popular and heavily used trail near the Sunrise Visitor Center, and rightfully so. There may be no easier or quicker way to get a view of Tahoma.

Sourdough Ridge Trail quickly climbs away from Sunrise Visitor Center into meadows. Every step leads to a better view. Of course The Mountain is impressively big, but the Cowlitz Chimneys and Sarvent Glaciers are seen best from this route. Those who survive the ascent of the first mile have seen the worst. The trail follows the ridge beneath Antler Peak and Dege Peak, the trail's highlight (a side trail leads to its summit). Look north over meadowy ridges to the Palisades and all the way up to Glacier Peak. This is a great hike for families visiting Sunrise; the trail gains less than 600 feet.

User Groups: Hikers only. No dogs, horses, or mountain bikes are allowed. No wheelchair access.

Permits: This area is usually accessible mid-June–September. A National Parks Pass is required to enter the park.

Maps: For a map of Mount Rainier National Park, contact the Outdoor Recreation Information Center at the downtown Seattle REI. For a topographic map, ask Green Trails

for No. 270, Mount Rainier East, or ask the USGS for Sunrise.

Directions: From Puyallup, drive east 52 miles on Highway 410 to Sunrise Road in Mount Rainier National Park. Turn right and drive 15 miles to the trailhead at Sunrise Visitor Center.

Contact: Mount Rainier National Park, White River Wilderness Information Center, 70004 Hwy. 410 E., Enumclaw, WA 98022, 360/569-2211 x6030.

27 BURROUGHS MOUNTAIN LOOP

5.5 mi/3.0 hr   🏃3   ⛰10

near Sunrise in Mount Rainier National Park

One of Mount Rainier's best day hikes, Burroughs Mountain is also one of its most challenging. Many hikers set out on this hike only to be turned back by snowfields that linger well into August. It's best to check in with the ranger at Sunrise and get a trail report. Snow or not, there's definitely lots to see along the way. You'll find meadows of flowers and marmots before reaching the tundralike expanses atop Burroughs Mountain. Add to it a lake for a lunch break and views of glaciers, and Burroughs Loop seems to have it all.

Burroughs Mountain Trail makes a 5-mile loop up to the high, rocky plateau of Burroughs Mountain. A clockwise direction is best, especially if the north side is still snowy. From the visitors center, the trail crosses over crystal streams and colorful meadows to Shadow Lake and an overlook of Emmons Glacier and the White River (1.4 miles). Hikers start dropping off as the trail climbs 900 feet to First Burroughs Mountain (2.8 miles). Guaranteed: Mount Rainier has never looked so big in your life.

Burroughs Mountain Trail wanders the wide, flat plateau and drops to Frozen Lake (3.6 miles). Snowfields like to linger along this northern half of the loop. These steep slopes can be crossed when snowy, but an ice ax is highly, highly recommended. The well-signed trail heads back to the visitors center.

User Groups: Hikers only. No dogs, horses, or mountain bikes are allowed. No wheelchair access.

Permits: This area is usually accessible July–September. A National Parks Pass is required to enter the park.

Maps: For a map of Mount Rainier National Park, contact the Outdoor Recreation Information Center at the downtown Seattle REI. For a topographic map, ask Green Trails for No. 270, Mount Rainier East, or ask the USGS for Sunrise.

Directions: From Puyallup, drive east 52 miles on Highway 410 to Sunrise Road in Mount Rainier National Park. Turn right and drive 15 miles to the trailhead at Sunrise Visitor Center.

Contact: Mount Rainier National Park, White River Wilderness Information Center, 70004 Hwy. 410 E., Enumclaw, WA 98022, 360/569-2211 x6030.

28 PALISADES LAKES
6.6 mi/3.5 hr-2 days

near Sunrise in Mount Rainier National Park

There is no easier lake hike in Mount Rainier National Park than Palisades Lakes Trail. It has no big views of Tahoma; those are blocked by the rugged Sourdough Mountains. But Palisades Lakes Trail offers seven subalpine lakes and many smaller tarns, each among acres of meadows and rocky ridges. The trail is up and down but never significantly, making this a perfect hike for younger hikers. The short length of the trail means it's easily hiked in an afternoon, but a pair of backcountry camps are enticing enough to warrant an overnight visit.

Palisades Lakes Trail leaves Sunrise Road and quickly climbs to Sunrise Lake (0.4 mile), where a short side trail leads to the small,

forested lake. Palisades Trail continues past Clover Lake (1.4 miles) and Hidden Lake (2.5 miles), each surrounded by subalpine groves and meadows. Another mile of trail through acres of meadows, brimming with wildflowers in early August, arrives at Upper Palisades Lake. The lake gets its name from the rocky ridge, known as the Palisades, framing the basin. Marmots and picas are sure to be heard whistling from the talus slopes, and mountain goats are residents of the area too. For an overnight stay, you must make camp at either Dicks Lake or Upper Palisades.

User Groups: Hikers only. No dogs, horses, or mountain bikes are allowed. No wheelchair access.

Permits: This area is usually accessible mid-June–September. A National Parks Pass is required to enter the park. Overnight stays within the national park require backcountry camping permits, which are available at Sunrise Visitor Center.

Maps: For a map of Mount Rainier National Park, contact the Outdoor Recreation Information Center at the downtown Seattle REI. For a topographic map, ask Green Trails for No. 270, Mount Rainier East, or ask the USGS for White River Park.

Directions: From Puyallup, drive east 52 miles on Highway 410 to Sunrise Road in Mount Rainier National Park. Turn right and drive 13 miles to Sunrise Point and the trailhead.

Contact: Mount Rainier National Park, White River Wilderness Information Center, 70004 Hwy. 410 E., Enumclaw, WA 98022, 360/569-2211 x6030.

29 CRYSTAL MOUNTAIN
9.0 mi/4.5 hr

near Crystal Mountain Ski Resort in Mount Baker-Snoqualmie National Forest

Better known for ski runs, Crystal Mountain features a good hiking trail. Getting there isn't quite as easy as using a ski lift, however, unless you actually ride the resort's chair lift, which is possible. Crystal Mountain Trail spends a fair amount of time in unimpressive woods before breaking out into miles of more-than-wonderful ridge hiking. This is a great place to view Mount Rainier and munch on huckleberries.

Crystal Mountain Trail begins with little flair, enduring clear-cuts and second-growth forest for 3 miles as it ascends 1,600 feet. That's the requirement to achieve Crystal Ridge and any notable rewards. At the ridge, Mount Rainier appears above the White River Valley. The trail climbs another 3 miles along the ridge through wide, rounded meadows mixed with steep, rocky slopes. Wildflowers are in full gear during early June while huckleberries make the trip twice as sweet in early August. Any place along the ridge makes for a good turnaround spot. Water is nonexistent, so carry an extra supply.

Crystal Mountain Trail can be completed several other ways, but they aren't as enjoyable. The trail forms a loop back to the ski resort, passing several small mountain lakes (a total of 13.8 miles, 2.5 on the road). An all-downhill version can be had by riding a ski lift up to the ridge and hiking back down.

User Groups: Hikers, leashed dogs, horses, and mountain bikes. No wheelchair access.

Permits: This trail is accessible June–September. A federal Northwest Forest Pass is required to park here.

Maps: For a map of Mount Baker–Snoqualmie National Forest, contact the Outdoor Recreation Information Center at the downtown Seattle REI. For topographic maps, ask Green Trails for No. 270, Mount Rainier East, and No. 271, Bumping Lake, or ask the USGS for Bumping Lake and White River.

Directions: From Puyallup, drive east 47 miles on State Highway 410 to Crystal Mountain Road (Forest Service Road 7190). Turn left (east) and drive 4.4 miles to Forest Service Road 7190-510. Turn right and drive 0.4 mile to Sand Flats camping area and the trailhead.

Contact: Mount Baker–Snoqualmie National Forest, Enumclaw Ranger Station, 450 Roosevelt Ave. E., Enumclaw, WA 98022, 360/825-6585.

30 NORSE PEAK
11.2-13.8 mi/6.0-7.5 hr

near Crystal Mountain Ski Resort in Mount Baker-Snoqualmie National Forest

Ignored by the masses at Mount Rainier, Norse Peak and Cascade Crest are equally deserving of attention. Although steep, Norse Peak Trail travels miles of meadows to a former lookout site west of Rainier. Conveniently, the trail offers a detour of even more meadowy hiking on the way. When in this region, it's often hard to justify not visiting the national park. Not here. Norse Peak is worth it.

Norse Peak Trail spends all of its time climbing, gaining 2,900 feet to the lookout. It's well laid out and never too steep, but it's certainly tiring under a hot summer sun. Most of the trail is exposed in high-country meadows, so bringing plenty of water and sunscreen are good ideas. Norse Peak Trail spends less than 2 miles in the forest before emerging into the open. As the trail climbs, Tahoma rises from behind Crystal Mountain. At 3.6 miles lies Goat Lake junction and at 4.9 miles is Norse Peak Lookout junction; stay to the right both times for the lookout, 6,856 feet of views. Tahoma is its usual magnificent self, but numerous other peaks are noteworthy too.

You can make a loop to visit beautiful Big Crow Basin. Descend from the lookout to the upper junction. Turn right and pass through the large basin of meadows to the Pacific Crest Trail (PCT) and back again via Goat Lake Trail. Even with a trip to the lookout, the loop is less than 14 miles.

User Groups: Hikers, leashed dogs, horses, and mountain bikes (no mountain bikes in Big Crow Basin). No wheelchair access.

HIKING

Permits: This trail is accessible mid-June–September. A federal Northwest Forest Pass is required to park here.

Maps: For a map of Mount Baker–Snoqualmie National Forest, contact the Outdoor Recreation Information Center at the downtown Seattle REI. For a topographic map, ask Green Trails for No. 271, Bumping Lake, or ask the USGS for Norse Peak.

Directions: From Puyallup, drive east 47 miles on State Highway 410 to Crystal Mountain Road (Forest Service Road 7190). Turn left (east) and drive 4 miles to Forest Service Road 7190-410. Parking is on the right side of Crystal Mountain Road (Forest Service Road 7190); the signed trailhead is several hundred yards up Forest Service Road 7190-410.

Contact: Mount Baker–Snoqualmie National Forest, Enumclaw Ranger Station, 450 Roosevelt Ave. E., Enumclaw, WA 98022, 360/825-6585.

31 CRYSTAL LAKES
6.0 mi/3.5 hr   👣3 ⛰9

near Sunrise in Mount Rainier National Park

Crystal Lakes Trail presents hikers a choice between two inspiring destinations. One route heads to Crystal Lakes, a pair of sublime subalpine lakes cloaked in wildflower meadows. As the lakes are in a large basin beneath Sourdough Gap and Crystal Peak, the distant views are limited (but hardly missed). The second option bypasses the two lakes and climbs to Crystal Peak Lookout. Naturally, the views of The Mountain are great. Either way, a great trip is assured.

Crystal Lakes Trail leaves Highway 410 and hastily climbs the valley wall within the forest. At 1.3 miles lies the decisive junction. Left for the lakes, right for the lookout. Crystal Lakes Trail keeps climbing, soon entering the open subalpine and Lower Crystal Lake (2.3 miles). Upper Crystal Lake is just a short climb away (3 miles). Acres of wildflowers light up the basins in early August. Backcountry camps are at each lake

and require a camping permit. For those itching to get to a high viewpoint, the Crystal Peak Trail climbs 2.5 miles from the junction along a dry, open slope to the lookout (elevation 6,615 feet). On a clear day, five Cascades volcanoes are within view, not to mention much of the national park and surrounding national forest.

User Groups: Hikers only. No dogs, horses, or mountain bikes are allowed. No wheelchair access.

Permits: This trail is usually accessible mid-July–September. A National Parks Pass is required to enter the park. Overnight stays within the national park require backcountry camping permits, which are available at Sunrise Visitor Center.

Maps: For a map of Mount Rainier National Park, contact the Outdoor Recreation Information Center at the downtown Seattle REI. For a topographic map, ask Green Trails for No. 270, Mount Rainier East, or ask the USGS for White River Park.

Directions: From Puyallup, drive east 51 miles on Highway 410 to Crystal Lakes Trailhead, just before the White River Wilderness Information Center.

Contact: Mount Rainier National Park, White River Wilderness Information Center, 70004 Hwy. 410 E., Enumclaw, WA 98022, 360/569-2211 x6030.

32 GLACIER BASIN
3.8-7.0 mi/2.0-3.5 hr   👣2 ⛰8

near Sunrise in Mount Rainier National Park

Mount Rainier may be known best for the immense glaciers covering its slopes. More than two dozen massive ice sheets radiate from the mountain's summit, sculpting entire valleys and ridges. Glacier Basin Trail provides a close look at two of Mount Rainier's glaciers, Emmons Glacier and Inter Glacier, hard at work. If you find glaciers boring, then shift your attention to the hillsides and look for mountain goats among the meadows.

Here's a little geology lesson first. Glaciers are massive sheets of ice produced over thousands of years. Snowfall slowly accumulates through the years and becomes compacted into a sheet of ice. Enter gravity, which slowly pulls the glacier down the valley, scraping and sculpting the terrain as it moves. It may take a while (millennia), but glaciers are heavy-duty landscapers. When glaciers retreat (melt faster than they form, as happens now), they leave a denuded valley filled with moraine (piles of rock and dirt), which you'll see here. Got it? You're ready for Glacier Basin Trail.

The trail has two forks: Glacier Basin Trail (7 miles round-trip) and Emmons Glacier Trail (3.8 miles). The trail departs White River Campground and gently climbs to the junction (0.9 mile): Head left for Emmons Glacier (the largest in the lower 48 states), right for Inter Glacier. Both trails provide great views of the glaciers. Being a glacier is dirty work, apparent from the enormous piles of rock and mud covering the ice. Glacier Basin is most popular with mountaineers seeking a summit of The Mountain.

User Groups: Hikers only. No dogs, horses, or mountain bikes are allowed. No wheelchair access.

Permits: This trail is usually accessible mid-July–September. A National Parks Pass is required to enter the park.

Maps: For a map of Mount Rainier National Park, contact the Outdoor Recreation Information Center at the downtown Seattle REI. For a topographic map, ask Green Trails for No. 270, Mount Rainier East, or ask the USGS for White River Park.

Directions: From Puyallup, drive east 52 miles on Highway 410 to Sunrise Road in Mount Rainier National Park. Turn right and drive 5.5 miles to White River Road. Turn left and drive 2 miles to White River Campground and signed trailhead.

Contact: Mount Rainier National Park, White River Wilderness Information Center, 70004 Hwy. 410 E., Enumclaw, WA 98022, 360/569-2211 x6030.

33 SUMMERLAND/ PANHANDLE GAP
8.6–11.4 mi/4.5–6.0 hr   🏃3   ⛰10

near Sunrise in Mount Rainier National Park

BEST (

Many hikers who have completed Wonderland Trail, a 93-mile trek around The Mountain, claim the country surrounding Panhandle Gap as their favorite. The meadows of Summerland and Ohanapecosh Park lie on either side of Panhandle Gap. Above, the ancient volcano of Little Tahoma stands before its big sister, Mount Rainier. Traveling this high country via Wonderland Trail at White River is a diverse and scenic trip.

The route leaves White River Campground and follows Wonderland through old-growth forest of large western hemlock, western red cedar, and Douglas fir. Little Tahoma, with Fryingpan Glacier hanging off its side, signals your arrival in the meadows and wildflowers of Summerland (4.3 miles). Large herds of mountain goats are frequently seen on the rocky slopes surrounding Summerland.

The curious and energetic can follow Wonderland Trail another 1.4 miles as it ascends steeply to the wind-swept terrain of Panhandle Gap. From this high point, the meadows of Ohanapecosh Park unfold beneath several high waterfalls. A word of caution: This high country is rocky and fairly barren. In many places, the trail is designated by rock cairns. No matter the season, be prepared for adverse weather. Tahoma has a system of its own, one that changes rapidly and unexpectedly, so bring warm clothes and know how to use your compass.

User Groups: Hikers only. No dogs, horses, or mountain bikes are allowed. No wheelchair access.

Permits: This area is usually accessible August–September. A National Parks Pass is required to enter the park.

Maps: For a map of Mount Rainier National Park, contact the Outdoor Recreation Information Center at the downtown Seattle

REI. For a topographic map, ask Green Trails for No. 270, Mount Rainier East, or ask the USGS for Sunrise and White River Park.

Directions: From Puyallup, drive east 52 miles on Highway 410 to Sunrise Road in Mount Rainier National Park. Turn right and drive 4.5 miles to Fryingpan Trailhead on the left.

Contact: Mount Rainier National Park, White River Wilderness Information Center, 70004 Hwy. 410 E., Enumclaw, WA 98022, 360/569-2211 x6030.

34 OWYHIGH LAKES

7.6 mi/4.0 hr

east of Tahoma in Mount Rainier National Park

With such a dominating presence, Mount Rainier makes it easy to miss some of the other outstanding scenery in the park. Plenty of great hiking is to be had that doesn't include bulky views of the massive volcano. Owyhigh Lakes Trail is one such hike, traveling up through old but dense forest to parkland lakes. Meadows of wildflowers surround the several lakes and light up the scenery during early August. If you're worried about missing out on seeing rocky peaks and ridges, don't fret. The lakes are situated between craggy Governors Ridge and stately Tamanos Mountain, home of four prominent pinnacles known as the Cowlitz Chimneys.

Adding to Owyhigh Trail's allure is its lack of people. When the crowds at the park visitors centers make you begin to think it's holiday shopping season at the mall, Owyhigh Lakes is likely to be vacant. Folks hoping to spend the night can pitch their shelters at Tamanos Creek Camp, 0.5 mile before the lakes; just remember to pick up your permit. The trail continues beyond the lakes, crests a pass, and drops 5 miles to Deer Creek Trailhead, requiring a car-drop. Day hikers should turn around at Owyhigh Lakes.

User Groups: Hikers only. No dogs, horses, or mountain bikes are allowed. No wheelchair access.

Permits: This trail is accessible mid-July–September. A National Parks Pass is required to enter the park.

Maps: For a map of Mount Rainier National Park, contact the Outdoor Recreation Information Center at the downtown Seattle REI. For a topographic map, ask Green Trails for No. 270, Mount Rainier East, or ask the USGS for White River Park and Chinook Pass.

Directions: From Puyallup, drive east 52 miles on Highway 410 to Sunrise Road in Mount Rainier National Park. Turn right and drive 3 miles to the signed trailhead on the left.

Contact: Mount Rainier National Park, White River Wilderness Information Center, 70004 Hwy. 410 E., Enumclaw, WA 98022, 360/569-2211 x6030.

35 CHINOOK PASS HIKES

1.0-13.0 mi/0.5-6.0 hr

at Chinook Pass in Mount Baker-Snoqualmie National Forest

Chinook Pass is one of the most beautiful of Washington's Cascade passes. So it comes as no surprise that it is a starting point for some amazing hiking. Three great hikes originate here, two of them routes along the famed PCT. Tipsoo Lake Trail is extremely easy, perfect for families with little ones. Naches Loop is longer but also easy, full of big-time views. Sourdough Gap and Pickhandle Point offer views and meadows along the PCT.

Tipsoo Lake is a short 1-mile walk around the high mountain lake. Wildflowers light up the meadows in July, with views of Mount Rainier. The trail around Tipsoo Lake is flat with many picnic sites.

Making a 4-mile loop around Naches Peak, the PCT connects to Naches Trail among acres of wildflower-filled meadows. The preferred route is clockwise, so as to keep Mount Rainier in front of you. The trail gains just 400 feet but is exposed and dry, becoming hot on summer afternoons.

A longer trip from Chinook Pass heads along the PCT to Sourdough Gap and Pickhandle Point. This is one of the PCT's most beautiful segments, traveling through open meadows to Sourdough Gap (3 miles one-way) and Pickhandle Point (6.5 miles). Pickhandle Point lies south and above the lifts of the local ski resort; skiers accustomed to a snowy landscape will be just as pleased with the summertime look.

User Groups: Hikers, leashed dogs, and horses. No mountain bikes are allowed. Tipsoo Lake Trail is wheelchair accessible.

Permits: This area is accessible June–mid-October. A federal Northwest Forest Pass is required to park here.

Maps: For a map of Mount Baker–Snoqualmie National Forest, contact the Outdoor Recreation Information Center at the downtown Seattle REI. For a topographic map, ask Green Trails for No. 270, Mount Rainier East, and No. 271, Bumping Lake, or ask the USGS for Chinook Pass.

Directions: From Puyallup, drive east 60 miles on Highway 410 to Tipsoo Lake Trailhead, on the west side of Chinook Pass.

Contact: Wenatchee National Forest, Naches Ranger Station, 10237 U.S. 12, Naches, WA 98937, 509/653-1401.

36 KLAPATCHE PARK
21.0 mi/2 days

near Longmire in Mount Rainier National Park

The one sure way to instantly turn a popular backcountry destination into a remote and lonely journey is to close the access road. That's exactly what happened to Klapatche Park, now mostly enjoyed by trekkers on Wonderland Trail. A washout on Westside Road extended a trip into Klapatche from 5 miles round-trip into 21 miles. That's 16 miles of road—but don't miss out on the miles of meadows and high country lakes of Klapatche Park. Instead, hop on a mountain bike and turn this into Washington's best ride and hike.

The best access to Klapatche Park is via Klapatche Ridge Trail, eight miles up Westside Road. The trail climbs through old-growth forest to the high meadows of Klapatche Park and Aurora Lake (2.5 miles). Mount Rainier towers above fields of lupine, aster, and penstemon. The giant meadows of St. Andrew's Park make for a must-do side trip, just a mile south on Wonderland Trail. This certainly qualifies as some of the park's best high country. Return back via Klapatche Ridge Trail or make a loop of it via South Puyallup Trail. Camping is allowed only at Klapatche Park Camp or South Puyallup Camp and requires reservations. Road or not, this is a gorgeous hike.

User Groups: Hikers and mountain bikes (mountain bikes on Westside Road). No dogs or horses are allowed. No wheelchair access.

Permits: This trail is accessible July–mid-October. A National Parks Pass is required to enter the park. Overnight stays within the national park require backcountry camping permits, which are available at Longmire Wilderness Information Center.

Maps: For a map of Mount Rainier National Park, contact the Outdoor Recreation Information Center at the downtown Seattle REI. For a topographic map, ask Green Trails for No. 269, Mount Rainier West, or ask the USGS for Mount Wow and Mount Rainier West.

Directions: From Tacoma, drive south 40 miles on Highway 7 to Elbe. Turn east on Highway 706 and drive 10 miles to the Nisqually Entrance Station. Continue 1 mile to Westside Road. Turn left and drive to the trailhead at the washout. Hike or bike 8 miles on the closed road to the trailhead on the right.

Contact: Mount Rainier National Park, Longmire Wilderness Information Center, Tahoma Woods, Star Route, Ashford, WA 98304, 360/569-4453.

37 EMERALD RIDGE LOOP
16.2 mi/1-2 days   ☆☆3 ◭10

near Longmire in Mount Rainier National Park

More remote and less accessible than other faces, Mount Rainier's western side features few trails outside of Mowich. And the trails that do explore The Mountain's western slopes are fading into obscurity thanks to the closure of Westside Road. That's a shame, as Emerald Ridge is a beauty of a trail. With old-growth forest, alpine meadows, and an almost-close-enough-to-touch encounter with Tahoma Glacier, there's little left to desire.

Westside Road once provided easy access to the trailheads. But after a washout, the Park Service decided not to reopen it. That has kept the crowds out and the animals wild. It also means some road walking, about 8.3 miles of road out of a 16.2-mile total loop. The park does allow mountain bikes on the road; the smart hiker bikes to the upper trailhead, hikes the loop, and coasts back to the car.

On the trail, the loop follows Round Pass Trail and South Emerald Ridge Trail up to Wonderland Trail (2.1 miles). An interesting outcrop of columnar basalt (hexagonal columns formed as erupted lava cooled) is found just before the junction. Wonderland Trail climbs to emerald meadows and Tahoma Glacier (4.3 miles). Glacier Island, encircled by glaciers as recently as the 1930s, stands before the towering bulk of Mount Rainier. The loop drops to Tahoma Creek Trail (5.8 miles) and to the lower trailhead (7.9 miles). Backpackers need to plan on setting up for the night at South Puyallup Camp (the only site along the trail), located at the junction of South Emerald Ridge and Wonderland Trails.

User Groups: Hikers and mountain bikes (mountain bikes on Westside Road). No dogs or horses are allowed. No wheelchair access.

Permits: This trail is accessible July–mid-October. A National Parks Pass is required to enter the park.

Maps: For a map of Mount Rainier National Park, contact the Outdoor Recreation Information Center at the downtown Seattle REI. For a topographic map, ask Green Trails for No. 269, Mount Rainier West, or ask the USGS for Mount Wow and Mount Rainier West.

Directions: From Tacoma, drive south 40 miles on Highway 7 to Elbe. Turn east on Highway 706 and drive 10 miles to the Nisqually Entrance Station. Continue 1 mile to Westside Road. Turn left and drive to the trailhead at the washout. Hike or bike 5 miles on the closed road to the trailhead on the right.

Contact: Mount Rainier National Park, Longmire Wilderness Information Center, Tahoma Woods, Star Route, Ashford, WA 98304, 360/569-4453.

38 GLACIER VIEW WILDERNESS
1.5-7.0 mi/1.0-3.5 hr   ☆☆1 ◭9

west of Mount Rainier in Glacier View Wilderness of Gifford Pinchot National Forest

Excluded from the national park but protected by wilderness designation, Glacier View Wilderness is a gem hidden from the masses. This small enclave on the west side of Mount Rainier National Park features several pristine mountain lakes and a pair of gorgeous viewpoints. When you want to see The Mountain in all its glory but don't want to bump elbows with the crowds at Sunrise or Paradise, head to Glacier View Wilderness.

The wilderness is bisected by Glacier View Trail, which runs north to south and has two trailheads. The southern trailhead provides easy access to Lake Christine. The trail climbs gently to the mountain lake (0.75 mile), cloaked by mountain hemlock and subalpine fir. There are several great campsites, and the fishing is supposedly not half bad either. From the lake, a side trail leads 1 mile to the summit of Mount Beljica, awash in big views of Rainier.

HIKING

The northern trailhead provides access to Glacier View Lookout. Glacier View Trail runs north along a forested ridge to Glacier View Lookout (2 miles; elevation 5,450). This high forest is chock-full of ancient trees and bear grass with its huge blooms. The lookout provides great views of Rainier and surrounding countryside. Beyond the lookout are Lake West (2.3 miles) and Lake Helen (3.5 miles). Both lakes have several campsites. You'll likely be able to count on one hand the people you run across.

User Groups: Hikers, leashed dogs, and horses are allowed. No mountain bikes are allowed. No wheelchair access.

Permits: This area is accessible mid-June–October. A federal Northwest Forest Pass is required to park here.

Maps: For a map of Gifford Pinchot National Forest, contact the Outdoor Recreation Information Center at the downtown Seattle REI. For a topographic map, ask Green Trails for No. 269, Mount Rainier West, or ask the USGS for Mount Wow.

Directions: From Tacoma, drive south 40 miles on Highway 7 to Elbe. Turn east on Highway 706 and drive to Copper Creek Road (Forest Service Road 59). Turn left and drive 4.5 miles to Forest Service Road 5920. Turn right and drive to the unsigned trailhead at road's end.

Contact: Gifford Pinchot National Forest, Cowlitz Valley Ranger Station, 10024 U.S. 12, Randle, WA 98377, 360/497-1100.

39 GOBBLER'S KNOB/ LAKE GEORGE

6.4-8.8 mi/3.5-4.5 hr 🏃2 ⛰10

west of Mount Rainier in Glacier View Wilderness and Mount Rainier National Park

Gobbler's Knob is the best deal in the Mount Rainier area. Pristine old-growth forest blankets this grand route as it passes a beautiful mountain lake on its way to the national park,

a viewpoint, and another impressive lake. From atop Gobbler's Knob, Mount Rainier looms large with its impressive stature. Lake George lies beneath Mount Wow. Wow means "goat" in the Salish, the language of local American Indians in the Puget Sound region, and it's likely what you'll be mouthing as you watch mountain goats rambling along the steep slopes.

The preferred route to Gobbler's Knob and Lake George crosses Glacier View Wilderness. A washout on Westside Road increased access via the national park by 3 miles (all on old road). Avoid park fees and an unsightly road walk by hiking through the wilderness. Puyallup Trail meanders through Beljica Meadows to the junction with Lake Christine Trail (0.9 mile). Head left as the trail drops through old-growth mountain hemlock and subalpine fir to Goat Lake (2.3 miles). Campsites are scattered around the lake and require no backcountry permits.

Puyallup Trail then climbs to a saddle between Gobbler's Knob and rocky Mount Wow (3.2 miles). A side trail leads to Gobbler's Knob Lookout and its drop-dead views of Mount Rainier and its glaciers. What a place to watch a sunset! Lake George lies 1,200 feet below, surrounded by forest and rocky slopes. Lake George Camp requires backcountry permits from the National Park Service. The trail continues 0.8 mile to the abandoned Westside Road.

User Groups: Hikers only. No dogs, horses, or mountain bikes are allowed. No wheelchair access.

Permits: This area is accessible mid-June–October. A federal Northwest Forest Pass is required to park here. Overnight stays within the national park require backcountry camping permits, which are available at Longmire Wilderness Information Center.

Maps: For a map of Mount Rainier National Park and Gifford Pinchot National Forest, contact the Outdoor Recreation Information Center at the downtown Seattle REI. For a topographic map, ask Green Trails for No.

269, Mount Rainier West, or ask the USGS for Mount Wow.

Directions: From Tacoma, drive south 40 miles on Highway 7 to Elbe. Turn east on Highway 706 and drive to Copper Creek Road (Forest Service Road 59). Turn left and drive 4.5 miles to Forest Service Road 5920. Turn right and drive to the unsigned trailhead at road's end. (For access via the national park, follow directions for the Emerald Ridge listing in this chapter.)

Contact: Mount Rainier National Park, Longmire Wilderness Information Center, Tahoma Woods, Star Route, Ashford, WA 98304, 360/569-4453.

40 INDIAN HENRY'S HUNTING GROUND

11.4 mi/7.0 hr   3 9

near Longmire in Mount Rainier National Park

Home to some of Mount Rainier's most beautiful scenery, Kautz Creek Trail to Indian Henry's Hunting Ground has it all. The trail passes through old-growth forest, where Douglas firs, western hemlocks, and western red cedars have been standing together for centuries. Upper sections of the route are enveloped in subalpine meadows, where bear, deer, and marmots roam the parkland. And of course, The Mountain makes a grand appearance, towering above the high country with rocky arms and glistening glaciers. It's a full day of hiking, but enjoyable every step of the way.

There are three ways into Indian Henry's Hunting Ground, the best being via Kautz Creek, described below. Other options include Wonderland Trail out of Longmire (an up-and-down 13.8 miles) and Tahoma Creek Trail (a steeper, less scenic 10 miles). Kautz Creek Trail quickly crosses its namesake on an old floodplain. The trail then climbs through stands of old-growth forest on its way to high-country meadows (3.5 miles).

The grade becomes more gentle in its final 2 miles, providing plenty of time to snack on huckleberries in the fall. A great side trip is Mirror Lakes (an extra 1.2 miles round-trip), where Tahoma reflects in the small subalpine tarns. At Indian Henry's Hunting Ground stands a historic patrol cabin still staffed by the Park Service. The only campground within the area is Devils Dream Camp (reservations required), usually full with Wonderland Trail trekkers.

User Groups: Hikers only. No dogs, horses, or mountain bikes are allowed. No wheelchair access.

Permits: This area is usually accessible year-round. A National Parks Pass is required to enter the park. Overnight stays within the national park require backcountry camping permits, which are available at Longmire Wilderness Information Center in Ashford.

Maps: For a map of Mount Rainier National Park, contact the Outdoor Recreation Information Center at the downtown Seattle REI. For a topographic map, ask Green Trails for No. 269, Mount Rainier West, and No. 301, Randle, or ask the USGS for Mount Rainier West.

Directions: From Tacoma, drive south 40 miles on Highway 7 to Elbe. Turn east on Highway 706 and drive 10 miles to the Nisqually Entrance Station. Continue 7 miles to Longmire Wilderness Information Center. The trailhead is across the street in Kautz Creek Picnic Area.

Contact: Mount Rainier National Park, Longmire Wilderness Information Center, Tahoma Woods, Star Route, Ashford, WA 98304, 360/569-4453.

41 RAMPART RIDGE LOOP

4.5 mi/2.5 hr   2 8

near Longmire in Mount Rainier National Park

Climbing atop one of Rainier's ancient lava flows, Rampart Ridge Trail delivers the requisite views and meadows needed in any hike. The trail offers some of the best views of Tahoma (Mount Rainier) from the Long-mire Visitor Center. Included in the deal are old-growth forests and some likely encounters with wildlife. Deer, grouse, squirrels, and woodpeckers are regular residents of the area. Gaining little more than 1,100 feet, it's a great trail for all hikers.

The loop is best done clockwise, hiking along the ridge toward the mountain. Rampart Ridge Trail begins on Trail of the Shadows, just 300 yards from the parking lot. From there, it switchbacks at a moderate but steady grade around the steep cliffs of Rampart Ridge. The forest here is great old-growth mountain hemlocks and subalpine firs, decked out in gowns of moss and lichens. The trail finds the top of the ridge (1.5 miles) and follows the level plateau for more than a mile. Forest is regularly broken up by meadows of wildflowers (try the month of July) and huckleberries (usually ripe in August). Although The Mountain dominates the skyline, Rampart Ridge offers a great view of the large, U-shaped Nisqually River Valley (thank you, glaciers). The trail circles back to Longmire via Wonderland Trail.

User Groups: Hikers only. No dogs, horses, or mountain bikes are allowed. No wheelchair access.

Permits: This trail is usually accessible July–mid-October. A National Parks Pass is required to enter the park.

Maps: For a map of Mount Rainier National Park, contact the Outdoor Recreation Information Center at the downtown Seattle REI. For a topographic map, ask Green Trails for No. 269, Mount Rainier West, or ask the USGS for Mount Rainier West.

Directions: From Tacoma, drive south 40 miles on Highway 7 to Elbe. Turn east on Highway 706 and drive 10 miles to the Nisqually Entrance Station. Continue 18 miles to the National Park Inn at Paradise. The trailhead is behind the inn.

Contact: Mount Rainier National Park,

Longmire Wilderness Information Center, Tahoma Woods, Star Route, Ashford, WA 98304, 360/569-4453.

42 COMET FALLS/ VAN TRUMP PARK

6.2 mi/3.5 hr   🏃3 ⛰10

near Longmire in Mount Rainier National Park

BEST (

Two of the most scenic spots in Mount Rainier National Park are conveniently on the same trail. One of Rainier's highest waterfalls, Comet Falls, plunges off a rocky cliff more than 320 feet. It's the largest of several cascades along the route. As great as Comet Falls may be, Van Trump Park is arguably even better. Acre upon acre of meadow unfolds beneath behemoth Tahoma, with wildflowers coloring the entire scene during the summer. That rumbling is just Kautz and Van Trump Glaciers doing their thing, cracking and breaking in the summer heat.

You can bet that with so much to see, the trail will be busy. In fact, this is one of the park's most popular hikes. Unfortunately, it has a small trailhead with no alternate parking; be ready to choose another hike if the parking lot is full. Van Trump Park Trail leaves the trailhead and briskly climbs alongside the constantly cascading Van Trump Creek. Christine Falls is a short 10-minute walk from the trailhead. Old-growth forest provides shade all the way to Comet Falls. Shutterbugs rejoice, but save some film for later. From the falls, Van Trump Park Trail switchbacks up to open meadows and prime views. Clear days reveal the Tatoosh Range, Mount Adams, and Mount St. Helens to the south. Be sure to stick to established trails; in such a heavily used area, meadows are quickly destroyed by wayward feet.

User Groups: Hikers only. No dogs, horses, or mountain bikes are allowed. No wheelchair access.

Permits: This trail is usually accessible

July–mid-October. A National Parks Pass is required to enter the park.

Maps: For a map of Mount Rainier National Park, contact the Outdoor Recreation Information Center at the downtown Seattle REI. For a topographic map, ask Green Trails for No. 269, Mount Rainier West, or ask the USGS for Mount Rainier West.

Directions: From Tacoma, drive south 40 miles on Highway 7 to Elbe. Turn east on Highway 706 and drive 10 miles to the Nisqually Entrance Station. Continue 12 miles to the signed trailhead on the left.

Contact: Mount Rainier National Park, Longmire Wilderness Information Center, Tahoma Woods, Star Route, Ashford, WA 98304, 360/569-4453.

43 EAGLE PEAK

7.2 mi/4.0 hr

near Longmire in Mount Rainier National Park

Directly out of Longmire, Eagle Peak Trail climbs skyward through old-growth forest and meadows to Eagle Peak Saddle on the north side of Tatoosh Range. At an elevation of 5,700 feet, Mount Rainier looms large while several other Cascade volcanoes are well within sight. The trail is fairly steep, gaining 2,700 feet in just 3.6 miles. Despite its close proximity to Longmire, the ascent keeps the trail less traveled than those near Sunrise or Paradise Visitor Centers.

Eagle Peak Trail climbs quickly and steeply through the mature forest. Douglas fir and mountain hemlock quickly give way to their relatives, mountain hemlock and subalpine fir. The forest covers the trail for 3 miles, keeping it relatively cool; the only water is found when the trail crosses a small stream (2 miles). The final 0.5 mile is a steep ascent in flower-clad meadows, with Eagle Peak towering above. The trail ends in a large saddle between Eagle and Chutla Peaks. Scrambles to either peak are recommended only for experienced and

outfitted climbers. From this outpost of the Tatoosh Range, miles and miles of surrounding countryside (some forested, some denuded) are revealed. Hikers who neglect to bring a camera never fail to regret it.

User Groups: Hikers only. No dogs, horses, or mountain bikes are allowed. No wheelchair access.

Permits: This area is usually accessible mid-July–September. A National Parks Pass is required to enter the park.

Maps: For a map of Mount Rainier National Park, contact the Outdoor Recreation Information Center at the downtown Seattle REI. For a topographic map, ask Green Trails for No. 269, Mount Rainier West, and No. 301, Randle, or ask the USGS for Mount Rainier West and Wahpenayo.

Directions: From Tacoma, drive south 40 miles on Highway 7 to Elbe. Turn east on Highway 706 and drive 10 miles to the Nisqually Entrance Station. Continue 7 miles to Longmire Museum for parking. The signed trailhead is on the opposite side of the suspension bridge crossing the Nisqually River, on the left.

Contact: Mount Rainier National Park, Longmire Wilderness Information Center, Tahoma Woods, Star Route, Ashford, WA 98304, 360/569-4453.

44 PARADISE NATURE TRAILS

1.5-2.8 mi/0.7-1.5 hr

near Paradise in Mount Rainier National Park

BEST (

World-famous and Mount Rainier's most visited setting, Paradise fails to disappoint even the highest expectations. Directly below The Mountain among acres of subalpine meadows, Paradise sports a striking visitors center as well as the historic Paradise Inn. Folks have been coming here to experience Mount Rainier for well over 100 years. And Paradise is a great place to become acquainted with Washington's tallest peak on a number of easy and highly scenic trails. From glacier viewpoints to wildflower rambles, the trails of Paradise easily put visitors into seventh heaven.

The large network of trails near Paradise may appear confusing on a map, but all junctions are well signed. The meadows of this high country are extremely fragile and wither away quickly under the stomp of a boot. Be sure to stick to designated trails at all times. For a view of enormous Nisqually Glacier and its expansive moraine, hike from the visitors center to Nisqually Vista (1.6 miles). This level and wide trail makes a loop (shaped like a lasso) and is perfect for hikers of any ability. Also accessible from the visitors center is Alta Vista Trail (1.5 miles), a gentle climb to a viewpoint. From this small knob, Rainier's bulk astounds even the most veteran of hikers. Look south to take in views of southern Washington's other volcanic peaks, Mount St. Helens and Mount Adams.

Paradise Inn also offers an array of trails, easily customized to any length desired. A good hike is to Golden Gate (2.8 miles) and the vast meadows of Edith Creek Basin. Also beginning in Paradise but long enough to warrant their own listings in this chapter are Skyline Loop, Mazama Ridge, and Paradise Glacier Trails (see next listings).

User Groups: Hikers only. No dogs, horses, or mountain bikes are allowed. No wheelchair access.

Permits: This area is accessible mid-June–October. A National Parks Pass is required to enter the park.

Maps: For a map of Mount Rainier National Park, contact the Outdoor Recreation Information Center at the downtown Seattle REI. For a topographic map, ask Green Trails for No. 270S, Paradise, or ask the USGS for Mount Rainier East.

Directions: From Tacoma, drive south 40 miles on Highway 7 to Elbe. Turn east on Highway 706 and drive 10 miles to the Nisqually Entrance Station. Continue 17.5 miles to the Henry M. Jackson Visitor Center

or 18 miles to the Paradise National Park Inn. The trails emanate from the visitors center and the lodge. Consult a map to see which trailhead to access.

Contact: Mount Rainier National Park, Longmire Wilderness Information Center, Tahoma Woods, Star Route, Ashford, WA 98304, 360/569-4453.

45 PARADISE GLACIER
6.0 mi/3.0 hr   2 9

near Paradise in Mount Rainier National Park

To discover what millions of tons of ice look and sound like, take scenic Paradise Glacier Trail, which gently climbs through wide, open meadows, rock fields, and snowfields to the living Paradise Glacier. Centuries of snowfall built up this massive block of ice slowly sliding down Mount Rainier. The upper reaches of the trail reveal the barren landscapes that are trademarks of retreating glaciers. Paradise Glacier Trail is the park's best chance to view up close the mountain's most famous features.

The route to Paradise Glacier follows Skyline Trail (counterclockwise from Paradise Inn) 1.9 miles to Paradise Glacier Trail junction, just above Sluiskin Falls. Also here is Stevens–Van Trump Historical Memorial, commemorating the 1870 ascent of Mount Rainier, one of the first by white men. Paradise Glacier Trail begins here and heads directly for the glacier (3 miles), cracking, creaking, and breaking apart before your very eyes and ears. Although the terrain appears barren, it is very fragile; be sure to stick to designated trails. The high country here is pretty close to true tundra, with tiny plants doing their best to survive on the barren slopes. Streams cascade all around. Paradise Glacier used to sport several large ice caves that could be explored, but warm weather through the last few decades has left them destroyed or unsafe. Walking on the glacier is also unsafe and prohibited.

User Groups: Hikers only. No dogs, horses, or

mountain bikes are allowed. No wheelchair access.

Permits: This trail is accessible mid-June–October. A National Parks Pass is required to enter the park.

Maps: For a map of Mount Rainier National Park, contact the Outdoor Recreation Information Center at the downtown Seattle REI. For a topographic map, ask Green Trails for No. 270S, Paradise, or ask the USGS for Mount Rainier East.

Directions: From Tacoma, drive south 40 miles on Highway 7 to Elbe. Turn east on Highway 706 and drive 10 miles to the Nisqually Entrance Station. Continue 18 miles to the National Park Inn at Paradise. The trailhead is behind the inn.

Contact: Mount Rainier National Park, Longmire Wilderness Information Center, Tahoma Woods, Star Route, Ashford, WA 98304, 360/569-4453.

46 MAZAMA RIDGE

5.4 mi/2.5 hr   👫2 ⛰10

near Paradise in Mount Rainier National Park

Walking away from The Mountain, Mazama Ridge avoids the mall-like crush of visitors along other Paradise trails. Such a beautiful hike still gets plenty of use, however, and for good reason. The easy trail spends its entirety wandering amid subalpine meadows with big views of the big mountain. To the south stands the jagged Tatoosh Range. And to cap it all off is a series of small tarns, idyllic spots for lunch.

The theme of Mazama Ridge Trail is meadows, meadows, meadows. The route leaves Paradise Inn and follows Skyline Trail 1.5 miles to a signed junction; to the right is Mazama Ridge Trail. The trail follows the wide, flat ridgeline south. During July, lupine, daisies, and countless other wildflowers add shrouds of color to green meadows.

The trail reaches a number of small lakes

and tarns (2.5 miles) along the flat top of Faraway Rock. Below its steep slopes lie Louise and Reflection Lakes and Wonderland Trail. With little elevation change, this is a great trail for families with little ones.

User Groups: Hikers only. No dogs, horses, or mountain bikes are allowed. No wheelchair access.

Permits: This trail is accessible mid-June–October. A National Parks Pass is required to enter the park.

Maps: For a map of Mount Rainier National Park, contact the Outdoor Recreation Information Center at the downtown Seattle REI. For a topographic map, ask Green Trails for No. 270S, Paradise, or ask the USGS for Mount Rainier East.

Directions: From Tacoma, drive south 40 miles on Highway 7 to Elbe. Turn east on Highway 706 and drive 10 miles to the Nisqually Entrance Station. Continue 18 miles to the National Park Inn at Paradise. The trailhead is behind the inn.

Contact: Mount Rainier National Park, Longmire Wilderness Information Center, Tahoma Woods, Star Route, Ashford, WA 98304, 360/569-4453.

47 SKYLINE LOOP

5.0 mi/3.0 hr   👫2 ⛰10

out of Paradise in Mount Rainier National Park

BEST (

Skyline Trail may well be the premier hike in Mount Rainier National Park. The trail delivers miles of alpine meadows, peers over the enormous Nisqually Glacier, and summits Panorama Point. This high vista is as close to The Mountain as you can get without ropes and a harness. Acres of blooming wildflowers line the trail in late July, and if big-time views bore you, several streams and waterfalls are thrown in for good measure. This is a popular trip for folks visiting the Paradise Visitor Center. The overall elevation gain is 1,400 feet, a respectable but not strenuous workout.

The best route is a clockwise one. Although numerous trails crisscross this area, Skyline Trail is well signed at every junction. Starting at Paradise, the trail skirts Alta Vista Peak and climbs through meadows to the ridge above Nisqually Glacier (1.3 miles). On hot summer days, the silence of the high country is broken only by whistling marmots and the cracking glacier.

Panorama Point (2.5 miles; elevation 6,800 feet) is an appropriate name for this high vista. Mount Rainier towers above the viewpoint, and the rocky and jagged Tatoosh Range stands to the south. On clear days, Mount Adams, Goat Rocks, Mount St. Helens, and even Mount Hood in Oregon make appearances. Panorama indeed! Because you definitely packed your camera, save some film for the last half of the trail. Descending to Paradise, Skyline Trail passes Stevens–Van Trump Memorial (commemorating an ascent of Mount Rainier), Sluiskin Falls, and Myrtle Falls. Camping is not permitted in the Paradise area.

User Groups: Hikers only. No dogs, horses, or mountain bikes are allowed. Part of the trail is wheelchair accessible (but somewhat steep).

Permits: This trail is accessible mid-July–September. A National Parks Pass is required to enter the park.

Maps: For a map of Mount Rainier National Park, contact the Outdoor Recreation Information Center at the downtown Seattle REI. For a topographic map, ask Green Trails for No. 270S, Paradise, or ask the USGS for Mount Rainier East.

Directions: From Tacoma, drive south 40 miles on Highway 7 to Elbe. Turn east on Highway 706 and drive 10 miles to the Nisqually Entrance Station. Continue 18 miles to the National Park Inn at Paradise. The trailhead is behind the inn.

Contact: Mount Rainier National Park, Longmire Wilderness Information Center, Tahoma Woods, Star Route, Ashford, WA 98304, 360/569-4453.

48 WONDERLAND TRAIL
93.0 mi/10 days   🏃5 ⛰10

around Tahoma in Mount Rainier National Park

Wonderland Trail is considered by many to be the be-all and end-all of Washington hiking. The long, demanding trek makes a full circle around the behemoth mountain, exploring old-growth forest, high alpine meadows, and everything in between. Tahoma (Mount Rainier's Native American name) is the center of attention at almost every turn, towering above the trail with massive glaciers and windswept snowfields. The Wonderland passes through the park's most beautiful terrain. Acres and acres of wildflower meadows dominate Spray Park, Indian Henry's Hunting Ground, and Summerland. Outstanding lakes and streams are repeat encounters, with Mowich Lake, Carbon River, and Martha Falls a sampling of many highlights.

Wonderland Trail is certainly one of the most demanding hikes in the state. The route repeatedly climbs out of low river valleys to high ridges radiating from Tahoma. Although some folks complete the hike in as few as seven or eight days, plan for at least 10 full days. This makes for a leisurely pace of about 10 miles per day. Besides, there's far too much to see to rush through it. The best starting points include Longmire, Sunrise, or Paradise Visitor Centers. Smart hikers plan carefully and leave a food cache at a visitors center halfway through the route. Because of the trail's popularity, the Park Service requires reservations for all backcountry camps (cross-country camping— that is, selecting a temporary site somewhere off-trail, is not allowed). Spots are limited and regularly fill up in April (reservations can be made after April 1). And finally, be prepared for adverse weather in any season. Tahoma creates its own weather systems, sometimes in just minutes. Set out upon this epic trail and you will not be disappointed, guaranteed!

HIKING

User Groups: Hikers only. No dogs, horses, or mountain bikes are allowed. No wheelchair access.

Permits: This trail is accessible mid-July–September. A National Parks Pass is required to enter the park. Overnight stays within the national park require backcountry camping permits, which are available at Longmire Wilderness Information Center in Ashford. Hikers doing the complete Wonderland Trail are limited to camping in designated camps only—the use of cross-country zones is not permitted.

Maps: For a map of Mount Rainier National Park, contact the Outdoor Recreation Information Center at the downtown Seattle REI. For a topographic map, ask Green Trails for No. 269, Mount Rainier West, and No. 270, Mount Rainier East, or ask the USGS for Mount Rainier West, Mount Rainier East, Mowich Lake, Sunrise, Golden Lakes, Mount Wow, White River Park, and Chinook Pass.

Directions: From Tacoma, drive south 40 miles on Highway 7 to Elbe. Turn east on Highway 706 and drive 10 miles to the Nisqually Entrance Station. Continue 18 miles to the National Park Inn at Paradise. The well-signed trailhead is beside the inn. Other access points include Sunrise Visitor Center or Mowich Lake.

Contact: Mount Rainier National Park, Longmire Wilderness Information Center, Tahoma Woods, Star Route, Ashford, WA 98304, 360/569-4453.

49 PINNACLE SADDLE
2.6 mi/2.5 hr   🏃4 ⛰9

near Paradise in Mount Rainier National Park

Pinnacle Peak Trail is one of the park's steepest trails. An elevation gain of 1,050 feet passes underfoot in a short 1.3 miles, delivering hikers to a wonderful viewpoint. The steep,

rocky path keeps the crowds at bay, leaving the route for only the most determined hikers and view junkies. Although it starts gently, much of the trail does little but climb skyward. Mount Rainier remains visible the entire way. Because the trail is situated on the north-facing slopes of the Tatoosh Range, snow lingers here late, sometimes into August. Marmots and picas whistle and scurry about the rocky meadows while mountain goats frequently patrol the jagged ridge. The trail eventually reaches Pinnacle Saddle, between Pinnacle and Denham Peaks, in the heart of the Tatoosh Range. To the north stands The Mountain, above Paradise Meadows; to the south, snowy Goat Rocks and Mount Adams are visible. The truly adventurous can undertake a rocky scramble to the summit of Pinnacle Peak. It's a gain of 600 feet, but few views are to be gained for the extra effort. Other than snowmelt, little water is to be found along the way; be sure to pack your own.

User Groups: Hikers only. No dogs, horses, or mountain bikes are allowed. No wheelchair access.

Permits: This area is accessible August–September. A National Parks Pass is required to enter the park.

Maps: For a map of Mount Rainier National Park, contact the Outdoor Recreation Information Center at the downtown Seattle REI. For a topographic map, ask Green Trails for No. 270, Mount Rainier East, or ask the USGS for Mount Rainier East.

Directions: From Tacoma, drive south 40 miles on Highway 7 to Elbe. Turn east on Highway 706 and drive 10 miles to the Nisqually Entrance Station. Continue 16 miles to Stevens Canyon Road. Turn right and drive 2.5 miles to the signed trailhead on the right.

Contact: Mount Rainier National Park, Longmire Wilderness Information Center, Tahoma Woods, Star Route, Ashford, WA 98304, 360/569-4453.

50 SNOW AND BENCH LAKES
2.6 mi/1.5 hr   🏃1 ⛰9

near Paradise in Mount Rainier National Park

BEST (

Short, flat, and beautiful best describe Snow Lake Trail. The perfect hike for folks young and old, Snow Lake Trail features a pair of subalpine lakes enclosed by meadows and rocky peaks. The total elevation gain is about 200 feet, practically unnoticeable. Away from the bustle of the Paradise area, Snow Lake offers visitors prime hiking without the crowds.

Snow Lake Trail leaves Stevens Canyon Road and quickly reaches The Bench, a wide, flat meadow with perfect views of Mount Rainier. Bear grass occupies the large meadows, sending its large blooms skyward during August. Bench Lake occupies part of the large meadow. The trail continues another 0.5 mile to Snow Lake, tucked away within a large basin. The lake got its name from the heavy snowpack that lingers around the lake (and on the trail) until late July. Craggy Unicorn Peak rises above the lake and talus slopes from the south. Visitors interested in spending the night will appreciate Snow Lake Camp, the park's most accessible backcountry campground (permits required).

User Groups: Hikers only. No dogs, horses, or mountain bikes are allowed. No wheelchair access.

Permits: This trail is usually accessible August–September. A National Parks Pass is required to enter the park. Overnight stays within the national park require backcountry camping permits, which are available at Sunrise Visitor Center.

Maps: For a map of Mount Rainier National Park, contact the Outdoor Recreation Information Center at the downtown Seattle REI. For a topographic map, ask Green Trails for No. 270, Mount Rainier East, or ask the USGS for Mount Rainier East.

Directions: From Tacoma, drive south 40 miles on Highway 7 to Elbe. Turn east on Highway 706 and drive 10 miles to the Nisqually Entrance Station. Continue 16 miles to Stevens Canyon Road. Turn right and drive 4 miles to the signed trailhead on the right.

Contact: Mount Rainier National Park, Longmire Wilderness Information Center, Tahoma Woods, Star Route, Ashford, WA 98304, 360/569-4453.

51 SHRINER PEAK LOOKOUT
8.4 mi/5.0 hr -2 days   🏃5 ⛰9

near Stevens Canyon entrance in Mount Rainier National Park

Probably nothing is more beautiful than waking to Mount Rainier basking in the glow of the rising sun. And probably there is no better place to behold such a sight than Shriner Peak. But this extraordinary place requires extraordinary effort. Shriner Peak Trail gains extensive elevation in open terrain, made hot by the afternoon sun. Easily done in a day, Shriner Camp invites hikers to spend the night and enjoy the daybreak view.

Shriner Peak Trail is not for the faint of heart. The trail gains more than 3,400 feet in just 4.2 miles, a steep ascent by any standard. Plus, much of the route lies on an exposed, south-facing slope (the hottest of them all). As you sweat and trudge uphill, keep in mind that nature rewards those who work the hardest. The trail winds its way through shady forest before entering an old burn area and eventually open meadows (2.5 miles). The upper half of the route is awash in views of Mount Rainier and surrounding valleys. Shriner Camp is just below the summit off a short side trail; unfortunately it's a dry camp. Shriner Peak is best undertaken early in the day, before the sun is high. Finally, be sure to carry extra water; even if it's cloudy and cool, you'll need it.

User Groups: Hikers only. No dogs, horses, or mountain bikes are allowed. No wheelchair access.

Permits: This area is accessible August–September. A National Parks Pass is required to enter the park. Overnight stays within the national park require backcountry camping permits, which are available at the Longmire and White River Wilderness Information Centers.

Maps: For a map of Mount Rainier National Park, contact the Outdoor Recreation Information Center at the downtown Seattle REI. For a topographic map, ask Green Trails for No. 270, Mount Rainier East, or ask the USGS for Chinook Pass.

Directions: From Puyallup, drive east 56 miles on Highway 410 to Highway 123. Turn right (south) and drive 7.5 miles to the trailhead on the left side of the road.

Contact: Mount Rainier National Park, White River Wilderness Information Center, 70004 Hwy. 410 E., Enumclaw, WA 98022, 360/569-2211 x6030.

52 LAUGHINGWATER CREEK
11.4 mi/6.0 hr-2 days 🥾2 ⛰️8

near Stevens Canyon entrance in Mount Rainier National Park

A rarity in this national park, Laughingwater Creek Trail forsakes mountain meadows and views of Mount Rainier. Instead, this lightly used trail makes a grand trip through old-growth forest to Three Lakes, set among open subalpine forest. The trail provides a quiet reintroduction to the Cascade Mountains after the crowds of Mount Rainier's visitors centers. The only sounds around these parts are the noisy rumbling of Laughingwater Creek and the bellows of elk.

Laughingwater Creek Trail gains more than 2,500 feet between the trailhead and Three Lakes. Most of the climb is spread moderately along the route, easy enough for hikers young and old. The trail sticks close to the creek and passes within view of a waterfall at 2.5 miles. Western hemlocks give way to mountain hemlocks and subalpine fir replaces Douglas fir as the trail nears the crest of the hike.

Three Lakes lie in a small basin atop the ridge. A wonderful backcountry camp is situated here with an aged shelter. This is an out-of-the-way section of the national park (if any remain these days), with few visitors spending the night at Three Lakes Camp. If you have an itch to see The Mountain, continue on the trail past Three Lakes toward the PCT and meadow vistas.

User Groups: Hikers and horses. No dogs or mountain bikes are allowed. No wheelchair access.

Permits: This area is usually accessible July–September. A National Parks Pass is required to enter the park. Overnight stays within the national park require backcountry camping permits, which are available at White River Wilderness Information Center in Enumclaw.

Maps: For a map of Mount Rainier National Park, contact the Outdoor Recreation Information Center at the downtown Seattle REI. For a topographic map, ask Green Trails for No. 270, Mount Rainier East, and No. 271, Bumping Lake, or ask the USGS for Chinook Pass.

Directions: From Puyallup, drive east 56 miles on Highway 410 to Highway 123. Turn right (south) and drive 10.5 miles to the trailhead on the left side of the road, just south of Stevens Canyon entrance.

Contact: Mount Rainier National Park, White River Wilderness Information Center, 70004 Hwy. 410 E., Enumclaw, WA 98022, 360/569-2211 x6030.

53 SILVER FALLS LOOP
3.0 mi/1.5 hr 🥾1 ⛰️8

out of Ohanapecosh in Mount Rainier National Park

Silver Falls Loop is one of Mount Rainier's best river trails, perfect for families and hikers of all abilities. The route is a gentle grade along the bustling river to one of the park's most impressive cascades. Silver Falls Trail follows Ohanapecosh River a gentle 1.5 miles to Silver Falls. Old-growth trees dominate the forest found along the route, making the trail a cool and shady respite from hot and sunny meadows. Squirrels and woodpeckers are often found scurrying among the timber while deer and elk browse the forest floor. Anglers are frequent visitors to the trail, thanks to its easy access to the trout-laden river.

Silver Falls is a thunderous waterfall, where the glacial-fed Ohanapecosh makes a series of cascades. The climax is a 70-foot drop into a large punch bowl. The trail crosses a deep gorge via a bridge immediately below the falls, showering hikers in mist when the river is roaring. Although beautiful, the falls are dangerous if explored off-trail. Keep a short leash on little ones and stick to the established trail. The loop heads directly back to Ohanapecosh Campground along the opposite bank of the river, a quick and easy outing.

User Groups: Hikers only. No dogs, horses, or mountain bikes are allowed. No wheelchair access.

Permits: This trail is accessible year-round. A National Parks Pass is required to enter the park.

Maps: For a map of Mount Rainier National Park, contact the Outdoor Recreation Information Center at the downtown Seattle REI. For a topographic map, ask Green Trails for No. 270, Mount Rainier East, or ask the USGS for Ohanapecosh Hot Springs and Chinook Pass.

Directions: From Puyallup, drive east 56 miles on Highway 410 to Highway 123. Turn right (south) and drive 13 miles to Ohanapecosh Campground. Turn left into the campground; the trailhead is near the visitor center.

Contact: Mount Rainier National Park, White River Wilderness Information Center, 70004 Hwy. 410 E., Enumclaw, WA 98022, 360/569-2211 x6030.

54 GROVE OF THE PATRIARCHS

1.5 mi/1.0 hr

near Stevens Canyon entrance in Mount Rainier National Park

BEST (

Competing with Olympic rainforests, here, in the low valley of the Ohanapecosh River, is one of Washington's most impressive stands of old-growth timber. On a small island in the middle of the river, this grove of Douglas fir, western hemlock, and western red cedar has been growing undisturbed for nearly 1,000 years. That's right, a full millennium. Isolated by the river from the surrounding forest, Grove of the Patriarchs has been able to avoid fire and other natural disturbances, living up to its full potential. This is a true climax forest. The trail to Grove of the Patriarchs is flat and easily navigated. The trail heads upstream for 0.5 mile through an impressive (yet comparatively small) forest. The trail crosses the river via bridge and loops around the island. Many of the trees measure more than 25 feet around the trunk, with one granddaddy fir rounding out at 35 feet in circumference. In this ancient place, the only hazard is a strained neck.

User Groups: Hikers only. No dogs, horses, or mountain bikes are allowed. No wheelchair access.

Permits: This area is accessible mid-May–October. A National Parks Pass is required to enter the park.

Maps: For a map of Mount Rainier National Park, contact the Outdoor Recreation Information Center at the downtown Seattle REI. For a topographic map, ask Green Trails for No. 270, Mount Rainier East, or ask the USGS for Ohanapecosh Hot Springs.

Directions: From Puyallup, drive east 56 miles on Highway 410 to Highway 123. Turn right (south) and drive 11 miles to Stevens Canyon Road/entrance. Turn right and the trailhead is just beyond the guard station on the right.

Contact: Mount Rainier National Park, White River Wilderness Information Center, 70004

HIKING

Hwy. 410 E., Enumclaw, WA 98022, 360/569-2211 x6030.

55 EAST SIDE TRAIL
3.0-5.0 mi/1.5-3.5 hr

near Stevens Canyon entrance in Mount Rainier National Park

East Side Trail follows Chinook Creek and Ohanopecosh River as they wind their ways through exceptional old-growth forests. The trail has three trailheads, including near Cayuse Pass and Ohanopecosh Campgrounds. The distance between these two endpoints is 12 miles. The best access, however, is via Deer Creek in the middle of the route. This 0.5-mile access trail joins East Side Trail within a mile of spectacular waterfalls to the north and south. Deer Creek Trail drops to East Side Trail at the backcountry camp of Deer Creek. The best option is to turn left (south) and follow the level trail 1 mile to where it crosses Chinook Creek. Here, the stream cascades through a narrow gorge directly below the footbridge. Bigger Stafford Falls is another mile down the trail. From Deer Creek Camp, the trail climbs kindly toward Cayuse Pass, passing more falls and cascades. This is a great trail for families with little ones; just keep a short leash on them near all stream crossings.

User Groups: Hikers only. No dogs, horses, or mountain bikes are allowed. No wheelchair access.

Permits: This area is usually accessible April–October. Permits are not required. Parking and access are free.

Maps: For a map of Mount Rainier National Park, contact the Outdoor Recreation Information Center at the downtown Seattle REI. For a topographic map, ask Green Trails for No. 270, Mount Rainier East, or ask the USGS for Ohanapecosh Hot Springs and Chinook Pass.

Directions: From Puyallup, drive east 56 miles

on Highway 410 to Highway 123. Turn right (south) and drive 4 miles to the signed trailhead on the right side of the road.

Contact: Mount Rainier National Park, White River Wilderness Information Center, 70004 Hwy. 410 E., Enumclaw, WA 98022, 360/569-2211 x6030.

56 AMERICAN RIDGE
10.2-26.2 mi/5.0 hr-3 days

in William O. Douglas Wilderness of Wenatchee National Forest

A major route bisecting the northern William O. Douglas Wilderness, American Ridge Trail offers hikers many options to customize a hike. From the Bumping River all the way up to the PCT, American Ridge stretches more than 26 miles. Eight different access trails, including the PCT, create a whole slew of opportunities. The eastern end is primarily high forests; the middle third reaches into high ridgeline meadows with lots of views; the western end offers access to a number of high-country lakes and meadows (see the next listing).

Four trails reach American Ridge from Highway 410, with Mesatchee Creek Trail a favorite. Mesatchee Trail climbs 5.3 miles and 2,200 feet through forest and intermittent meadows to the ridge. East of this junction delivers more than 5 miles of meadows. Also from Highway 410, Goat Peak Trail climbs 3,000 feet in 4 miles to a lookout.

Three trails reach the ridge from Bumping River, Goose Prairie Trail being the preferred route. This is a 5.1-mile ascent to the ridge. Hike west for tiny Kettle Lake and miles of meadows. All of these trails are very hot in the late summer and always lack any water, an important consideration. They're also lonely routes into a beautiful backcountry.

User Groups: Hikers, leashed dogs, and horses. No mountain bikes are allowed. No wheelchair access.

Permits: This trail is accessible April–October.

A federal Northwest Forest Pass is required to park here.

Maps: For a map of Wenatchee National Forest, contact the Outdoor Recreation Information Center at the downtown Seattle REI. For a topographic map, ask Green Trails for No. 271, Bumping Lake, and No. 272, Old Scab Mountain, or ask the USGS for Norse Peak, Cougar Peak, Bumping Lake, Goose Prairie, and Old Scab Mountain.

Directions: From Yakima, drive west on Highway 410 to Forest Service Road 460, just west of Lodgepole Campground. Turn left and drive 0.3 mile to the trailhead at road's end.

Contact: Wenatchee National Forest, Naches Ranger Station, 10237 U.S. 12, Naches, WA 98937, 509/653-1401.

57 COUGAR LAKES
12.0-20.0 mi/6.0 hr-2 days

in William O. Douglas Wilderness of Wenatchee National Forest

Cougar Lakes lie at the western end of American Ridge, directly below the Cascade Crest. They make a great day hike or easy overnighter. Also in the area is the PCT, which lends itself to an excellent loop hike connecting to Cougar Lakes. This is a great weekend hike, encompassing one of the best sections of PCT in southern Washington. Meadows and mountain lakes are prominent themes on both routes. Each route is great for hikers of all abilities, gaining moderate elevation gently.

To reach Cougar Lakes, the route begins with Swamp Lake Trail, a gradual, forested ascent to Swamp Lake (4 miles) and American Ridge Trail (4.6 miles). Hike west toward PCT; Cougar Lakes junction (5.2 miles) cuts south to the two lakes (6 miles). Around the lakes, subalpine meadows unfold beneath tall, rocky cliffs. Numerous campsites are around the basin. Whether on a day hike or

overnighter, be sure to scramble the crest for a view of Mount Rainier.

To hike the longer loop on PCT, continue west on American Ridge Trail toward PCT (6.7 miles). The loop route goes south on PCT, passing Two Lakes, Crag Lake, and Buck Lake. This is meadow country with prime viewing of Mount Rainier and many other mountains. The route intersects Bumping River Trail (13.1 miles) and turns east to return to the trailhead (20 miles). All lakes along the way offer camping and are the sole sources of water.

User Groups: Hikers, leashed dogs, and horses. No mountain bikes are allowed. No wheelchair access.

Permits: This trail is accessible June–mid-October. A federal Northwest Forest Pass is required to park here.

Maps: For a map of Wenatchee National Forest, contact the Outdoor Recreation Information Center at the downtown Seattle REI. For a topographic map, ask Green Trails for No. 271, Bumping Lake, or ask the USGS for Cougar Lake.

Directions: From Yakima, drive west on Highway 410 to Bumping Lake Road (Forest Service Road 1800). Turn left and drive 17 miles to the trailhead at road's end.

Contact: Wenatchee National Forest, Naches Ranger Station, 10237 U.S. 12, Naches, WA 98937, 509/653-1401.

58 MOUNT AIX
11.0 mi/6.0 hr

in William O. Douglas Wilderness of Wenatchee National Forest

Steep, rocky, and downright treacherous at times, Mount Aix does its best to discourage visitors. It stands at 7,766 feet, and hikers must scale 4,000 feet in just 5.5 miles to reach the summit. And the mountain offers no water to aid the trek, a harsh slight on the hot, exposed slopes. Demanding as it may be, Mount Aix rewards with much

HIKING

more than it asks. Miles of meadows chock-full of wildflowers highlight the upper half as do exceptional views of Mount Rainier and surrounding mountains. Mount Aix is definitely best for seasoned hikers who are looking for a good workout.

Mount Aix Trail rests on the east side of the Cascade Crest, meaning the route receives less snow than trails just a few miles west. This is one of the earliest high-country routes to open in the state. Switchbacks are the name of the game, rising out of the forest into the open meadows. At 3.7 miles is a junction with Nelson Ridge Trail. This is a nice option, offering several miles of ridgeline meadows before dozens of miles in the William O. Douglas Wilderness. Head right and climb another 2 miles to the summit. This last effort to the trail's climax is rocky and sometimes a scramble.

User Groups: Hikers, leashed dogs, and horses. No mountain bikes are allowed. No wheelchair access.

Permits: This trail is accessible mid-May–mid-October. A federal Northwest Forest Pass is required to park here.

Maps: For a map of Wenatchee National Forest, contact the Outdoor Recreation Information Center at the downtown Seattle REI. For a topographic map, ask Green Trails for No. 271, Bumping Lake, or ask the USGS for Timberwolf Mountain and Bumping Lake.

Directions: From Yakima, drive west on Highway 410 to Bumping Lake Road (Forest Service Road 1800). Turn left and drive 14 miles to Forest Service Road 1808. Turn left and drive 1.5 miles to the signed trailhead on the left side.

Contact: Wenatchee National Forest, Naches Ranger Station, 10237 U.S. 12, Naches, WA 98937, 509/653-1401.

59 SAWTOOTH LAKES

7.0 mi/4.0 hr

south of Mount Rainier in Gifford Pinchot National Forest

Along the north side of Sawtooth Ridge lie four high lakes among forest and meadows. Just outside the national park boundary, these lakes are highly ignored by the masses headed for Mount Rainier. That's good news for peace and quiet, at least until July 1. After that date motorcycles are allowed on the trail. Visit here in late May or June, and you'll have these great swimming holes all to yourself. Old forest and peek-a-boo views of The Mountain vie for attention along the way. And to cap off the hike is a neck-straining view of High Rock's 600-foot vertical cliff.

The best route to Sawtooth Lakes is via Teeley Creek Trail. After a quick climb past Pothole Lake, the trail levels out completely. At Osborne Mountain Trail junction (0.7 mile), stay left on Teeley Creek Trail and soon reach the two largest and best lakes, Bertha May (1.2 miles) and Granite (1.8 miles). The trail continues along the north side of Sawtooth Ridge to meadows directly beneath the cliffs of High Rock (3.1 miles). Although the trail continues 2 miles to Cora Lake and additional trailheads, the meadows below High Rock are a great turnaround. On hot summer days, a dip in the lakes will be calling your name.

User Groups: Hikers, leashed dogs, horses, mountain bikes, and motorcycles (motorcycles allowed after June 30). No wheelchair access.

Permits: This trail is accessible mid-June–October. No permits are required. Parking and access are free.

Maps: For a map of Gifford Pinchot National Forest, contact the Outdoor Recreation Information Center at the downtown Seattle REI. For a topographic map, ask Green Trails for No. 301, Randle, or ask the USGS for Sawtooth Ridge.

Directions: From Tacoma, drive south 40

miles on Highway 7 to Elbe. Turn east on Highway 706 and drive 7 miles to Forest Service Road 52. Turn right and drive 4.5 miles to Forest Service Road 84. Turn right and drive 1.5 miles to Forest Service Road 8410. Turn right and drive 4.5 miles to the trailhead on the left.

Contact: Gifford Pinchot National Forest, Cowlitz Valley Ranger Station, 10024 U.S. 12, Randle, WA 98377, 360/497-1100.

60 HIGH ROCK LOOKOUT
3.2 mi/2.0 hr

south of Mount Rainier in Gifford Pinchot National Forest

Towering over the adjacent Sawtooth Ridge at 5,685 feet, this peak is certainly high. And with a sheer 600-foot drop on its north face, it definitely qualifies as a rock. And yet the name is an understatement. High Rock might be an imposing sight from below, but the Forest Service Lookout stationed on the summit boasts some of the best views in the Gifford Pinchot. The mountain is separated from Mount Rainier National Park only by Nisqually Valley. Thus, broad views but sparse crowds.

Atop the tallest peak in Sawtooth Range, High Rock Lookout Trail endures a short but sharp climb: 1,600 feet in just 1.5 miles. It wastes little time reaching high meadows and glorious views along High Rock's southern arm. Southern-oriented meadows means sunny, exposed, and dry. Bring water. The lookout stands at 5,685 feet and revels in views of Goat Rocks, Mount Adams, and Mount St. Helens. That enormous mountain just a stone's throw away is Mount Rainier. The northern edge is a sharp drop, so watch your step. Over the edge lie three high lakes along Sawtooth Ridge (see previous listing).

User Groups: Hikers and leashed dogs. No horses or mountain bikes are allowed. No wheelchair access.

Permits: This trail is accessible mid-June–October. No permits are required. Parking and access are free.

Maps: For a map of Gifford Pinchot National Forest, contact the Outdoor Recreation Information Center at the downtown Seattle REI. For a topographic map, ask Green Trails for No. 301, Randle, or ask the USGS for Sawtooth Ridge.

Directions: From Tacoma, drive south 40 miles on Highway 7 to Elbe. Turn east on Highway 706 and drive 7 miles to Forest Service Road 52. Turn right and drive 1 mile to Forest Service Road 85. Continue straight and drive 5 miles to Forest Service Road 8440. Stay to the left and drive 4.5 miles to the trailhead on the left at Towhead Gap.

Contact: Gifford Pinchot National Forest, Cowlitz Valley Ranger Station, 10024 U.S. 12, Randle, WA 98377, 360/497-1100.

61 TATOOSH RIDGE
5.0 mi/3.5 hr

south of Mount Rainier in Tatoosh Wilderness of Gifford Pinchot National Forest

Tatoosh Range stands less than 10 miles from Mount Rainier (as the crow flies), practically a smaller sister to the dominating mountain. And Tatoosh Ridge Trail boasts incredible views of The Mountain, yet it seems so far away—far away from the crowds in the national park, that is. Just south of the park boundary but protected by its own wilderness, Tatoosh Range receives just a fraction of the visitors that trails inside the park do. It's good habitat for lonely views, high lakes, and mountain meadows.

Tatoosh Ridge Trail runs along the southern spine of Tatoosh Ridge, with trailheads at either end. Both ends are steep switchback shuffles, but the northern trailhead offers access to much more scenic terrain. Tackle 2,600 feet of elevation in just 2 miles before reaching Tatoosh Lakes junction. This side trail (1 mile round-trip) leads up to a saddle of epic views and down to Tatoosh Lakes, lying among rocky slopes and meadows. Several great camps are found along the lakeshore.

From the first junction, Tatoosh Ridge Trail continues over rocky and exposed terrain to another junction (3.9 miles), this time leading up to Tatoosh Lookout. At 6,310 feet, here are your epic views. The trail drops from the second junction, below Butter Peak and to the southern trailhead (9 miles one-way). Pack sunscreen and extra water, as the trail is hot, often exposed, and without water, save for the lakes.

User Groups: Hikers and horses only. No dogs or mountain bikes are allowed. No wheelchair access.

Permits: This trail is accessible July–September. No permits are required. Parking and access are free.

Maps: For a map of Gifford Pinchot National Forest, contact the Outdoor Recreation Information Center at the downtown Seattle REI. For a topographic map, ask Green Trails for No. 302, Packwood, or ask the USGS for Tatoosh Lakes.

Directions: To the northern trailhead: From Packwood, drive north 4 miles on Skate Creek Road (Forest Service Road 52) to Forest Service Road 5270. Turn right and drive 6 miles to the signed trailhead on the right.

To the southern trailhead: From Packwood, drive north on Skate Creek Road and turn right on Forest Service Road 5290. Drive 5 miles, staying on the main gravel road, then veer left, remaining on Forest Service Road 5290 for 3.5 miles to the trailhead at road's end.

Contact: Gifford Pinchot National Forest, Cowlitz Valley Ranger Station, 10024 U.S. 12, Randle, WA 98377, 360/497-1100.

62 CLEAR FORK
19.2 mi/8.0 hr

east of Packwood in Goat Rocks Wilderness of Gifford Pinchot National Forest

Clear Fork Trail offers something rarely found south of the North Cascades: a long, undisturbed river valley hike up to the PCT. Although many river valleys in the area were logged long ago, the upper Clear Fork of Cowlitz River survived the ax and saw. That's a good thing, for the bubbling water of this stream makes for a serene scene. This is an ideal hike for families, with lots to see and very little elevation change in the first 7 miles.

Clear Fork Trail begins on a level, timbered plateau above the river. Situated in an open meadow, Lily Lake (1.5 miles) makes a great swimming hole and turnaround for hikers seeking a shorter hike. Beyond, Clear Fork rambles through old-growth forest and meets the river (5.5 miles). Anglers will note that trout inhabit this wild, rarely fished water. The forests are full of deer and elk, and maybe even a black bear or two. The trail eventually fords the river (7 miles) and climbs to the PCT (9.6 miles).

User Groups: Hikers, and horses only. No dogs or mountain bikes are allowed. No wheelchair access.

Permits: This trail is accessible year-round. No permits are required. Parking and access are free.

Maps: For a map of Gifford Pinchot National Forest, contact the Outdoor Recreation Information Center at the downtown Seattle REI. For a topographic map, ask Green Trails for No. 303, White Pass, or ask the USGS for White Pass and Packwood.

Directions: From Randle, drive east 21 miles on Highway 12 to Forest Service Road 46. Turn right (south) and drive 9 miles to the trailhead at road's end.

Contact: Gifford Pinchot National Forest, Cowlitz Valley Ranger Station, 10024 U.S. 12, Randle, WA 98377, 360/497-1100.

63 BLUFF LAKE
3.0-13.2 mi/2.0-8.0 hr

east of Packwood in Goat Rocks Wilderness
of Gifford Pinchot National Forest

On the map, Bluff Lake fails to muster much excitement, appearing as nothing more than a small body of water atop a low ridge. Once boots hit trail, however, it's apparent that a great trip is in store. Bluff Lake Trail climbs to its namesake and beyond, running 6.6 miles along the crest of Coal Creek Mountain. Old-growth forest gives way to subalpine meadows. No map mentions that your most likely traveling companions will be deer, elk, and mountain goats. And the map's biggest secret is huckleberries, acres of them.

Bluff Lake Trail gets under way in a mean way, quickly rising 1,000 feet to Bluff Lake (1.5 miles) in the forest atop the ridge. The lake is a good place to turn around for a short hike, but the best is yet to come. The trail maintains its ascent to the crest of Coal Creek Mountain and mellows out along the ridge. The forest grows increasingly sparse, giving way to meadows full of views and huckleberries. This is a good place to see the Goat Rocks, several miles to the southeast. At 6.6 miles, Bluff Lake Trail ends atop a high butte, at a junction with Clear Lost Trail (dropping to Lost Hat Lake, 1 mile) and Packwood Lake Trail (dropping to Lost Lake, 1.4 miles). Trips to these lakes can make your hike slightly longer. Other than Bluff Lake, there's no water to be found along the route.

User Groups: Hikers and horses only. No dogs or mountain bikes are allowed. No wheelchair access.

Permits: This trail is accessible mid-May–October. No permits are required. Parking and access are free.

Maps: For a map of Gifford Pinchot National Forest, contact the Outdoor Recreation Information Center at the downtown Seattle REI. For a topographic map, ask Green Trails

for No. 302, Packwood, or ask the USGS for Ohanapecosh.

Directions: From Randle, drive east 21 miles on Highway 12 to Forest Service Road 46. Turn right (south) and drive 2 miles to Forest Service Road 4610. Turn right and drive 2 miles to Forest Service Road 4612. Turn left and drive 3 miles to the trailhead at a sharp left turn in the road.

Contact: Gifford Pinchot National Forest, Cowlitz Valley Ranger Station, 10024 U.S. 12, Randle, WA 98377, 360/497-1100.

64 DUMBBELL LAKE LOOP
15.8 mi/2 days

southeast of Mount Rainier in William O.
Douglas Wilderness of Gifford Pinchot
National Forest

Dumbbell Lake knows how to treat a hiker well. It offers not only beautiful scenery but the opportunity for lots of exploring. It's situated on a high plateau, where the firs are plentiful and form a nice surrounding forest. On the north side, a connected chain of small islands extends into the lake and encourages lots of investigation.

The hike to Dumbbell begins along the PCT out of White Pass. Follow PCT for 6.5 miles as it climbs gently onto the plateau. The trail passes small Sand Lake before dropping to Buesch Lake, where good camping is to be had. Abandon PCT and join Trail 56, where Dumbbell lies just 0.5 mile away. The best camping is found near the middle of the lake on the north side, beyond the burned section at the west end. The trail continues past Cramer Lake while gradually dropping elevation back to the trailhead.

On these high flatlands, dense groves of subalpine firs and mountain hemlocks frequently give way to open meadows. The many small lakes and large open meadows on this high plateau make for great day excursions. If you try this hike in the summer, expect

HIKING

people and bugs. Both can be pesky, but don't miss this hike.

User Groups: Hikers and horses only. No dogs or mountain bikes are allowed. No wheelchair access.

Permits: This trail is usually accessible July–mid-October. No permits are required. Parking and access are free.

Maps: For a map of Gifford Pinchot National Forest, contact the Outdoor Recreation Information Center at the downtown Seattle REI. For topographic maps, ask Green Trails for No. 303, White Pass, or ask the USGS for White Pass and Spiral Lake.

Directions: From Randle, drive east on Highway 12 to White Pass Campground, on the north side of the highway just east of the pass. The trailhead is located just before the campground entrance and is signed as the Pacific Crest Trail.

Contact: Gifford Pinchot National Forest, Cowlitz Valley Ranger Station, 10024 U.S. 12, Randle, WA 98377, 360/497-1100.

65 TWIN SISTERS
2.4 mi/1.5 hr

southeast of Mount Rainier in William O. Douglas Wilderness of Gifford Pinchot National Forest

It's almost too easy to get to Twin Sisters. A place so beautiful usually loses out when access is so easy, and that's nearly the case here. A pair of large, stunning high lakes are the Twin Sisters, surrounded by a wilderness of firs and hemlocks. The lakes are popular destinations for folks of all types because of their easy accessibility, great camping, and extensive opportunities for side trips, including the great Tumac Mountain.

This hike serves well both as a day hike or as an extended backpacking trip. The grade up Deep Creek is short and never taxing. The lakes are surrounded by forests of subalpine fir and mountain hemlock. To the north, almost

between the lakes, lies a small butte. Most of the terrain in this area is gentle, rolling hills. At the lakes, excessive use through the years created numerous campsites. Camping must now be at least 200 feet from the lakeshore to keep damage to a minimum. If the crowds feel too thick at Twin Sisters, many other small lakes are worth seeking out.

A necessary side trip is Tumac Mountain, a relatively small and young High Cascades volcano. Just 2 miles from the east lake, the 6,340-foot summit of Tumac includes a crater and stunning views of Mount Rainier. Other easy expeditions are to Fryingpan Lake, Snow Lake, or Blakenship Lakes, and the PCT is not far.

User Groups: Hikers, leashed dogs, and horses. No mountain bikes are allowed. No wheelchair access.

Permits: This area is usually accessible July–early October. A federal Northwest Forest Pass is required to park here.

Maps: For a map of Gifford Pinchot National Forest, contact the Outdoor Recreation Information Center at the downtown Seattle REI. For a topographic map, ask Green Trails for No. 303, White Pass, or ask the USGS for Spiral Lake, Bumping Lake, and White Pass.

Directions: From Yakima, drive west on Highway 410 to Bumping Lake Road (Forest Service Road 1800). Turn left and drive 13 miles to Forest Service Road 1808. Turn left and drive 6.5 miles to Deer Creek Campground and the trailhead at road's end.

Contact: Gifford Pinchot National Forest, Cowlitz Valley Ranger Station, 10024 U.S. 12, Randle, WA 98377, 360/497-1100.

66 SPIRAL BUTTE
12.0 mi/6.0 hr

southeast of Mount Rainier in William O. Douglas Wilderness of Gifford Pinchot National Forest

Forget all the gear, time, and trouble it takes to summit Mount Rainier or Mount Adams.

Getting atop a High Cascades volcano can be done in a day with nothing more than a sturdy pair of hiking boots. That's the allure of Spiral Butte, a small peak just north of Highway 12 near White Pass. The scene from the top is panoramic, offering views of Mount Rainier, Goat Rocks, and other surrounding peaks and ridges.

The trail is a steady climb nearly all the way, gaining 2,500 feet. Sand Ridge Trail climbs through a typical east-side forest. Take a left onto Shellrock Lake Trail (3 miles) and another left on Spiral Butte Trail (4 miles). Here, western larches begin to appear and add some needed color on autumn days. Spiral Butte is so named because of a long, twisting arm of the mountain that swings out from the north. It is on this arm that the trail climbs, providing a great alternative to switchbacks but nevertheless gaining 1,100 feet in the final 2 miles.

Spiral Butte is relatively young, about one million years old, and consists of andesite, a volcanic rock that breaks into large and beautiful gray chunks. Large slopes of talus are visible, revealing the difficulty vegetation can encounter when trying to pioneer such tough terrain.

User Groups: Hikers, leashed dogs, mountain bikes, and horses. No wheelchair access.

Permits: This trail is usually accessible mid-June–early October. A federal Northwest Forest Pass is required to park here.

Maps: For a map of Gifford Pinchot National Forest, contact the Outdoor Recreation Information Center at the downtown Seattle REI. For topographic maps, ask Green Trails for No. 303, White Pass, or ask the USGS for Spiral Butte.

Directions: From Randle, drive east on Highway 12 to White Pass. Continue east on Highway 12 for 6 miles to the trailhead (signed "Sand Ridge") on the north side of the highway.

Contact: Gifford Pinchot National Forest, Cowlitz Valley Ranger Station, 10024 U.S. 12, Randle, WA 98377, 360/497-1100.

67 IRONSTONE MOUNTAIN
11.0 mi/6.0 hr 🚶2 ⛰9

north of White Pass in William O. Douglas Wilderness of Wenatchee National Forest

Aided by a high trailhead (elevation 6,300 feet), Ironstone Mountain presents the easiest ridge hike in the area. Sparse, open forest regularly gives way to open meadows and great views. Ironstone Mountain Trail leaves Forest Service Road 199 and follows the ups and downs of the ridge to Ironstone Mountain. Along the way are several trail junctions, including Burnt Mountain Trail (2.5 miles) and Shellrock Peak (4.5 miles). These two side trails can be combined to form a loop option down (way down) to Rattlesnake Creek and back. A full trip out to Ironstone Mountain is nearly 20 miles round-trip. The best option is to hike the ridge to Shellrock Peak Trail and head north on this trail. Within a mile is easy access to Shellrock Peak, a panoramic vista at 6,835 feet. This is a great viewpoint to see Mount Rainier, the Cascade Crest, and Goat Rocks. Remember to carry plenty of water. This trail is on the east side of the Cascades and can be extremely hot and dry.

User Groups: Hikers, leashed dogs, and horses. No mountain bikes are allowed. No wheelchair access.

Permits: This trail is accessible June–October. A federal Northwest Forest Pass is required to park here.

Maps: For a map of Wenatchee National Forest, contact the Outdoor Recreation Information Center at the downtown Seattle REI. For a topographic map, ask Green Trails for No. 304, Rimrock, or ask the USGS for Spiral Butte and Rimrock Lake.

Directions: From White Pass, drive east 18 miles to Bethel Ridge Road (Forest Service Road 1500) at Bethel Ridge Sno-Park. Turn left and drive 9.5 miles to Forest Service Road 199. Turn left and drive 2.5 miles to the trailhead at road's end.

Contact: Wenatchee National Forest, Naches

HIKING

Ranger Station, 10237 U.S. 12, Naches, WA 98937, 509/653-1401.

68 ROUND MOUNTAIN
5.0 mi/3.0 hr

south of White Pass in Goat Rocks Wilderness of Wenatchee National Forest

Short but steep, Round Mountain Trail climbs to an abandoned lookout and onward over Twin Peaks to the PCT. This rugged trail shows few qualms about reaching its destination, gaining 1,600 feet in just 2.5 miles. Round Mountain Trail begins in open forest, but the timber gives way to rocky meadows near the top of Round Mountain. This is a good place to see elk and deer foraging in the forest. At the summit, 5,970 feet, stands an old, shuttered lookout no longer in use by the Forest Service. The views, looking out over miles of the Cascade Crest, are grand—north to Spiral Butte and Mount Rainier and south to Goat Rocks. Beyond the summit, Round Mountain Trail continues over Twin Peaks (4.5 miles) to the PCT (6.5 miles). Be sure to carry plenty of water and sunscreen, as this is a hot and dry trail.

User Groups: Hikers, leashed dogs, and horses. No mountain bikes are allowed. No wheelchair access.

Permits: This trail is accessible June–October. A federal Northwest Forest Pass is required to park here.

Maps: For a map of Gifford Pinchot National Forest, contact the Outdoor Recreation Information Center at the downtown Seattle REI. For a topographic map, ask Green Trails for No. 303, White Pass, or ask the USGS for Spiral Butte.

Directions: From White Pass, drive east 7.5 miles on Highway 12 to Tieton Road (Forest Service Road 1200). Turn right (south) and drive 3 miles to Forest Service Road 830. Turn right and drive 4.5 miles to the trailhead on the left side.

Contact: Wenatchee National Forest, Naches Ranger Station, 10237 U.S. 12, Naches, WA 98937, 509/653-1401.

69 SHOE LAKE
13.5 mi/8.0 hr

south of White Pass in Goat Rocks Wilderness of Gifford Pinchot National Forest

Some of the best stretches of the PCT are here in Goat Rocks Wilderness. Though not as celebrated as the rocky crags of the Goat Rocks peaks, Shoe Lake is a scenic hike and certainly carries its own weight. Starting directly from Highway 12, the PCT traverses 7 miles of open forest and wide open meadows to reach refreshing Shoe Lake.

The PCT leaves White Pass and progressively climbs through open forest, passing small Ginette Lake (2.2 miles). The PCT eventually finds itself swamped in meadows (5 miles) and awash in wildflower color in late June. For those who have made it this far, the best is still to come. Mount Rainier comes into view as the PCT skirts Hogback Mountain and ascends to a high saddle (6.3 miles) overlooking the basin of Shoe Lake with Pinegrass Ridge in the distance. Reaching Shoe Lake requires a steep, short drop into the basin.

The hike to Shoe Lake is very hot and dry, especially during late summer. Until you reach the lake, water is nonexistent, an important consideration when packing before your trip. Camping is highly discouraged in Shoe Lake Basin because of heavy use in the past. Overnight hikers must continue to Hidden Spring (8.5 miles) or cross-country camp more than 200 yards from the trail.

User Groups: Hikers, leashed dogs, and horses. No mountain bikes are allowed. No wheelchair access.

Permits: This trail is accessible June–October. A federal Northwest Forest Pass is required to park here.

Maps: For a map of Gifford Pinchot National

Forest, contact the Outdoor Recreation Information Center at the downtown Seattle REI. For a topographic map, ask Green Trails for No. 303, White Pass, or ask the USGS for White Pass.

Directions: From White Pass, drive east 0.7 mile on Highway 12 to the Pacific Crest Trailhead at White Pass Campground. Park here, on the north side of the highway. The trailhead is on the south side.

Contact: Gifford Pinchot National Forest, Cowlitz Valley Ranger Station, 10024 U.S. 12, Randle, WA 98377, 360/497-1100.

70 NORTH FORK TIETON
14.0 mi/1-2 days

south of White Pass in Goat Rocks Wilderness of Wenatchee National Forest

North Fork Tieton Trail makes a terrific run up to the PCT and an amazing basin below the glaciers of Goat Rocks. This is one of the best ways to reach PCT, just before it climbs into the Goat Rocks. Although this isn't Mount Rainier, Goat Rocks still gets fairly crowded on a summer weekend. This northern side of Goat Rocks, however, sees a fraction of the use compared to the western side.

North Fork Tieton Trail climbs at a steady grade before making a steep rise to Tieton Pass (4.9 miles). Old-growth forests line the trail, with large timber despite being east of the Cascade Crest. Along the way are views of enormous Tieton Valley, ringed by tall, snowy peaks. Gilbert Peak and Old Snowy tower from the heart of the Goat Rocks, at the head of the basin. To the east stand the rugged, rocky slopes of Tieton Peak and Devils Horns.

The PCT runs north-south from Tieton Pass. Head south to reach a junction for McCall Basin (6.5 miles). Break south along McCall Basin Trail and wander into a subalpine wonderland. Acres of meadows run into rocky slopes. Large herds of mountain goats

are regular visitors in the area. Since McCall Basin makes a long day hike, campsites are scattered about, ideal for Leave-No-Trace camping.

User Groups: Hikers, leashed dogs, and horses. No mountain bikes are allowed. No wheelchair access.

Permits: This trail is accessible mid-June–mid-October. A federal Northwest Forest Pass is required to park here.

Maps: For a map of Wenatchee National Forest, contact the Outdoor Recreation Information Center at the downtown Seattle REI. For a topographic map, ask Green Trails for No. 303, White Pass, or ask the USGS for Pinegrass Ridge and Old Snowy Mountain.

Directions: From White Pass, drive east 7.5 miles on Highway 12 to Tieton Road (Forest Service Road 1200). Turn right (south) and drive 3 miles to Forest Service Road 1207. Continue straight onto Road 1207 and drive 4.5 miles to the trailhead at road's end.

Contact: Wenatchee National Forest, Naches Ranger Station, 10237 U.S. 12, Naches, WA 98937, 509/653-1401.

71 BEAR CREEK MOUNTAIN
12.8 mi/8.0 hr

southeast of White Pass in Goat Rocks Wilderness of Wenatchee National Forest

As far as forgotten and ignored trails in the Goat Rocks go, this is it. Bear Creek Mountain Trail makes a steep trip to the summit along the ridge dividing the North and South Fork Tieton Rivers. Because of an elevation gain of more than 3,000 feet, most hikers select other trails in the area. That's a shame, because high-country meadows full of wildflowers, maybe even mountain goats, reward those who make the trip.

Bear Creek Mountain Trail wastes little time before starting a steep ascent out of the South Fork Tieton Valley. The trees are big, but this being the east side of the Cascade

Crest, the forest is open. Meadows begin to appear as the trail reaches a junction with Tieton Meadows Trail (5.4 miles). The views are grand from this north-facing vista, including Mount Rainier, which outshines any other peak.

To gain panoramic views, one must turn south and scramble nearly 1,000 feet in 1 mile to the summit of Bear Creek Mountain. To say the least, this is an impressive location from which to study Goat Rocks. Hikers who pack a pair of binoculars this far will be glad they did. Bear Creek Mountain Trail passes no water along the way, so plan to carry plenty.

User Groups: Hikers, leashed dogs, and horses, and mountain bikes are allowed. No wheelchair access.

Permits: This trail is accessible July–October. A federal Northwest Forest Pass is required to park here.

Maps: For a map of Wenatchee National Forest, contact the Outdoor Recreation Information Center at the downtown Seattle REI. For a topographic map, ask Green Trails for No. 303, White Pass, or ask the USGS for Pinegrass Ridge.

Directions: From White Pass, drive east 7.5 miles on Highway 12 to Tieton Road (Forest Service Road 1200). Turn right (south) and drive 12 miles to Forest Service Road 1000. Turn right and drive 12 miles to the trailhead at road's end.

Contact: Wenatchee National Forest, Naches Ranger Station, 10237 U.S. 12, Naches, WA 98937, 509/653-1401.

72 SOUTH FORK TIETON RIVER

13.9 mi/1-2 days

southeast of White Pass in Goat Rocks Wilderness of Wenatchee National Forest

Free from the crowds that pack much of the Goat Rocks Wilderness in summer, South Fork Tieton River Trail offers access to one of the mountains' most beautiful basins. The trail follows the river upstream before splitting to make a loop around the top of the expansive basin. The beauty of this trail layout (it's shaped like a lasso) is that very little of the trail is walked twice. Rocky peaks of Gilbert Peak and Klickitat Divide loom over the loop, home to fields of wildflowers and herds of mountain goats.

South Fork Tieton Trail remains exceptionally level and easy for the first several miles. Open Conrad Meadows features some very large timber. Elk and deer are common. The trail comes to a junction (4.3 miles), where the loop begins. This is also where the climbing starts. Either side of the loop climbs quickly to the upper slopes of the basin before leveling out. Long, narrow Surprise Lake is truly a surprise along the forested slopes, and it makes a great place to pitch camp. Mountain goats are frequent along the rocky rim bordering the basin. Hikers can make great excursions among the rocky meadows to the crest of Klickitat Divide for views of the surrounding Goat Rocks.

User Groups: Hikers, leashed dogs, and horses. No mountain bikes are allowed. No wheelchair access.

Permits: This trail is accessible July–October. A federal Northwest Forest Pass is required to park here.

Maps: For a map of Wenatchee National Forest, contact the Outdoor Recreation Information Center at the downtown Seattle REI. For a topographic map, ask Green Trails for No. 303, White Pass, or No. 335, Walupt Lake, or ask the USGS for Jennies Butte and Pinegrass Ridge.

Directions: From White Pass, drive east 7.5 miles on Highway 12 to Tieton Road (Forest Service Road 1200). Turn right (south) and drive 12 miles to Forest Service Road 1000. Turn right and drive 12 miles to the trailhead at road's end.

Contact: Wenatchee National Forest, Naches Ranger Station, 10237 U.S. 12, Naches, WA 98937, 509/653-1401.

73 PURCELL MOUNTAIN

7.4-15.4 mi/4.0-8.0 hr   🥾4 ⛰9

north of Randle in Gifford Pinchot National Forest

Conveniently situated along Highway 12 near Randle, Purcell Mountain reaches into the high country and snags meadows and views. It's not an easy trip, however, despite two separate access trails. Expect some significant climbing along either end, with switchbacks the name of the game. The reward for such efforts? Expansive meadows of flowers spread before vast mountain vistas.

Purcell Mountain Trail runs the ridge of the long mountain, almost 8 miles from end to end with a total elevation gain of 4,500 feet. From Highway 12, the trail wastes no time and quickly climbs among old timber. The forest provides welcome shade but breaks occasionally for valley views. Meadows appear before Prairie Mountain (5 miles) and dominate the eastern slopes at Little Paradise (6 miles). The trail ends atop Purcell Mountain (7.7 miles).

A shorter but more strenuous option is Purcell Lookout Trail to the upper ridge. The trail climbs from a logging road to the top of Purcell Mountain (elevation 5,442 feet), gaining 2,400 feet in 3.7 miles. The lookout is long gone, but the views stuck around. Across miles of logged national forest land, Mount Rainier, Mount St. Helens, and Goat Rocks make inspiring neighbors.

On either route, water is a scarce commodity; be sure to carry adequate supplies. Campsites are also scarce, but a couple may be found below Little Paradise Meadows and at the two trails' junction.

User Groups: Hikers, leashed dogs, horses, and mountain bikes. No wheelchair access.

Permits: This trail is accessible mid-June–October. A federal Northwest Forest Pass is required to park here.

Maps: For a map of Gifford Pinchot National Forest, contact the Outdoor Recreation Information Center at the downtown Seattle REI. For a topographic map, ask Green Trails for No. 301, Randle, or ask the USGS for Randle.

Directions: Lower trailhead: From Randle, drive east 6 miles on Highway 12 to the signed trailhead, on the left (north) side.

Upper trailhead: From Randle, drive east 6 miles to Davis Creek Road. Turn left and drive 1 mile to Forest Service Road 63. Turn left and drive 4.5 miles to Forest Service Road 6310. Turn left and drive 1 mile to the trailhead on the right.

Contact: Gifford Pinchot National Forest, Cowlitz Valley Ranger Station, 10024 U.S. 12, Randle, WA 98377, 360/497-1100.

74 POMPEY PEAK

3.2 mi/2.0 hr   🥾3 ⛰8

southwest of Packwood in Gifford Pinchot National Forest

Pompey Peak Trail offers a quick, beautiful, but steep trip to a high viewpoint overlooking the Cowlitz River Valley. The trailhead actually bisects the trail, eliminating 2,500 feet of knee-knocking elevation gain along Kilborn Creek. That sounds good. From Kilborn Springs at the trailhead, Pompey Peak Trail climbs quickly and steadily through shady old-growth forest. Douglas fir and western hemlock give way to silver fir as the trail climbs. A social trail breaks off from the main trail (1.5 miles) and makes a short scramble to the summit (elevation 5,180 feet). Mount Rainier towers above the Tatoosh Range, while the peaks of Goat Rocks peek out from the east. Those with a hankering to put more trail underfoot can wander along Pompey Peak Trail another 2.8 miles along the ridge to Klickitat Trail, near Twin Sisters Mountain. And for a bit of history: Pompey Peak was named for a pack mule belonging to an old settler. The mule fell to its death on the upper part of the trail in the 1890s.

HIKING

HIKING

User Groups: Hikers, leashed dogs, horses, and mountain bikes. No wheelchair access.

Permits: This trail is accessible June–October. No permits are required. Parking and access are free.

Maps: For a map of Gifford Pinchot National Forest, contact the Outdoor Recreation Information Center at the downtown Seattle REI. For a topographic map, ask Green Trails for No. 301, Randle, or ask the USGS for Purcell Mountain.

Directions: From Randle, drive south 1 mile on Highway 131 to Forest Service Road 23. Turn left and drive 3.5 miles to Forest Service Road 2404. Turn left and drive to the trailhead at road's end.

Contact: Gifford Pinchot National Forest, Cowlitz Valley Ranger Station, 10024 U.S. 12, Randle, WA 98377, 360/497-1100.

75 PACKWOOD LAKE

9.2 mi/5.0 hr

east of Packwood in Goat Rocks Wilderness of Gifford Pinchot National Forest

Here's a hike the whole family can enjoy. Packwood Lake Trail skirts the base of Snyder Mountain through a forest of big trees to the large, scenic lake. Peaks of the Goat Rocks are visible to the south and Mount Rainier's summit to the north. The lake's crystal-blue water is inviting to swimmers and anglers alike; it holds a healthy population of trout. Elk are frequent visitors during the winter. The idyllic setting is punctuated by a small forested island in the middle.

Although Packwood Lake Trail is forested and shady, little water is to be found along the way. The elevation gain of 900 feet is barely noticeable, well spread over the 4.6 miles of trail. Clear-cuts and second-growth forests are quickly passed by before you enter stands of old timber. The lake is a favorite overnight destination for families, with campsites found around the shores of the lake. A trail winds

around the east shore, with trails leading to Mosquito (6.8 miles) and Lost Lakes (8.8 miles).

User Groups: Hikers and horses only. No dogs or mountain bikes are allowed. No wheelchair access.

Permits: This trail is accessible year-round. A federal Northwest Forest Pass is required to park here.

Maps: For a map of Gifford Pinchot National Forest, contact the Outdoor Recreation Information Center at the downtown Seattle REI. For a topographic map, ask Green Trails for No. 302, Packwood, or ask the USGS for Packwood.

Directions: From Randle, drive east 16 miles to Packwood. Turn right on Forest Service Road 1260 (near the ranger station) and drive south 5 miles to the trailhead at road's end.

Contact: Gifford Pinchot National Forest, Cowlitz Valley Ranger Station, 10024 U.S. 12, Randle, WA 98377, 360/497-1100.

76 LILY BASIN

12.0 mi/6.0 hr

south of Mount Rainier in Goat Rocks Wilderness of Gifford Pinchot National Forest

Lily Basin Trail is full of great views of the South Cascade volcanoes and blooming wildflowers. Contouring around the head of Glacier Creek, the trail gives a bird's-eye view of Lily Basin, where bugling elk and howling coyotes are frequently heard. Johnson Peak towers above the trail before Heart Lake, set within subalpine meadows, comes into view below the trail. Many hikers leave with a camera full of great pictures.

The trail begins quite high, at 4,200 feet, and quickly enters Goat Rocks Wilderness. The trees along the ridge fight the heavy winter snowpack to attain large girths. The trail follows the ridge for 4 miles before arriving high above Lily Basin. Large populations of elk often graze in Lily Basin. The trail becomes tricky as it contours around the basin through avalanche chutes and talus. The slope falls away quickly, and hikers should take care when tackling this section. Wildflowers are abundant in these high open slopes.

At 6 miles is the junction with Angry Mountain Trail. From here, one can gaze down onto either side of the ridge, and no fewer than three of the major volcanoes are within view. A couple of possible camps lie along the trail, with the best camping a quick descent to Heart Lake.

User Groups: Hikers, leashed dogs, and horses (horses may have difficulty navigating the last couple of miles around the basin). No mountain bikes are allowed. No wheelchair access.

Permits: This area is accessible July–October. A federal Northwest Forest Pass is required to park here.

Maps: For a map of Gifford Pinchot National Forest, contact the Outdoor Recreation Information Center at the downtown Seattle REI. For a topographic map, ask Green Trails for No. 302, Packwood, or ask the USGS for Packwood.

Directions: From Randle, drive east 14 miles on Highway 12 to Forest Service Road 48. Turn right (south) and drive 9.5 miles to the trailhead on the right. This is shortly after a sharp left-hand turn in a creek bottom.

Contact: Gifford Pinchot National Forest, Cowlitz Valley Ranger Station, 10024 U.S. 12, Randle, WA 98377, 360/497-1100.

77 SOUTH POINT LOOKOUT
7.0 mi/4.0 hr

south of Randle in Gifford Pinchot National Forest

The lookout may be long gone, but the far-reaching views remain. South Point Lookout Trail makes a rugged assault on South Point Mountain, gaining 3,200 feet in just 3.5 miles. That's steep by anyone's standards. The payoff

is grand, though, with views of Mount Rainier, Mount St. Helens, and Goat Rocks, not to mention many surrounding ridges and peaks. Much of the trail climbs within an open forest burned long ago. The resulting forest of snags provides increasingly better vistas along the ascent but also makes the hike a hot one (and dry, so bring extra water). The trail ends at the summit, where the lookout once stood. Adventurous folk will enjoy scrambling south along the rocky, meadowy ridge.

User Groups: Hikers, leashed dogs, horses, and mountain bikes. No wheelchair access.

Permits: This trail is accessible June–October. No permits are required. Parking and access are free.

Maps: For a map of Gifford Pinchot National Forest, contact the Outdoor Recreation Information Center at the downtown Seattle REI. For a topographic map, ask Green Trails for No. 302, Packwood, or ask the USGS for Packwood.

Directions: From Randle, drive east 11 miles on Highway 12 to Forest Service Road 20. Turn right (south) and drive 4 miles (crossing Smith Creek) to the signed trailhead on the left.

Contact: Gifford Pinchot National Forest, Cowlitz Valley Ranger Station, 10024 U.S. 12, Randle, WA 98377, 360/497-1100.

78 GLACIER LAKE
4.0 mi/2.0 hr

south of Mount Rainier in Goat Rocks Wilderness of Gifford Pinchot National Forest

The trail to Glacier Lake is short, has just 800 feet of gain, and leads to a great lake full of trout. The name is misleading, as there are no glaciers near the lake. Instead, beautiful forests of old-growth fir and hemlock encase the lake with a small meadow at the west end making for a great picnicking spot. Elk roam Lily Basin farther up the creek and often make it down to the lake.

Glacier Lake Trail starts off from the trailhead in a young forest logged several decades ago. Within a mile the trail enters the wilderness and virgin forests. The trail is well maintained and never very steep, making easy access for all. A footpath skirts the large lake for exploration by anglers and families alike. **User Groups:** Hikers, leashed dogs, and horses. No mountain bikes are allowed. No wheelchair access.

Permits: This trail is accessible May–November. A federal Northwest Forest Pass is required to park here.

Maps: For a map of Gifford Pinchot National Forest, contact the Outdoor Recreation Information Center at the downtown Seattle REI. For a topographic map, ask Green Trails for No. 302, Packwood, or ask the USGS for Packwood.

Directions: From Randle, drive east 12 miles on Highway 12 to Forest Service Road 21. Turn right (south) and drive 5 miles to Forest Service Road 2110. Turn left and drive 0.5 mile to the trailhead on the right.

Contact: Gifford Pinchot National Forest, Cowlitz Valley Ranger Station, 10024 U.S. 12, Randle, WA 98377, 360/497-1100.

79 ANGRY MOUNTAIN
16.8 mi/8.0 hr   4 7

south of Mount Rainier in Goat Rocks
Wilderness of Gifford Pinchot National Forest

Despite the name of the mountain, few people leave Angry Mountain in a foul mood. Out of breath and quite tired, but angry, not likely. The trail climbs 3,400 feet along the long ridge of the mountain with the help of plenty of switchbacks. Mount Rainier seems never to be far off, constantly in view to the north. The route ventures deep into the Goat Rocks Wilderness, ending at Heart Lake, a beautiful high lake sure to calm flared tempers and sore feet.

Angry Mountain Trail is difficult from the get-go. It quickly switchbacks up the west end

of the mountain through nice forests of Douglas fir and hemlock. The forest soon opens, with large trees spaced farther apart because of heavy winter snowpacks. The trail follows the ridge, which drops steeply to the south. The severe cliffs along the south side of the mountain are a likely source of the name Angry Mountain. Or maybe it's the steep ascent.

Angry Mountain Trail continues by making another series of steep switchbacks, nearing the high point of the mountain and a viewpoint. The trail enters its prime from here, meandering along the ridge. Wildflowers go crazy during June and July. The trail eventually connects to Lily Basin Trail, near the head of Jordan Basin. A great overnight stay is found at Heart Lake (9 miles). **User Groups:** Hikers, leashed dogs, and horses. No mountain bikes are allowed. No wheelchair access.

Permits: This area is usually accessible mid-June–October. A federal Northwest Forest Pass is required to park here.

Maps: For a map of Gifford Pinchot National Forest, contact the Outdoor Recreation Information Center at the downtown Seattle REI. For topographic maps, ask Green Trails for No. 302, Packwood, or ask the USGS for Packwood Lake.

Directions: From Randle, drive east 12 miles on Highway 12 to Forest Service Road 21. Turn right (south) and drive 7.5 miles to Forest Service Road 2120. Turn left and drive 0.5 mile to the trailhead on the right.

Contact: Gifford Pinchot National Forest, Cowlitz Valley Ranger Station, 10024 U.S. 12, Randle, WA 98377, 360/497-1100.

80 GOAT RIDGE
11.0 mi/6.0 hr   3 9

south of Mount Rainier in Goat Rocks Wilderness of Gifford Pinchot National Forest

BEST (

This is one of the most popular trails in Goat Rocks and for good reason. After climbing into

© SCOTT LEONARD

HIKING

Mount Adams from Goat Lake

the subalpine with miles of views, the trail finds the beautiful but cold Goat Lake. Guarantees are rare, but it's likely that you'll see mountain goats on the high ridges surrounding the lake in the evening. So if you're after goats, wildflowers, or views, Goat Ridge is your hike.

The trail begins from Berry Patch Trailhead and climbs quickly through the forest. A loop option is available (1.2 miles) and is highly recommended. It climbs to the site of a former lookout, where three Cascade volcanoes sit close by. The loop returns to the main Goat Ridge Trail and adds little distance to the hike.

Scaling the slopes of Jordan Basin, the trail passes through wide-open meadows that ignite with wildflower blooms in the summer. The trail intercepts Jordan Basin Trail (5.1 miles), a great side trip. Goat Lake lies another 0.5 mile on Goat Ridge Trail, set deep among high alpine ridges, home to white fuzzy goats.

Goat Ridge makes a great loop. Beyond Goat Lake, hike to Snowgrass Flats (7.8 miles), where hikers can drop back to the trailhead (13.3 miles) via Snowgrass Trail. This is an outstanding overnight trip.

User Groups: Hikers, leashed dogs, and horses. No mountain bikes are allowed. No wheelchair access.

Permits: This trail is usually accessible July–September. A federal Northwest Forest Pass is required to park here.

Maps: For a map of Gifford Pinchot National Forest, contact the Outdoor Recreation Information Center at the downtown Seattle REI. For topographic maps, ask Green Trails for No. 334, Blue Lake, and No. 303, White Pass, or ask the USGS for Hamilton Butte and Old Snowy Mountain.

Directions: From Randle, drive east 12 miles on Highway 12 to Forest Service Road 21. Turn right (south) and drive 13 miles to Forest Service Road 2150 (the second left). Turn left and drive 3.5 miles. Stay left at the first Chambers Lake sign, stay right at the Chambers Lake turnoff, and then left to the north Berry Patch Trailhead. (There are two trailheads named Berry Patch—check signboards to verify you're at the one you want.)

Contact: Gifford Pinchot National Forest, Cowlitz Valley Ranger Station, 10024 U.S. 12, Randle, WA 98377, 360/497-1100.

81 SNOWGRASS FLATS

8.4 mi/5.0 hr   🏃3 ⛰10

south of Mount Rainier in Goat Rocks
Wilderness of Gifford Pinchot National Forest

Some trails feature smile-inducing views or open vistas. Others showcase beautiful vegetation or wildlife. When a trail delivers both, it enters a realm reserved for few hikes. Snowgrass Flats is one of those hikes. The trail starts with a diverse forest featuring trees of inspiring size. Next are a pair of beautiful streams. And at the top lies Snowgrass Flats, a wide-open parkland featuring more than acres of meadow. And last, the towering peaks of the Goat Rocks.

Snowgrass Trail leaves Berry Patch Trailhead and climbs over the end of Goat Ridge. It crosses Goat Creek on a nice bridge, where the stream cascades and courses over bedrock. Giant yellow cedars, Douglas firs, silver firs, and mountain hemlocks grow here. The trail passes another cascading stream, and the scenery only gets better. Numerous trees cost hikers time on the trail to ponder their ages.

After fairly steady climbing, the trail reaches Snowgrass Flats. This is open parkland for the most part, with meadows spreading far and wide. Here the trail runs into the PCT. Hiking about 2 miles south on PCT is well worth the effort, as the trail climbs to the base of Old Snowy and the views north become wide open. Old Snowy, at almost 8,000 feet, beckons you to climb farther with a very steep but trouble-free way trail to the summit. This is a hike to remember. Unfortunately, camping is prohibited within Snowgrass Flats.

User Groups: Hikers, and horses only. No dogs or mountain bikes are allowed. No wheelchair access.

Permits: This trail is usually accessible July–September. No permits are required. Parking and access are free.

Maps: For a map of Gifford Pinchot National Forest, contact the Outdoor Recreation Information Center at the downtown Seattle REI.

For topographic maps, ask Green Trails for No. 334, Blue Lake, No. 335, Walupt Lake, and No. 303, White Pass, or ask the USGS for Hamilton Butte and Walupt Lake.

Directions: From Randle, drive east 12 miles on Highway 12 to Forest Service Road 21. Turn right (south) and drive 14 miles to Forest Service Road 2150. Turn left and drive 3.5 miles. Stay right at Chambers Lake turnoff and then right on Forest Service Road 2150-405, toward the south Berry Patch Trailhead. (There are two trailheads named Berry Patch—check signboards to verify you're at the one you want.)

Contact: Gifford Pinchot National Forest, Cowlitz Valley Ranger Station, 10024 U.S. 12, Randle, WA 98377, 360/497-1100.

82 CISPUS BRAILLE

0.5 mi/0.5 hr   🏃1 ⛰8

south of Randle in Gifford Pinchot
National Forest

This nature trail at the Cispus Environmental Learning Center investigates a forest recovering from fire. The trail is level and easy to negotiate, an ideal outing for families or those using a wheelchair. Interpretive signs lead the way and describe the flora and fauna helping to recreate a forest. The folks at the Learning Center have also designed this trail to be accessible to the visually impaired, with Braille markings and roping to guide hikers around the loop. This is a wonderful place to find elk or deer grazing the understory, especially in the winter when the high country lies under several feet of wet snow.

User Groups: Hikers, leashed dogs, horses, and mountain bikes are allowed. No wheelchair access.

Permits: This trail is accessible year-round. No permits are required. Parking and access are free.

Maps: For a map of Gifford Pinchot National Forest, contact the Outdoor Recreation

Information Center at the downtown Seattle REI. For a topographic map, ask Green Trails for No. 333, McCoy Peak, or ask the USGS for Tower Rock.

Directions: From Randle, drive south 1 mile on Highway 131 to Forest Service Road 23. Veer left and drive 8 miles to Forest Service Road 28. Turn right and drive 1.5 miles to Forest Service Road 76. Stay to the right and drive 1 mile to the Cispus Environmental Learning Center. The trailhead is on the opposite side of Road 76.

Contact: Gifford Pinchot National Forest, Cowlitz Valley Ranger Station, 10024 U.S. 12, Randle, WA 98377, 360/497-1100.

83 KLICKITAT TRAIL
17.1 mi one-way/9.0 hr 4 ⚠9

south of Packwood in Gifford Pinchot National Forest

Following an ancient Native American trail through the high country, Klickitat Trail makes an excellent ridge run. Bathed in summer sun, with miles of huckleberry bushes and mountain views, Klickitat Trail makes for an ideal day (or two) in the Gifford Pinchot. The length and orientation of the trail make an out-and-back hike very unappealing; a car-drop is best if it can be arranged. If not, the two trailheads are supplemented with several additional access points. Although the trail starts and ends high, the route encounters numerous ups and downs, making for some challenging elevation changes. Because much of the trail rides the crest of a ridge, snowfields are common on north slopes well into August.

From west to east, the trail skirts the rocky masses of Twin Sisters and Castle Butte. A side trail leads to the summit of Cispus Lookout (3.2 miles). Huckleberries and views of Mount Rainier dominate the scenery on the way to Horseshoe Point (7.5 miles), Cold Spring Butte (9 miles), and Mission Mountain (12.4 miles).

The ridge (and trail) head south to the eastern trailhead, below Elk Peak (17.1 miles). The trail is dry except for Jackpot Lake (4.4 miles) and St. Michael Lake (off-trail below Cold Springs Butte).

User Groups: Hikers, leashed dogs, horses, and mountain bikes. No wheelchair access.

Permits: This trail is accessible mid-July–October. A federal Northwest Forest Pass is required to park here.

Maps: For a map of Gifford Pinchot National Forest, contact the Outdoor Recreation Information Center at the downtown Seattle REI. For a topographic map, ask Green Trails for No. 334, Blue Lake, or ask the USGS for Tower Rock, Hamilton Butte, and Blue Lake.

Directions: From Randle, drive south 1 mile on Highway 131 to Forest Service Road 25. Stay to the right and drive 21 miles to Forest Service Road 28. Turn left and drive 2.5 miles to the signed trailhead.

Contact: Gifford Pinchot National Forest, Cowlitz Valley Ranger Station, 10024 U.S. 12, Randle, WA 98377, 360/497-1100.

84 HAMILTON BUTTES
5.6 mi/3.0 hr 🥾2 ⚠8

south of Randle in Gifford Pinchot National Forest

Hamilton Buttes Trail features a pair of trailheads, one low and one high. Pick the starting location that's right for you, but the upper trailhead is 1.5 miles shorter and saves 1,000 feet of elevation gain. Hamilton Buttes Trail leads to the twin peaks on a route primarily cloaked in carpets of wildflower meadows and huckleberries.

From the upper trailhead, Hamilton Buttes Trail scales the side of a forested basin to reach a small ridgeline and junction (2.2 miles). Turning right drops to the lower trailhead, so don't do that. Head left, uphill, and climb to the top of the two peaks. This is divine country, with outstanding views of Goat Rocks and Mount Adams. August is the prime month to find ripe huckleberries. Carry plenty of water, as none is to be found once you leave the car.

User Groups: Hikers, leashed dogs, horses, mountain bikes, and motorcycles. No wheelchair access.

Permits: This trail is accessible June–October. No permits are required. Parking and access are free.

Maps: For a map of Gifford Pinchot National Forest, contact the Outdoor Recreation Information Center at the downtown Seattle REI. For a topographic map, ask Green Trails for No. 334, Blue Lake, or ask the USGS for Hamilton Butte.

Directions: From Randle, drive south 1 mile on Highway 131 to Forest Service Road 23. Veer left and drive 12 miles to Forest Service Road 22. Turn left and drive 6 miles to Forest Service Road 78. Turn right and drive 8.5 miles to the trailhead at the pass.

Contact: Gifford Pinchot National Forest, Cowlitz Valley Ranger Station, 10024 U.S. 12, Randle, WA 98377, 360/497-1100.

85 YOZOO
8.0 mi/4.0 hr
🚶2 ⛰8

south of Randle in Gifford Pinchot National Forest

Don't ask where the name came from, just enjoy the huckleberries and views of Mount Rainier. That's easy enough, because Yozoo Trail spends a big chunk of its length in open meadows along the high ridge. Through large, old forest, the trail skirts a ridge and climbs through the small valley of Grouse Creek (1.5 miles). This is the last chance for water before Yozoo Trail enters the high country with open meadows of small trees and huckleberry bushes. The trail runs just below the rim of Yozoo Basin, where views of Mount Rainier are constant. Several peaks frame the basin

and make great scrambles to even bigger views. Mountain goats, elk, and black bear are all regular visitors to this area during the summer and early fall. Just be mindful of the most annoying of beasts, roaring motorbikes. Yozoo Trail ends at Bishop Ridge Trail (4 miles), overlooking the sparkling and tempting water of Blue Lake.

User Groups: Hikers, leashed dogs, horses, mountain bikes, and motorcycles. No wheelchair access.

Permits: This trail is accessible April–October. No permits are required. Parking and access are free.

Maps: For a map of Gifford Pinchot National Forest, contact the Outdoor Recreation Information Center at the downtown Seattle REI. For a topographic map, ask Green Trails for No. 334, Blue Lake, or ask the USGS for Hamilton Butte.

Directions: From Randle, drive south 1 mile on Highway 131 to Forest Service Road 23. Veer left on Forest Service Road 23 and drive 12 miles to Forest Service Road 22. Turn left and drive 6 miles to Forest Service Road 78. Turn right and drive 5 miles to the signed trailhead.

Contact: Gifford Pinchot National Forest, Cowlitz Valley Ranger Station, 10024 U.S. 12, Randle, WA 98377, 360/497-1100.

86 NANNIE RIDGE
9.0 mi/5.5 hr
🚶3 ⛰9

south of White Pass in Goat Rocks Wilderness of Gifford Pinchot National Forest

Nannie Ridge Trail, in the southern Goat Rocks Wilderness, makes a scenic trip along the high crest. Nannie Ridge is between the craggy peaks of Goat Rocks and the commanding presence of Mount Adams. The trail passes an old lookout site on its way to the meadows of Sheep Lake and the PCT. Understandably, Nannie Ridge is a popular trail in the Gifford Pinchot.

Beginning from the shores of Walupt Lake, Nannie Ridge Trail climbs steadily and steeply to the crest of the ridge. A social trail leads to Nannie Peak (2.5 miles, elevation 6,106), the first but not last opportunity for expansive views. The trail traverses the ridge beneath tall, rocky cliffs and over open meadows of heather. This is hot and dry country, demanding that hikers pack extra water and sunscreen. Nannie Ridge Trail ends at Sheep Lake, a favorite campsite and swimming hole for hikers passing through on the PCT. If Sheep Lake doesn't tempt you into the water, Walupt Lake will.

User Groups: Hikers and horses only. No dogs or mountain bikes are allowed. No wheelchair access.

Permits: This trail is accessible June–October. No permits are required. Parking and access are free.

Maps: For a map of Gifford Pinchot National Forest, contact the Outdoor Recreation Information Center at the downtown Seattle REI. For a topographic map, ask Green Trails for No. 335, Walupt Lake, or ask the USGS for Walupt Lake.

Directions: From Randle, drive east 12 miles on Highway 12 to Forest Service Road 21. Turn right (south) and drive 18.5 miles to Forest Service Road 2160. Turn left and drive 5.5 miles to Walupt Lake Trailhead.

Contact: Gifford Pinchot National Forest, Cowlitz Valley Ranger Station, 10024 U.S. 12, Randle, WA 98377, 360/497-1100.

87 WALUPT CREEK

8.6-13.5 mi/4.5 hr-2 days 2 ⛰8

south of White Pass in Goat Rocks Wilderness of Gifford Pinchot National Forest

Short, easy, and not exceptionally scenic, Walupt Creek Trail is about more than just the creek. The up-and-back along the trail is a great hike, with pleasant forest and meadows, and even a few high tarns thrown in at the end. But more importantly, Walupt Creek Trail provides two great loops along the PCT.

Walupt Creek Trail provides great access to the PCT, gaining just 1,000 feet in more than 4 miles. The trail spends its first 1.5 miles along the shores of Walupt Lake. Good luck getting past here on a hot summer day without a quick dip to cool off. The trail briefly follows the creek before leaving it to climb out of the glacially shaped valley (notice the U shape) to a large, flat basin. Here are your open subalpine meadows and small tarns. Campsites are found along Walupt Creek and here, near the tarns and PCT.

Walupt Creek is the starting leg to a pair of great loops. From the end of Walupt Creek Trail, head north on the PCT to Sheep Lake and along Nannie Ridge (see previous listing) to Walupt Lake (12.3 miles). This route has the most views, especially along Nannie Ridge. Or head south on the PCT (13.5 miles), through a large basin and the meadows of Coleman Weedpatch. Both loops turn Walupt Creek from mundane into terrific.

User Groups: Hikers and horses only. No dogs or mountain bikes are allowed. No wheelchair access.

Permits: This trail is accessible June–October. No permits are required. Parking and access are free.

Maps: For a map of Gifford Pinchot National Forest, contact the Outdoor Recreation Information Center at the downtown Seattle REI. For a topographic map, ask Green Trails for No. 335, Walupt Lake, or ask the USGS for Walupt Lake.

Directions: From Randle, drive east 12 miles on Highway 12 to Forest Service Road 21. Turn right (south) and drive 18.5 miles to Forest Service Road 2160. Turn left and drive 5.5 miles to Walupt Lake Trailhead.

Contact: Gifford Pinchot National Forest, Cowlitz Valley Ranger Station, 10024 U.S. 12, Randle, WA 98377, 360/497-1100.

HIKING

HIKING

88 LANGILLE RIDGE
8.4 mi/5.0 hr

south of Randle in Gifford Pinchot
National Forest

In the heart of Gifford Pinchot National Forest, Langille Ridge stands as a lonely place. Because of a road washout at one end and a steep, rocky access trail, few hikers have the pleasure of hiking this high ridge. Thus the spoils of Langille Ridge are left to the few, a tantalizing prospect for hikers looking for solitude. The jagged ridge runs more than 10 miles from end to end, but the best spots are close to the car.

With the washout of the northern trailhead, Langille Ridge Trail is best reached via Rough Trail. Appropriately named, Rough Trail climbs 2,000 feet over a rocky path to Langille Ridge Trail (1.7 miles). This is the worst of it, however. From the junction, Langille Ridge Trail runs north and south, making some ups and downs along the jagged ridge. A hike south travels through rocky meadows, complete with huckleberries, to Boundary Trail (5.6 miles one-way).

The preferred option is to head north from the Rough Trail junction along Langille Ridge to McCoy Peak (4.2 miles) and Langille Peak (5.9 miles). Both peaks offer panoramic views of the surrounding countryside and forests. The northern half of Langille Ridge features uninterrupted views of Juniper Ridge and Mount Adams. This is a great place to see mountain goats along the rocky slopes and to hear elk bellowing from the basins below. Plan on packing plenty of water, as much of the ridge is exposed and dry.

User Groups: Hikers, leashed dogs, horses, mountain bikes, and motorcycles. No wheelchair access.

Permits: This trail is accessible May–October. No permits are required. Parking and access are free.

Maps: For a map of Gifford Pinchot National Forest, contact the Outdoor Recreation Information Center at the downtown Seattle REI.

For a topographic map, ask Green Trails for No. 333, McCoy Peak, or ask the USGS for Tower Rock and McCoy Peak.

Directions: From Randle, drive south 1 mile on Highway 131 to Forest Service Road 23. Veer left on Forest Service Road 23 and drive 8 miles to Forest Service Road 28. Turn right and drive 1.5 miles to Forest Service Road 29. Turn left and drive 12 miles to Forest Service Road 29-116. Turn right and drive 0.5 mile to the signed trailhead.

Contact: Gifford Pinchot National Forest, Cowlitz Valley Ranger Station, 10024 U.S. 12, Randle, WA 98377, 360/497-1100.

89 TONGUE MOUNTAIN
3.4 mi/2.0 hr

south of Randle in Gifford Pinchot
National Forest

Standing slightly apart from Juniper Ridge, Tongue Mountain towers over lush Cispus River Valley. Although the peak looks as if it belongs to the neighboring ridge, Tongue Mountain is actually the remains of an old volcano. Tongue Mountain Trail makes a gentle climb through old-growth forest to an open saddle (1 mile). Folks interested in views but not a workout can enjoy looking out over the valley to Mount Adams and Mount Rainier from here. More determined hikers can make the sharp and steep ascent to the peak's summit (1.7 miles, elevation 4,838 feet). This section of trail is a tough climb, but it's over quickly and is certainly rewarding. Cascades volcanoes tower over the Gifford Pinchot, and the noisy Cispus River roars from below. Lucky hikers will spot fluffy white mountain goats along the peaks' sheer cliffs.

User Groups: Hikers, leashed dogs, horses, mountain bikes, and motorcycles. No wheelchair access.

Permits: This trail is accessible April–October. No permits are required. Parking and access are free.

Maps: For a map of Gifford Pinchot National Forest, contact the Outdoor Recreation Information Center at the downtown Seattle REI. For a topographic map, ask Green Trails for No. 333, McCoy Peak, or ask the USGS for Tower Rock.

Directions: From Randle, drive south 1 mile on Highway 131 to Forest Service Road 23. Veer left on Forest Service Road 23 and drive 8 miles to Forest Service Road 28. Turn right and drive 1.5 miles to Forest Service Road 29. Turn left and drive 4 miles to Forest Service Road 2904. Turn left and drive 4 miles to the signed trailhead.

Contact: Gifford Pinchot National Forest, Cowlitz Valley Ranger Station, 10024 U.S. 12, Randle, WA 98377, 360/497-1100.

90 BADGER PEAK
2.0 mi/1.5 hr

south of Randle in Gifford Pinchot National Forest

Such easy access to a former lookout point is hard to come by, but Badger Ridge Trail delivers. It's just one short mile to the summit of Badger Peak (elevation 5,664 feet), where a lookout stood until the 1960s. Even harder to find is a refreshing lake nearby to enjoy after the climb to the summit, but that is found here also. Badger Ridge Trail starts high and climbs to the crest of Badger Ridge (0.6 mile). Already, the views of Mount St. Helens are grand. They have competition, however, from fields of huckleberries. The trail now splits, dropping slightly to Badger Lake or climbing to Badger Peak. From the summit, volcanoes new and old dominate the landscape. Mount St. Helens, Mount Rainier, and Mount Adams represent the new school, still busy at building themselves up. Older, extinct volcanoes include craggy Pinto Rock, jagged Langille Ridge, and other surrounding peaks. Your best bet is to climb the summit before dipping into Badger Lake.

User Groups: Hikers, leashed dogs, horses, mountain bikes, and motorcycles. No wheelchair access.

Permits: This trail is accessible May–October. No permits are required. Parking and access are free.

Maps: For a map of Gifford Pinchot National Forest, contact the Outdoor Recreation Information Center at the downtown Seattle REI. For a topographic map, ask Green Trails for No. 333, McCoy Peak, or ask the USGS for French Butte.

Directions: From Randle, drive south 1 mile on Highway 131 to Forest Service Road 25. Stay to the right and drive 21 miles to Forest Service Road 28. Turn left (east) and drive 2.5 miles to Forest Service Road 2816 (a bit rocky). Turn right and drive 5 miles to the trailhead at road's end.

Contact: Gifford Pinchot National Forest, Cowlitz Valley Ranger Station, 10024 U.S. 12, Randle, WA 98377, 360/497-1100.

91 JUNIPER RIDGE
6.4-8.8 mi/5.0 hr

south of Randle in Gifford Pinchot National Forest

BEST

High, open, and awash in huckleberries and views, Juniper Ridge Trail is a southern Washington favorite. The long ridge run follows the crest of Juniper Ridge over Juniper, Sunrise, and Jumbo Peaks. The hiker's reward is miles of huckleberries and views of Mount Adams, Mount Rainier, Mount St. Helens, and even Mount Hood. Between gazing and grazing, be sure not to bump into the numerous elk, mountain goats, deer, or bear that live here. Juniper Ridge is tremendously scenic and wild (except for the occasional dirt bike roaring through).

Juniper Ridge Trail runs 11.4 miles along the crest of the high ridge. Fortunately, the trail is bisected by Sunrise Trail, a short access trail (1.4 miles) conveniently starting at

4,500 feet. From Sunrise, hikers have options to head north to two separate peaks or south to miles of huckleberry meadows. Backpackers thinking of spending the night here will need to pack extra water; the ridge is dry.

The southern half of Juniper Ridge is certainly the best. The route is one big meadow ramble. Huckleberries are ripest in August. Juniper Ridge Trail skirts Jumbo Peak (3.2 miles), a good turnaround, before dropping to Dark Meadows and Boundary Trail.

The northern half of Juniper Ridge Trail leaves Sunrise Trailhead and climbs Sunrise Peak (1.4 miles), a steep but manageable endeavor. This is Juniper Ridge's highest point. The trail follows the rocky ridge north to Juniper Peak (4.4 miles), a good turnaround, before dropping into clear-cuts.

User Groups: Hikers, leashed dogs, horses, mountain bikes, and motorcycles. No wheelchair access.

Permits: This trail is accessible May–October. No permits are required. Parking and access are free.

Maps: For a map of Gifford Pinchot National Forest, contact the Outdoor Recreation Information Center at the downtown Seattle REI. For a topographic map, ask Green Trails for No. 333, McCoy Peak, and No. 334, Blue Lake, or ask the USGS for McCoy Peak and Tower Rock.

Directions: From Randle, drive south 1 mile on Highway 131 to Forest Service Road 23. Veer left on Forest Service Road 23 and drive 24 miles to Forest Service Road 2324. Turn right and drive 5 miles to Forest Service Road 2324-063. Turn left and drive 0.3 mile to the trailhead at road's end.

Contact: Gifford Pinchot National Forest, Cowlitz Valley Ranger Station, 10024 U.S. 12, Randle, WA 98377, 360/497-1100.

92 YELLOWJACKET PASS/ HAT ROCK

5.4 mi/3.0 hr

south of Randle in Gifford Pinchot National Forest

Hat Rock is but one of many things to see or travel to from this trailhead. Yellowjacket Trail is merely a shortcut to other trails, heading in every direction through the high country. This is also known as a cheater trail; that is, quick and easy access to terrain normally approached by longer, more traditional routes. In this instance, Yellowjacket Trail provides a quick route to Boundary Trail's scenic eastern segment and Langille Ridge.

Yellowjacket Trail climbs sharply to Boundary Trail, gaining 800 feet in just 1 mile. Head left for Langille Ridge junction (1.2 miles from the trailhead) or to follow Boundary Trail to the huckleberry riches of Dark Meadow. Turning right from Yellowjacket Trail leads through open meadows with stunning views of Mount Adams to Hat Rock (2.4 miles from the trailhead) and Yellowjacket Pass (2.7 miles). A boot-beaten path leads to the top of Hat Rock (elevation 5,599 feet) and a remarkable view of Badger Peak, Craggy Peak, Langille Ridge, and Juniper Ridge. The flattened top of Mount St. Helens rises to the west. Although short, this is an exposed and dry hike; remember plenty of water.

User Groups: Hikers, leashed dogs, horses, mountain bikes, and motorcycles. No wheelchair access.

Permits: This trail is accessible June–October. No permits are required. Parking and access are free.

Maps: For a map of Gifford Pinchot National Forest, contact the Outdoor Recreation Information Center at the downtown Seattle REI. For a topographic map, ask Green Trails for No. 333, McCoy, or ask the USGS for McCoy Peak.

Directions: From Randle, drive south 1 mile on Highway 131 to Forest Service Road 23.

Veer left on Forest Service Road 23 and drive 8 miles to Forest Service Road 28. Turn right and drive 11 miles to Forest Service Road 2810. Stay to the left and drive 9 miles to trailhead at road's end.

Contact: Gifford Pinchot National Forest, Mount St. Helens National Volcanic Monument, 42218 NE Yale Bridge Rd., Amboy, WA 98601, 360/449-7871.

93 CRAGGY PEAK
8.8 mi/5.0 hr   🚶2 ⛰9

northeast of Cougar in Gifford Pinchot National Forest

Craggy Peak Trail makes a great ridge run in the heart of the Gifford Pinchot, with meadow views to craggy peaks (including Craggy Peak!) and distant volcanoes. Enjoy the virgin forest shading the trail before it breaks out into spectacular meadows. Craggy Peak Trail also offers great access to Boundary Trail. With lots of campsites, this is a great day hike or an easy overnighter. Elk, deer, and mountain goats are frequent visitors to the area, and black bears appear in late summer to browse the huckleberries.

Craggy Peak Trail gets most of the climbing done early, ascending through an old forest of fir trees, dominated on the ground by bear grass. Quick glimpses of Mount Adams can be had through the trees, but the real views are reserved until the meadows (3 miles). The trail continues through prime huckleberry habitat to Boundary Trail, at the base of Craggy Peak (4.4 miles). Exploration along Boundary Trail is a meadow delight, north to Shark Rock or east to Yellowjacket Pass. The peaks tower over the deep, glaciated valleys, lush with old forests. Great campsites are situated along the trail, often down faint boot-worn paths to big views. Basin Camp is 0.5 mile east on Boundary Trail. Just be prepared for a dry trip with extra packed water.

User Groups: Hikers, leashed dogs, horses, mountain bikes, and motorcycles. No wheelchair access.

Permits: This trail is accessible June–October. A federal Northwest Forest Pass is required to park here.

Maps: For a map of Gifford Pinchot National Forest, contact the Outdoor Recreation Information Center at the downtown Seattle REI. For a topographic map, ask Green Trails for No. 333, McCoy Peak, and No. 365, Lone Butte, or ask the USGS for Spencer Butte, Quartz Creek, and McCoy Peak.

Directions: From Vancouver, drive north on I-5 to Highway 503 (Woodland, exit 21). Drive east 45 miles to Forest Service Road 25. Continue straight on Forest Service Road 25 and drive 6 miles to Forest Service Road 93, just beyond the Muddy River. Turn right and drive 13 miles to Forest Service Road 93-040. Turn left and drive 0.5 mile to the signed trailhead on the right.

Contact: Gifford Pinchot National Forest, Mount St. Helens National Volcanic Monument, 42218 NE Yale Bridge Rd., Amboy, WA 98601, 360/449-7871.

94 SUMMIT PRAIRIE
17.8 mi/1-2 days   🚶4 ⛰9

northeast of Cougar in Gifford Pinchot National Forest

Miles from the nearest trailhead, Summit Prairie is isolated, to say the least. Access to the open meadows, chock-full of huckleberry bushes, requires a long climb of nearly 3,000 feet. That keeps the crowds out of Summit Prairie and the wildlife wild, despite the occasional motorbike (they're still allowed in this "roadless" area). Herds of elk and mountain goats live in Quartz Creek Ridge and Summit Prairie, one of the Gifford Pinchot's most remote places.

In honor of full disclosure, a cheater trail does offer access to Summit Prairie (Boundary Trail, via Table Mountain). It's a little shorter, but nowhere near as scenic. Better access is via Summit Prairie Trail, which climbs Quartz Creek Ridge and runs the long, open ridgeline to Summit Prairie. Leaving from Forest Service Road 90, Summit Prairie Trail climbs harshly to the ridgeline (4 miles). The only water on the route is found in this first segment. Open subalpine forest and frequent meadows cover the ridge to Summit Prairie (8.9 miles) and Boundary Trail.

This is a tough trip to complete in one day, but campsites are few and far between. Overnight campers should plan on cross-country camping without a water source. If you've made it this far, the best option is to turn the trip into a 20.7-mile loop on Boundary Trail, Quartz Creek Trail (see listing in this chapter), and Quartz Creek Butte Trail (a 1.5-mile trail that serves as connector between Summit Prairie and Quartz Creek Big Trees).

User Groups: Hikers, leashed dogs, horses, mountain bikes, and motorcycles. No wheelchair access.

Permits: This trail is accessible mid-June–October. A federal Northwest Forest Pass is required to park here.

Maps: For a map of Gifford Pinchot National Forest, contact the Outdoor Recreation Information Center at the downtown Seattle REI. For a topographic map, ask Green Trails for No. 334, Blue Lake, No. 365, Lone Butte, and No. 366, Mount Adams West, or ask the USGS for Steamboat Mountain and East Canyon Ridge.

Directions: From Vancouver, drive north on I-5 to Highway 503 (Woodland, exit 21). Drive east 45 miles to Pine Creek Information Center. Turn right and continue on Forest Service Road 90 for 25 miles to the signed trailhead on the left (1.5 miles before Forest Service Road 88).

Contact: Gifford Pinchot National Forest, Mount St. Helens National Volcanic Monument, 42218 NE Yale Bridge Rd., Amboy, WA 98601, 360/449-7871.

95 DARK MEADOW

8.4 mi/4.5 hr

south of Randle in Gifford Pinchot National Forest

BEST (

Yet another locale with an ill-fitting name, the only thing dark in Dark Meadows are black huckleberries, juicy and ripe in August. In fact, these open meadows are lit up with summer sun, revealing great views of Jumbo Peak, Langille Ridge, and Mount Adams. Dark Meadow Trail endures several miles of shady forest before emerging into the dueling glories of huckleberry fields and vistas.

Dark Meadow Trail begins by gently wandering up the level valley of Dark Creek. The forest here is old Douglas fir and western hemlock, a perfect home for elk. After 1 mile, the trail climbs steeply to a junction with Juniper Ridge Trail (3.2 miles). The forest opens occasionally to reveal views of the valleys below. A short mile south on Juniper Ridge Trail finds Dark Meadow. Black huckleberry bushes fill the open meadows, attracting hikers and black bears alike. A short footpath leads through the meadow to the summit of Dark Mountain for a panoramic viewpoint (Mount Adams, wow!).

User Groups: Hikers, leashed dogs, horses, mountain bikes, and motorcycles. No wheelchair access.

Permits: This trail is accessible May–October. No permits are required. Parking and access are free.

Maps: For a map of Gifford Pinchot National Forest, contact the Outdoor Recreation Information Center at the downtown Seattle REI. For a topographic map, ask Green Trails for No. 333, McCoy Peak, and No. 334, Blue Lake, or ask the USGS for McCoy Peak and East Canyon Ridge.

Directions: From Randle, drive south 1 mile on Highway 131 to Forest Service Road 23. Veer left on Forest Service Road 23 and drive 25 miles to the signed trailhead on the right.

Contact: Gifford Pinchot National Forest, Cowlitz Valley Ranger Station, 10024 U.S. 12, Randle, WA 98377, 360/497-1100.

96 QUARTZ CREEK
21.2 mi/1-2 days   👫3 ⛺9

northeast of Cougar in Gifford Pinchot National Forest

Lesser known for old-growth forests than other forests of Washington, Gifford Pinchot features forests as magnificent as any other. Quartz Creek Trail is a wonderful example of these ancient timberlands, where towering Douglas fir, western hemlock, and western red cedar grow to immense proportions. Quartz Creek Trail spends more than 10 miles wandering up the valley. Numerous streams enter Quartz Creek, including Straight Creek and its waterfalls. Regardless of how far one ventures up Quartz Creek Trail, the trip is sure to be grand.

Although Quartz Creek Trail gains 2,500 feet net elevation, numerous ups and downs make total elevation change more than twice that amount. The trail encounters Straight Creek (2 miles), home to a beautiful series of waterfalls. The occasional sections of logged forest are worth tolerating, balanced by the many miles of ancient old-growth forest. Campsites dot the trail as it wanders up the valley, passing Quartz Creek Butte Trail (a 1.5-mile connector between Summit Prairie and Quartz Creek Big Trees) junction at 4.5 miles. The upper section of the trail passes through forest burned long ago and now replaced by a subalpine setting. The trail connects to Boundary Trail (10.6 miles).

Folks who decide to hike the length of the trail are well advised to turn the trip into a loop. Summit Prairie Trail (see listing in this chapter) traverses Quartz Creek Ridge, awash in distant views and berry bushes. At the junction with Boundary Trail, hike east 2.3 miles to Summit Prairie Trail and turn south

toward Quartz Creek Butte Trail, descending to Quartz Creek. Total mileage is 22 miles.

User Groups: Hikers only. Wheelchair accessible the first 0.3 miles of trail.

Permits: This trail is accessible mid-June–October. A federal Northwest Forest Pass is required to park here.

Maps: For a map of Gifford Pinchot National Forest, contact the Outdoor Recreation Information Center at the downtown Seattle REI. For a topographic map, ask Green Trails for No. 333, McCoy Peak, No. 334, Blue Lake, No. 365, Lone Butte, and No. 366, Mount Adams West, or ask the USGS for Quartz Creek Butte, East Canyon Ridge, and Steamboat Mountain.

Directions: From Vancouver, drive north on I-5 to Highway 503 (Woodland, exit 21). Drive east 45 miles to Pine Creek Information Center. Turn right and continue on Forest Service Road 90 for 20 miles to the signed trailhead on the left (just beyond Forest Service Road 93).

Contact: Gifford Pinchot National Forest, Mount St. Helens National Volcanic Monument, 42218 NE Yale Bridge Rd., Amboy, WA 98601, 360/449-7871.

97 HIGH LAKES
8.0 mi/3.5 hr   👫2 ⛺9

south of Packwood in Gifford Pinchot National Forest

Take much of what is great about the Gifford Pinchot, combine it into one trail, and High Lakes Trail is the result. The trail does indeed visit several high, meadow-rimmed lakes along the way. Views of Mount Adams make regular appearances along the route. And during the later summer, delicious, ripe huckleberries make this trip an appetizing day hike.

High Lakes Trail connects Olallie and Horseshoe Lakes. Save for a small segment in the middle, much of the route is easy to negotiate with little elevation gain. From the western end, the trail travels the dense forest around Olallie Lake to the open forest and meadows of Chain Lakes (1.3 miles). The trail crosses a large lava flow punctuating the valley of Adams Creek (2.8 miles) and climbs to Horseshoe Lake and campground. August is usually the best month to harvest mouthfuls of huckleberries along the way. These juicy berries constitute a large part of the summer diets for local black bears.

User Groups: Hikers, leashed dogs, horses, mountain bikes, and motorcycles. No wheelchair access.

Permits: This trail is accessible May–November. No permits are required. Parking and access are free.

Maps: For a map of Gifford Pinchot National Forest, contact the Outdoor Recreation Information Center at the downtown Seattle REI. For a topographic map, ask Green Trails for No. 334, Blue Lake, or ask the USGS for Green Mountain.

Directions: From Randle, drive south 1 mile on Highway 131 to Forest Service Road 23. Veer left on Forest Service Road 23 and drive 33 miles to Forest Service Road 2329. Turn left and drive 1 mile to the signed trailhead on the left.

Contact: Gifford Pinchot National Forest, Cowlitz Valley Ranger Station, 10024 U.S. 12, Randle, WA 98377, 360/497-1100.

98 TAKHLAKH LAKE AND MEADOWS

2.6 mi/1.5 hr   🏃1 ⛰8

north of Trout Lake in Gifford Pinchot National Forest

Families on the lookout for an easy but scenic hike will want to pay attention to this one. Two trails combine to enjoy Takhlakh Lake, a 1.1-mile loop, and Takhlakh Meadows, a 1.5-mile loop situated off the first trail (imagine a figure eight). Both trails are flat and extremely level, perfect for hikers of any age. The trails are even barrier free, making them accessible for folks in wheelchairs, although in a few sections assistance will be appreciated. Both trails enjoy views of Mount Adams to the southeast. Takhlakh Lake Trail loops around the lake. From the southeast part of this loop, Takhlakh Meadows Trail makes a separate loop. In August, these open meadows are full of delicious, ripe huckleberries.

User Groups: Hikers and leashed dogs. No horses or mountain bikes are allowed. These trails are wheelchair accessible.

Permits: This trail is accessible May–November. No permits are required. Parking and access are free.

Maps: For a map of Gifford Pinchot National Forest, contact the Outdoor Recreation Information Center at the downtown Seattle REI. For a topographic map, ask Green Trails for No. 334, Blue Lake, or ask the USGS for Green Mountain.

Directions: From Randle, drive south 1 mile on Highway 131 to Forest Service Road 23. Veer left on Forest Service Road 23 and drive 33 miles to Forest Service Road 2329. Turn left and drive 2 miles to the signed trailhead at road's end.

Contact: Gifford Pinchot National Forest, Mount Adams Ranger District, 2455 Highway 141, Trout Lake, WA 98650, 509/395-3400.

99 SPENCER BUTTE

3.8 mi/2.0 hr   🏃2 ⛰8

north of Cougar in Gifford Pinchot National Forest

Spencer Butte Trail leads to one of the most beautiful views of a volcano you're likely to find anywhere. From atop Spencer Butte, a natural rock arch frames Mount St. Helens, a memorable and picturesque view. Short and accessible, with trailheads at either end of the 3-mile route, Spencer Butte is a great trip for folks looking for views on a quick day hike.

The best access is from the upper (north) trailhead in Spencer Meadows. It's not unlikely that you'll spot a herd of elk before you've even hit the trail. Spencer Butte Trail climbs steadily from the open meadows along a wide ridge. White pines give way to noble fir as the trail ascends through an open forest with regular views of the surrounding valleys. The trail crests atop Spencer Butte (elevation 4,247 feet). On the south side, a side trail drops slightly to a cold-water spring and the natural archway. Bring a camera, and you'll have a picture to display for years.

User Groups: Hikers, leashed dogs, horses, mountain bikes, and motorcycles. No wheelchair access.

Permits: This trail is accessible May–November. A federal Northwest Forest Pass is required to park here.

Maps: For a map of Gifford Pinchot National Forest, contact the Outdoor Recreation Information Center at the downtown Seattle REI. For a topographic map, ask Green Trails for No. 365, Lone Butte, or ask the USGS for Spencer Butte.

Directions: From Vancouver, drive north on I-5 to Highway 503 (Woodland, exit 21). Drive east 45 miles to Forest Service Road 25. Continue straight on Forest Service Road 25 and drive 6 miles to Forest Service Road 93, just beyond the Muddy River. Turn right and drive 9 miles to the signed trailhead on the left. This road is accessible for a passenger car but a high-clearance vehicle is recommended.

Contact: Gifford Pinchot National Forest, Mount St. Helens National Volcanic Monument, 42218 NE Yale Bridge Rd., Amboy, WA 98601, 360/449-7871.

100 BIG CREEK FALLS
1.4 mi/0.5 hr

north of Cougar in Gifford Pinchot National Forest

This is one of the best and easiest trails in the Gifford Pinchot National Forest. Big Creek Falls Trail follows the steep cliffs alongside Big Creek to an overlook with an excellent view of the 110-foot cascade. Big Creek is exactly that, a thunderous gusher of a stream. The sound alone of Big Creek dropping into a pool beside the Lewis River is impressive, not to say anything of the enormous cloud of mist the fall generates. The trail has some interpretive signs discussing the old-growth forest through which the trail travels. Granddaddy Douglas firs and western hemlocks dominate the forest, draped in shrouds of ferns and mosses. The trail ends at a viewpoint over the falls, overlooking the Lewis River and Hemlock Falls on the opposite side. This is an ideal trail for young hikers-in-training.

User Groups: Hikers, leashed dogs, horses, mountain bikes and motorcycles (no motorized use March to July) are allowed. Part of this trail (a loop to a viewpoint) is wheelchair accessible.

Permits: This trail is accessible year-round. No permits are required. Parking and access are free.

Maps: For a map of Gifford Pinchot National Forest, contact the Outdoor Recreation Information Center at the downtown Seattle REI. For a topographic map, ask Green Trails for No. 365, Lone Butte, or ask the USGS for Burnt Peak.

Directions: From Vancouver, drive north on I-5 to Highway 503 (Woodland, exit 21). Drive east 45 miles to Pine Creek Information Center. Turn right and continue on Forest Service Road 90 for 11 miles to the signed trailhead on the left.

Contact: Gifford Pinchot National Forest, Mount St. Helens National Volcanic Monument, 42218 NE Yale Bridge Rd., Amboy, WA 98601, 360/449-7871.

HIKING

HIKING

101 THOMAS LAKE
6.6 mi/3.0 hr

north of Carson in Indian Heaven Wilderness
of Gifford Pinchot National Forest

The high country of Indian Heaven is covered by small lakes in beautiful subalpine settings. Thomas Lake Trail encounters more of these lakes than any other trail in Indian Heaven Wilderness. It's also one of the easiest trails here, gaining just 600 feet in 3 miles. That makes Thomas Lake Trail a popular route into the huckleberry fields and wildflower meadows that characterize this high, volcanic plateau.

Thomas Lake Trail gets much of the work out of the way early, quickly climbing through dense forest to Thomas, Dee, and Heather Lakes (0.6 mile). The forest begins to break frequently, revealing meadows full of lupine and huckleberries in August. Elk and deer are frequently seen in this area, grazing in the meadows or wallowing in the small lakes and tarns. The trail ascends gently through meadows, passing yet more lakes. It crests at Rock Lake before dropping slightly to Blue Lake and the PCT. Although the trail is easily accomplished in a morning, it's advisable to plan on spending a full day exploring the many meadows and lakes. Just remember a fly rod or swimsuit.

User Groups: Hikers, leashed dogs, and horses. No mountain bikes are allowed. No wheelchair access.

Permits: This trail is accessible July–October. A federal Northwest Forest Pass is required to park here.

Maps: For a map of Gifford Pinchot National Forest, contact the Outdoor Recreation Information Center at the downtown Seattle REI. For a topographic map, ask Green Trails for No. 365S, Indian Heaven, or ask the USGS for Gifford Peak and Lone Butte.

Directions: From Vancouver, drive east 55 miles on Highway 14 to the town of Carson. Turn north on Wind River Road and drive 5 miles to Forest Service Road 65. Turn right

and drive 17 miles to the signed trailhead on the right.

Contact: Gifford Pinchot National Forest, Mount Adams Ranger District, 2455 Hwy. 141, Trout Lake, WA 98650, 509/395-3400.

102 HIDDEN LAKES
0.4 mi/0.5 hr

west of Trout Lake in Indian Heaven
Wilderness of Gifford Pinchot National Forest

Hidden Lakes is a short and easy hike for everyone. Traveling around several small subalpine lakes, Hidden Lakes Trail provides a great sampler of this scenic area. On the northeast side of Indian Heaven Wilderness, the lakes are home to a primitive car campground. Small forest and open meadows dominate this area of the Gifford Pinchot National Forest, famous for its berry fields. Hidden Lakes is no different, basking in large fields of huckleberries, with peak season typically arriving in early August. Enjoy the berries, but leave some for others. A view of Mount Adams completes the scene.

User Groups: Hikers, leashed dogs, mountain bikes, and horses. No wheelchair access.

Permits: This trail is accessible June–October. No permits are required. Parking and access are free.

Maps: For a map of Gifford Pinchot National Forest, contact the Outdoor Recreation Information Center at the downtown Seattle REI. For a topographic map, ask Green Trails for No. 365S, Indian Heaven, or ask the USGS for Sleeping Lady.

Directions: From Vancouver, drive east 70 miles on Highway 14 to Highway 141. Turn north and drive 22 miles to Trout Lake. Continue north on Highway 141 as it becomes Forest Service Road 24 for 16 miles (past Little Goose Campground) to the trailhead on the right.

Contact: Gifford Pinchot National Forest, Mount Adams Ranger District, 2455 Hwy. 141, Trout Lake, WA 98650, 509/395-3400.

103 INDIAN HEAVEN
6.6 mi/3.5 hr   🏃2 ⛰10

west of Trout Lake in Indian Heaven
Wilderness of Gifford Pinchot National Forest

BEST (

Strewn with high country lakes and subalpine meadows, Indian Heaven is heavenly indeed. A visit to this volcanic highland in August is divine, when ripe black huckleberries are ubiquitous. Indian Heaven Trail is the best way to the meadows and lakes of this subalpine playground. The short and accessible trail delivers every step of the way, whether it be old-growth forest, wildflower meadows, or scenic vistas.

Indian Heaven Trail wastes no time in reaching the high plateau of Indian Heaven. The trail climbs steadily through superb old-growth forest of subalpine fir, mountain hemlock, Englemann spruce, and white pine. Peek-a-boo views of Mount Adams whet the appetite for the meadows to come. The arrival into the high country is signaled when the trail reaches Cultus Lake, directly next to the trail (2.3 miles). A signed side trail leads a few hundred yards to Deep Lake. The trail junctions with Lemei Trail (2.5 miles) and bypasses Clear Lake before continuing to the PCT (3.3 miles). Rambling along any of these trails is well recommended.

Hikers looking for a little variety can turn Indian Heaven Trail into part of a great loop. The 6.7-mile loop uses the PCT to encircle Bird Mountain, passing numerous lakes along the way. Hike east on Indian Heaven Trail to the PCT (3.3 miles). Turn north and hike to Cultus Creek Trail (5.2 miles), which quickly descends back to Cultus Creek Campground and trailhead.

User Groups: Hikers, leashed dogs, and horses. No mountain bikes are allowed. No wheelchair access.

Permits: This trail is accessible June–October. A federal Northwest Forest Pass is required to park here.

Maps: For a map of Gifford Pinchot National Forest, contact the Outdoor Recreation Information Center at the downtown Seattle REI. For a topographic map, ask Green Trails for No. 365S, Indian Heaven, or ask the USGS for Lone Butte.

Directions: From Vancouver, drive east 70 miles on Highway 14 to Highway 141. Turn north and drive 22 miles to Trout Lake. Continue north on Highway 141 as it becomes Forest Service Road 24 for 18 miles to the signed trailhead within Cultus Creek Campground.

Contact: Gifford Pinchot National Forest, Mount Adams Ranger District, 2455 Hwy. 141, Trout Lake, WA 98650, 509/395-3400.

104 LEMEI
10.6 mi/5.0 hr   🏃2 ⛰9

west of Trout Lake in Indian Heaven
Wilderness of Gifford Pinchot National Forest

Lemei Trail provides a scenic route to the volcanic plateau of Indian Heaven Wilderness. The trail is a decent workout, ascending through much of its length. Views, huckleberries, and lakes are ample reward for the effort. After enjoying the meadows teeming with wildflower displays and feasting on August-ripe huckleberries, hikers will find that the waters of Lake Wapiki make a refreshing dip. One of the prettiest lakes in the high country of Indian Heaven, Lake Wapiki is enclosed by the area's tallest peak, jagged Lemei Rock.

Lemei Trail spends its first mile in dense second-growth forest. As the trail enters the wilderness (1 mile), the timber becomes old and large, in a more open forest. An understory of huckleberry bushes helps to ease the sting of the continuous climb. A side trail (3 miles) leads 0.5 mile to Lake Wapiki in the basin of Lemei Rock. Small forest and meadow fill the basin under craggy Lemei Rock. Lemei Trail continues beyond the junction to Indian Heaven Trail (5.3 miles) and miles of meadow exploration.

User Groups: Hikers, leashed dogs, and horses. No mountain bikes are allowed. No wheelchair access.

Permits: This trail is accessible mid-July–October. A federal Northwest Forest Pass is required to park here.

Maps: For a map of Gifford Pinchot National Forest, contact the Outdoor Recreation Information Center at the downtown Seattle REI. For a topographic map, ask Green Trails for No. 365S, Indian Heaven, or ask the USGS for Sleeping Beauty and Lone Butte.

Directions: From Vancouver, drive east 70 miles on Highway 14 to Highway 141. Turn north and drive 22 miles to Trout Lake. Continue north on Highway 141 as it becomes Forest Service Road 24 for 13 miles to the trailhead on the left (before Little Goose Campground).

Contact: Gifford Pinchot National Forest, Mount Adams Ranger District, 2455 Hwy. 141, Trout Lake, WA 98650, 509/395-3400.

105 RACE TRACK

6.2 mi/3.5 hr

west of Trout Lake in Indian Heaven
Wilderness of Gifford Pinchot National Forest

BEST (

Huckleberries and history are the story of this trail. Race Track Trail delves into the southern section of Indian Heaven Wilderness, a former meeting place for Native Americans. Each year, thousands of people from Yakama, Klickitat, and Columbia River nations gathered here during the height of the berry-harvesting season (August). The huckleberry bushes that flourish in this volcanic soil were a major source of food for Native Americans. And as it's situated along an important cross-Cascades trade route, it's easy to see how this area came to be known as an "Indian Heaven." During their time here, Native Americans entertained themselves by staging pony races, hence the name Race Track. The dirt track they used is still visible today within an open meadow.

A popular trail into the wilderness, Race Track Trail climbs steadily but gently, emerging from large timber to open subalpine meadows. During August, huckleberries will be sure to be

the main attraction. But don't let them keep you from spotting the abundant wildlife, including deer, elk, hawk, and even black bear. Race Track Trail reaches Race Track Lake (2.3 miles), where the dirt track can be seen, and then ascends to the peak of Red Mountain. This lofty peak with big views is home to one of Gifford Pinchot's three remaining fire lookouts.

User Groups: Hikers, leashed dogs, and horses. No mountain bikes are allowed. No wheelchair access.

Permits: This trail is accessible June–October. A federal Northwest Forest Pass is required to park here.

Maps: For a map of Gifford Pinchot National Forest, contact the Outdoor Recreation Information Center at the downtown Seattle REI. For a topographic map, ask Green Trails for No. 365S, Indian Heaven, or ask the USGS for Gifford Peak.

Directions: From Vancouver, drive east 55 miles on Highway 14 to the town of Carson. Turn north on Wind River Road and drive 5 miles to Forest Service Road 65. Turn right and drive 13 miles to the signed trailhead at Falls Creek Horse Camp.

Contact: Gifford Pinchot National Forest, Mount Adams Ranger District, 2455 Hwy. 141, Trout Lake, WA 98650, 509/395-3400.

106 SLEEPING BEAUTY

2.8 mi/2.0 hr

north of Trout Lake in Gifford Pinchot National Forest

As close to Mount Adams as one can be without actually scaling its slopes, Sleeping Beauty offers a grand view of the mountain. A tall outcrop of craggy rock sticking out above the surrounding forest, Sleeping Beauty gazes at the mass of Mount Adams from just 8 miles distant. Access to the rocky peak is a steep but quick trip through dense second-growth forest. The trail finds the edge of logging and enjoys old timber for a short time. Any views are reserved until the very end.

Sleeping Beauty is so named because it apparently resembles the profile of a sleeping woman; we'll let you decide. All personifications aside, the view from the top is spectacular. Rainier, St. Helens, and Hood dot the distant horizons. The peaks of Indian Heaven rise on the western skyline. The peak was formerly home to a Forest Service lookout.

User Groups: Hikers and leashed dogs. No horses or mountain bikes are allowed. No wheelchair access.

Permits: This trail is accessible May–November. No permits are required. Parking and access are free.

Maps: For a map of Gifford Pinchot National Forest, contact the Outdoor Recreation Information Center at the downtown Seattle REI. For a topographic map, ask Green Trails for No. 366, Mount Adams West, or ask the USGS for Sleeping Beauty.

Directions: From Vancouver, drive east 70 miles on Highway 14 to Highway 141. Turn north and drive 22 miles to Forest Service Road 88, just beyond the town of Trout Lake. Turn right on Forest Service Road 88 and drive 5 miles to Forest Service Road 8810. Turn right and drive 5 miles to Forest Service Road 8810-040. Turn right and drive 0.5 mile to the trailhead on the left.

Contact: Gifford Pinchot National Forest, Mount Adams Ranger District, 2455 Hwy. 141, Trout Lake, WA 98650, 509/395-3400.

107 STAGMAN RIDGE

8.0-12.8 mi/4.0-7.0 hr

north of Trout Lake in Mount Adams Wilderness of Gifford Pinchot National Forest

Stagman Ridge Trail provides great access to the high-country meadows flanking the western slopes of Mount Adams. The trail steadily but gently climbs to Horseshoe Meadows, home of juicy huckleberries, roaming mountain goats, and some pretty spectacular views. A trip to Horseshoe Meadows is indeed a great day, but hikers looking to throw in a subalpine lake (think refreshing swim) can continue an extra 2.4 miles to Lookingglass Lake.

Stagman Ridge Trail begins at a lofty elevation of 4,200 feet and gains about 1,600 feet over 4 miles. The forested trail quickly opens to reveal tremendous views of the mountain. It crosses several small streams, and Stagman Ridge Trail intersects the PCT (4 miles) on the lower slopes of Horseshoe Meadows. Although you could turn around here, hikers are well advised to continue on the PCT in either direction for at least a mile; the meadows are full of huckleberries in late summer and offer outstanding views year-round.

If the cold and refreshing water of Lookingglass Lake entices you to continue (it's well worth it), turn right on PCT, turn right again on Round the Mountain Trail (4.4 miles), and one more right turn onto Lookingglass Trail (5.5 miles). The lake (6.4 miles) is situated within high meadows, underneath the mountain.

User Groups: Hikers, leashed dogs, and horses. No mountain bikes are allowed. No wheelchair access.

Permits: This trail is accessible June–October. A federal Northwest Forest Pass is required to park here.

Maps: For a map of Gifford Pinchot National Forest, contact the Outdoor Recreation Information Center at the downtown Seattle REI. For a topographic map, ask Green Trails for No. 367S, Mount Adams, or ask the USGS for Mount Adams West.

Directions: From Vancouver, drive east 70 miles on Highway 14 to Highway 141. Turn north and drive 22 miles to Forest Service Road 23 (Buck Creek Road), near the town of Trout Lake. Turn right and drive 8 miles to Forest Service Road 8031. Turn right and drive 0.5 mile to Forest Service Road 070. Turn left and drive 3.5 miles to Forest Service Road 120. Turn right and drive 0.5 mile to the trailhead at road's end.

Contact: Gifford Pinchot National Forest, Mount Adams Ranger District, 2455 Hwy. 141, Trout Lake, WA 98650, 509/395-3400.

108 ROUND-THE-MOUNTAIN

22.2 mi one-way/2 days

north of Trout Lake in Mount Adams
Wilderness of Gifford Pinchot National Forest

Like Washington's other big volcanoes, Mount Adams is circumnavigated by a long, demanding trail. Set high in the subalpine meadows gracing the slopes of Mount Adams, Round-the-Mountain Trail is the best way to fully experience Washington's second-tallest peak. Here's the catch. The east side of Mount Adams is managed by the Yakima Indian Nation, and special permits are required to hike within the reservation (a vexing process). Additionally, this section of trail is extremely difficult. East-side streams turn into dangerous glacial torrents during the summer, and no maintained trail exists over enormous lava fields. Thus, Round-the-Mountain is best completed as a through-hike, along the western side of Mount Adams.

Round-the-Mountain Trail is best begun from Cold Springs on the south side of Mount Adams. Hike South Climb Trail to Round-the-Mountain Trail (1.3 miles) and turn north. The scenery is supreme every step of the way, with alpine meadows and distant mountain views the norm. Expect to see an abundance of wildflowers in midsummer and huckleberries in early fall. The trail encounters the PCT (7 miles) and follows it to Muddy Meadows Trail (19.8 miles). Turn north to reach the northern trailhead at Keenee Campground (22.2 miles).

Highlights along the way include Lookingglass Lake (5.9 miles), Horseshoe Meadows (7 miles), Sheep Lake (11 miles), and Adams Meadows (14.5 miles, below Adams Glacier). Campsites are frequent along the route; stick to already established sites to minimize damage to fragile meadows. The views of Mount Adams improve with progress around the peak, with great looks at the glaciers. If a true circumnavigation of the mountain is an unshakable goal, please contact the Mount Adams Ranger Station for full details on trail conditions.

User Groups: Hikers, leashed dogs, and horses. No mountain bikes are allowed. No wheelchair access.

Permits: This trail is accessible mid-July–October. A federal Northwest Forest Pass is required to park here.

Maps: For a map of Gifford Pinchot National Forest, contact the Outdoor Recreation Information Center at the downtown Seattle REI. For a topographic map, ask Green Trails for No. 367S, Mount Adams, or ask the USGS for Mount Adams West, Mount Adams East, and Green Mountain.

Directions: From Vancouver, drive east 70 miles on Highway 14 to Highway 141. Turn north and drive 22 miles to Forest Service Road 23 (Buck Creek Road), near the town of Trout Lake. Turn right and drive 3 miles to Forest Service Road 82. Turn right and drive 0.5 mile to Forest Service Road 80. Turn left and drive 4 miles to Forest Service Road 8040. Continue 5 miles on Road 8040 to Morrison Creek Campground and Forest Service Road 500. Turn right and drive 2 miles to the trailhead at road's end.

Contact: Gifford Pinchot National Forest, Mount Adams Ranger District, 2455 Hwy. 141, Trout Lake, WA 98650, 509/395-3400.

109 KILLEN CREEK

6.2 mi/4.0 hr

north of Trout Lake in Mount Adams
Wilderness of Gifford Pinchot National Forest

By the time the first views of Mount Adams emerge (which is quickly), hikers on Killen Creek Trail know they've selected a beauty of a hike. This popular route on the north side of Mount Adams climbs steadily through open forest to wide-open meadows beneath towering glaciers. This is undoubtedly great rambling country, where the hike gets better every step of the way. Day hikes this grand are hard to come by in southern Washington, and this is one of the best in the state.

Killen Creek Trail starts high (4,600 feet) and climbs slowly but steadily to the PCT (3.1 miles). Much of the trail traverses open forest with repeated views of Mount Adams, but the last mile or so revels in meadows. Wildflowers take turns blooming throughout the summer. Rambling in either direction along the PCT is highly recommended to soak up the scenery. Hikers hoping to approach even closer to the mountain are welcome to do so along High Camp Trail, a continuation of Killen Creek Trail on the uphill side of the PCT. This is a 1-mile trail to High Camp, one of Adams' best, among rocky meadows and glacier moraine.

User Groups: Hikers, leashed dogs, and horses. No mountain bikes are allowed. No wheelchair access.

Permits: This trail is accessible mid-July–mid-October. A federal Northwest Forest Pass is required to park here.

Maps: For a map of Gifford Pinchot National Forest, contact the Outdoor Recreation Information Center at the downtown Seattle REI. For a topographic map, ask Green Trails for No. 367S, Mount Adams, or ask the USGS for Green Mountain and Mount Adams West.

Directions: From Vancouver, drive east 70 miles on Highway 14 to Highway 141. Turn north and drive 22 miles to Forest Service Road 23 (Buck Creek Road), near the town of Trout Lake. Turn right and drive about 30 miles to Forest Service Road 2329. Turn right and drive 5 miles (around Takhlakh Lake) to the trailhead on the right.

Contact: Gifford Pinchot National Forest, Mount Adams Ranger District, 2455 Hwy. 141, Trout Lake, WA 98650, 509/395-3400.

110 SOUTH CLIMB
6.8 mi/4.5 hr   4   9

north of Trout Lake in Mount Adams Wilderness of Gifford Pinchot National Forest

Not for the faint of heart, South Climb is exactly what the name implies: an ascent of Mount Adams from the south side. The summit needn't be one's goal to embark on this beautiful trail, but well-conditioned legs certainly are always helpful. South Climb Trail assaults the mountain straight on and reaches 8,500 feet of elevation before petering out beside Crescent Glacier. From here, it's a mad scramble to the top. Stopping at Crescent Glacier reveals spectacular views of the surrounding valleys, forests, and distant mountain ridges. If the wildflower meadows alongside the trail and beautiful views don't take your breath away, the steep pitch of South Climb will.

Should a summit of Mount Adams be on your wish list, keep several things in mind. One, it's steep as hell and strenuous. Experienced climbers take at least 6–8 hours to reach the summit from Cold Springs, an elevation gain of 6,700 feet. Visibility decreases after early morning, so smart mountaineers camp at Cold Springs Car Campground and hit the trail by 3 A.M. That's 3 o'clock in the morning. And the climb requires permits from the ranger station in Trout Lake. The summit is certainly achievable and is relatively easy compared to Mount Hood or Mount Rainier. Novices frequently reach the peak. At the top are views conceivable only if you've been there.

User Groups: Hikers, leashed dogs, and horses. No mountain bikes are allowed. No wheelchair access.

Permits: This trail is accessible July–September. A federal Northwest Forest Pass is required to park here. Climbing permits are required for summits of Mount Adams. The $15 permits are available at Trout Lake Ranger Station.

Maps: For a map of Gifford Pinchot National

HIKING

Forest, contact the Outdoor Recreation Information Center at the downtown Seattle REI. For a topographic map, ask Green Trails for No. 367S, Mount Adams, or ask the USGS for Mount Adams West.

Directions: From Vancouver, drive east 70 miles on Highway 14 to Highway 141. Turn north and drive 22 miles to Forest Service Road 23 (Buck Creek Road), near the town of Trout Lake. Turn right and drive 3 miles to Forest Service Road 82. Turn right and drive 0.5 mile to Forest Service Road 80. Turn left and drive 4 miles to Forest Service Road 8040. Continue 5 miles on Road 8040 to Morrison Creek Campground and Forest Service Road 500. Turn right and drive 2 miles to the trailhead at road's end.

Contact: Gifford Pinchot National Forest, Mount Adams Ranger District, 2455 Hwy. 141, Trout Lake, WA 98650, 509/395-3400.

⑪ BATTLE GROUND LAKE LOOP
7.0 mi/3.5 hr   🥾1 ⛰9

north of Vancouver in Battle Ground Lake
State Park

There's no need to drive all the way to southern Oregon to see Crater Lake. Washington has its own miniature version here in Battle Ground Lake. Like Crater Lake, Battle Ground Lake was created by a massive volcanic explosion. The resulting crater filled with spring water and created Battle Ground Lake. Today, conifer forests of Douglas fir and western hemlock surround the lake, creating peaceful and quiet surroundings. The trail circles the lake within the shady forest, never venturing far from the lakeshore. Anglers will appreciate the access to solitary fishing holes, where monster trout hide out. The state park has a large car campground, but it fills quickly on summer weekends.

User Groups: Hikers, leashed dogs, and horses. No mountain bikes are allowed. No wheelchair access.

Permits: This trail is accessible year-round.

No permits are required. Parking and access are free.

Maps: For a topographic map, ask the USGS for Battleground and Wacolt.

Directions: From Vancouver, drive north on I-5 to exit 14. Turn right on Northeast 179th Street and drive to the city of Battle Ground. Drive to the east end of town and turn left on Grace Avenue. Drive 3 miles to Battle Ground Lake State Park. The signed trailhead is near the day-use area within the park.

Contact: Battle Ground Lake State Park, 18002 NE 249th St., Battle Ground, WA, 98604, 360/687-4621.

⑫ BEACON ROCK
2.0 mi/2.0 hr   🥾3 ⛰9

east of Vancouver in Beacon Rock State Park

Visible from miles away and towering over the Columbia River, Beacon Rock offers an unbeatable view of the Columbia River Gorge. Geologically speaking, Beacon Rock is a true rock. That is, it's one solid piece of rock, not a conglomeration of different types of rock like many mountains are. That makes Beacon Rock the second tallest "rock" in the world! Beacon Rock is actually the core of an old volcano, exposed when the Missoula Floods eroded softer rock encasing it. The resulting hulk towers 848 feet over the mighty Columbia. It's quite a perch from the top.

Beacon Rock State Park offers nearly 20 miles of trail and road to explore, but the most popular and scenic is the trail to the summit. It's a little under 1 mile to the top, but don't let the short distance fool you. It's a steep climb every step of the way. Old forest shades the trail where trees can find a small ledge to grow, but many areas are on steep, exposed cliffs. Boardwalks, stairways, and handrails have been installed to present a safer experience. The summit is an ideal picnic spot, with great views of the gorge and Mount Hood.

User Groups: Hikers and leashed dogs. No

horses or mountain bikes are allowed. No wheelchair access.

Permits: This trail is accessible March–November. No permits are required. Parking and access are free.

Maps: For a topographic map, ask the USGS for Bonneville Dam and Tanner Butte.

Directions: From Vancouver, drive east on Highway 14 to Beacon Rock State Park (near Mile Marker 35). The trailhead is on the right side of the highway.

Contact: Beacon Rock State Park, 34841 State Road 14, Stevenson, WA, 98648-6081, 509/427-8265.

113 SIOUXON

8.0 mi/4.0 hr

east of Cougar in Gifford Pinchot National Forest

Deep within old forest, Siouxon Trail journeys alongside the noisy creek. Waterfalls and deep pools are regular highlights, making this a great winter hike when higher routes are closed due to snow. Siouxon Trail quickly descends from the trailhead to the creek. Large and gushing West Creek is crossed by a large wooden bridge (0.5 mile). Peer downstream to see the first of many waterfalls. The trail encounters another cascade on Siouxon Creek (4 miles), where the creek empties into a large emerald pool. During the summer, good luck avoiding the urge for a quick dip in the cold water. This is a common turnaround point for many day hikers, but Siouxon Trail travels along the creek for a total of 5.5 miles through grand forest the entire length. This is a great place to spend a night with little ones or first-time backpackers. Numerous campsites are on the stream banks, where the noisy stream lulls one to sleep.

User Groups: Hikers, leashed dogs, horses, and mountain bikes. No wheelchair access.

Permits: This trail is accessible year-round. No permits are required. Parking and access are free.

Maps: For a map of Gifford Pinchot National

Forest, contact the Outdoor Recreation Information Center at the downtown Seattle REI. For a topographic map, ask Green Trails for No. 396, Lookout Mountain, or ask the USGS for Siouxon Peak and Bear Mountain.

Directions: From Vancouver, drive north on I-5 to Highway 503 (Woodland, exit 21). Drive east 45 miles to Pine Creek Information Center. Turn right and continue on Forest Service Road 90 to Northeast Healy Road, in the town of Clehatchie. Turn right and drive 10 miles to Forest Service Road 57. Turn left and drive 1.5 miles to Forest Service Road 5701. Turn left and drive 4 miles to the trailhead at road's end.

Contact: Gifford Pinchot National Forest, Mount Adams Ranger District, 2455 Hwy. 141, Trout Lake, WA 98650, 509/395-3400.

114 LOWER FALLS CREEK

3.4 mi/2.0 hr

north of Carson in Gifford Pinchot National Forest

About the only thing keeping the masses from Lower Falls Creek is the short length of the trail. It's not a destination in itself. But anyone visiting the town of Carson should certainly spend the time to visit Lower Falls Creek. The trail follows this beautiful stream as it passes through a narrow gorge and ends at the base of a large waterfall. On hot summer days, the forest is cool and shady, and the water of Falls Creek is especially appealing.

Lower Falls Creek Trail climbs gently throughout its short length. Deer and elk are frequently seen browsing in the forest, filled with the sounds of woodpeckers and wrens. The trail crosses Falls Creek as it gushes through a rock gorge; fortunately, a suspension bridge spans the gap. Falls Creek Trail ends at the base of a large waterfall, where Falls Creek cascades down a steep wall.

User Groups: Hikers, leashed dogs, and mountain bikes. No horses are allowed. No wheelchair access.

Permits: This trail is accessible year-round. A federal Northwest Forest Pass is required to park here.

Maps: For a map of Gifford Pinchot National Forest, contact the Outdoor Recreation Information Center at the downtown Seattle REI. For a topographic map, ask Green Trails for No. 397, Wind River, or ask the USGS for Termination Point.

Directions: From Vancouver, drive east 55 miles on Highway 14 to the town of Carson. Turn north on Wind River Road and drive 9 miles to Forest Service Road 30. Turn right and drive 3 miles to the signed trailhead on the right.

Contact: Gifford Pinchot National Forest, Mount Adams Ranger District, 2455 Hwy. 141, Trout Lake, WA 98650, 509/395-3400.

115 TRAPPER CREEK
9.5 mi/4.5 hr

north of Carson in Trapper Creek Wilderness of Gifford Pinchot National Forest

Any opportunity to hike in old-growth forest should be seized, sooner rather than later. Trapper Creek, one of the least-known wildernesses in the state of Washington, preserves a small chunk of ancient timberland just north of the Columbia River Gorge. Trapper Creek Trail makes a full immersion into the wilderness, following the beautiful, restless creek to its headwaters as it flows over waterfalls and through narrow gorges. Trapper Creek Trail connects to Observation Trail (see next listing), so if you're itching for views, you can have them by making a large loop.

Trapper Creek Trail spends much of its length alongside the noisy creek. The forest is a diverse mix of giants, with Douglas fir, western hemlock, and western red cedar, all draped with mosses and lichens, growing to immense proportions. Trapper Creek Trail junctions with Observation Peak Trail (1 mile) but continues alongside the creek. The creek is a long sequence of cascades and pools, but Trapper Creek Falls

(4.5 miles) are the highlight of the trip and a good turnaround point. The trail ends at another junction with Observation Trail, the option for a loop trip (about 12 miles).

User Groups: Hikers, leashed dogs, and horses. No mountain bikes are allowed. No wheelchair access.

Permits: This trail is accessible year-round. A federal Northwest Forest Pass is required to park here.

Maps: For a map of Gifford Pinchot National Forest, contact the Outdoor Recreation Information Center at the downtown Seattle REI. For a topographic map, ask the USGS for Bare Mountain.

Directions: From Vancouver, drive east 55 miles on Highway 14 to the town of Carson. Turn north on Wind River Road and drive 10 miles to Forest Service Road 3065. Turn left and drive 1.5 miles to the signed trailhead at Government Mineral Springs.

Contact: Gifford Pinchot National Forest, Mount Adams Ranger District, 2455 Hwy. 141, Trout Lake, WA 98650, 509/395-3400.

116 OBSERVATION PEAK
6.0-13.0 mi/3.0-7.0 hr   2 10

north of Carson in Trapper Creek Wilderness of Gifford Pinchot National Forest

Options, options, options. Observation Peak provides great views from the heart of Trapper Creek Wilderness, over lush, green valleys out to several snowcapped volcanic peaks. Best of all, there are several ways to enjoy this pristine and unlogged section of the Gifford Pinchot. A trip to Observation Peak can be a short hike (5.6 miles), a long up and down (13 miles), or one of two loop trips (12 miles). These loops are by far the best way to experience the wilderness, where misty forests are full of ancient timber.

Observation Trail runs from the valley bottom up along a high ridge to Observation Peak and out to Forest Service Road 58. For a short hike, park on Forest Service Road 58 and hike south through Sister Rocks Natural Area (big trees!) to the peak (2.8 miles). Reaching Observation Peak from the south is certainly longer and more strenuous, but remember that rule: no pain, no gain.

From Government Mineral Springs, Observation Trail climbs steadily from old-growth lowland forest into a mix of subalpine trees. Views are frequent along the lightly forested ridge, as are huckleberries and deer. Hearty hikers can pass the peak and descend back to the trailhead via Trapper Creek Trail (see previous listing) or Dry Creek (Big Hollow Trail, another big tree and beautiful creek route).

User Groups: Hikers, leashed dogs, and horses. No mountain bikes are allowed. No wheelchair access.

Permits: This trail is accessible July–October. A federal Northwest Forest Pass is required to park here.

Maps: For a map of Gifford Pinchot National Forest, contact the Outdoor Recreation Information Center at the downtown Seattle REI. For a topographic map, ask Green Trails for No. 396, Lookout Mountain, and No. 397, Wind River, or ask the USGS for Bare Mountain.

Directions: From Vancouver, drive east 55 miles on Highway 14 to the town of Carson. Turn north on Wind River Road and drive 10 miles to Forest Service Road 3065. Turn left and drive 1.5 miles to the signed trailhead at Government Mineral Springs.

Contact: Gifford Pinchot National Forest, Mount Adams Ranger District, 2455 Hwy. 141, Trout Lake, WA 98650, 509/395-3400.

117 BUNKER HILL
3.6 mi/1.5 hr   2 7

north of Carson in Gifford Pinchot National Forest

Great for folks in Carson with a couple of hours to kill, Bunker Hill Trail is a quick but strenuous climb to the summit. The first

0.5 mile of the route follows the PCT north. Most folks on the PCT are through-hikers coming from Oregon and on their way to big, grand country in the coming months. Turn left onto Bunker Hill Trail and do the switchback shuffle up to the summit. Views are reserved until the very top, where a fire lookout once stood. Views of the Wind River Valley are revealed, as are numerous surrounding ridges.

User Groups: Hikers and leashed dogs. No horses or mountain bikes are allowed. No wheelchair access.

Permits: This trail is accessible April–December. No permits are required. Parking and access are free.

Maps: For a map of Gifford Pinchot National Forest, contact the Outdoor Recreation Information Center at the downtown Seattle REI. For a topographic map, ask Green Trails for No. 397, Wind River, or ask the USGS for Stabler.

Directions: From Vancouver, drive east 55 miles on Highway 14 to the town of Carson. Drive north 5.5 miles on Wind River Road to Hemlock Road. Turn left and drive 1.5 miles to Forest Service Road 43. Turn right and drive 0.5 mile to Forest Service Road 43-417. Turn right and drive 0.2 mile to the Pacific Crest Trailhead. Head to the right (north) on the PCT.

Contact: Gifford Pinchot National Forest, Mount Adams Ranger District, 2455 Hwy. 141, Trout Lake, WA 98650, 509/395-3400.

118 LITTLE HUCKLEBERRY
5.0 mi/3.0 hr   3 9

west of Trout Lake in Gifford Pinchot National Forest

One of the more accessible viewpoints from Highway 14, Little Huckleberry Trail makes a quick and at times steep trip to an old lookout site. Views of Mount Adams and Mount Hood, across the Columbia River, are quite nice. And a feast of huckleberries along the way sweetens the deal on August trips to the mountain. This is a nice trail for a weekend morning, if you're coming from Vancouver or Portland.

Little Huckleberry Trail gains 1,800 feet in just 2.5 miles, a steady and soon tiring ascent within a small draw. Enjoy the old forest and take your time. Early in the summer, a cold-water spring runs (2 miles), offering a great place to break. The final 0.5 mile climbs through open berry fields and rock slopes to the summit. A lookout once stood atop this rounded top, perched over a wide expanse of the Gifford Pinchot. With room for a tent, this is a fun overnighter for beginning backpackers (think of the stars).

User Groups: Hikers, leashed dogs, horses, and mountain bikes. No wheelchair access.

Permits: This trail is accessible April–November. A federal Northwest Forest Pass is required to park here.

Maps: For a map of Gifford Pinchot National Forest, contact the Outdoor Recreation Information Center at the downtown Seattle REI. For a topographic map, ask Green Trails for No. 398, Willard, or ask the USGS for Sleeping Beauty.

Directions: From Vancouver, drive east 70 miles on Highway 14 to Highway 141. Turn north and drive 22 miles to Trout Lake. Continue north on Highway 141 as it becomes Forest Service Road 24 for 10 miles to Forest Service Road 66. Turn left (south) and drive 5 miles to the trailhead on the left.

Contact: Gifford Pinchot National Forest, Mount Adams Ranger District, 2455 Hwy. 141, Trout Lake, WA 98650, 509/395-3400.

⬛119 DOG MOUNTAIN
6.0 mi/3.5 hr 3 9

east of Carson in Gifford Pinchot National Forest

Getting to Dog Mountain, with a trailhead directly on Highway 14, is no problem. Getting up Dog Mountain is a bit more of a workout, however. Dense forest mixes with open wildflower meadows along the trail, cresting at the open summit of Dog Mountain. The views of the Columbia River Gorge are outstanding, with snowcapped Mount Hood standing across the way. This is a very popular hike with folks coming from Vancouver or Portland, especially on the weekends. Expect to see a neighbor or two.

Dog Mountain Trail makes the best of what it has been given, forming a loop instead of a straight up and down. The loop is arranged like a lasso. Climb steeply to the loop junction (0.5 mile). Head to the right for a more gradual and scenic route to the top. Regular breaks in the forest provide room for open meadows of wildflowers (May is a great month here). This is dry country, meaning water is nonexistent; pack plenty, because overall elevation gain is 2,700 feet. Do be on the lookout for poison oak and rattlesnakes, things that most hikers don't care to mess with. The summit is the former home to a Forest Service lookout. The loop returns to the junction via a steep, densely forested route.

User Groups: Hikers and leashed dogs. No horses or mountain bikes are allowed. No wheelchair access.

Permits: This trail is accessible March–December. No permits are required. A federal Northwest Forest Pass is required to park here, and access is free.

Maps: For a map of Gifford Pinchot National Forest, contact the Outdoor Recreation Information Center at the downtown Seattle REI. For a topographic map, ask the USGS for Mount Defiance.

Directions: From Vancouver, drive east on Highway 14 to Mile Marker 53 and the signed trailhead.

Contact: Gifford Pinchot National Forest, Mount Adams Ranger District, 2455 Hwy. 141, Trout Lake, WA 98650, 509/395-3400.

Index

www.moon.com

DESTINATIONS | ACTIVITIES | BLOGS | MAPS | BOOKS

MOON.COM is ready to help plan your next trip! Filled with fresh trip ideas and strategies, author interviews, informative travel blogs, a detailed map library, and descriptions of all the Moon guidebooks, Moon.com is all you need to get out and explore the world—or even places in your own backyard. While at Moon.com, sign up for our monthly e-newsletter for updates on new releases, travel tips, and expert advice from our on-the-go Moon authors. As always, when you travel with Moon, expect an experience that is uncommon and truly unique.

MOON IS ON FACEBOOK—BECOME A FAN!
JOIN THE MOON PHOTO GROUP ON FLICKR

 OUTDOORS

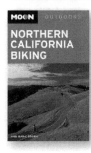

"Well written, thoroughly researched, and packed full of useful information and advice, these guides really do get you into the outdoors."

—GORP.COM

MOON WASHINGTON'S COLUMBIA RIVER GORGE CAMPING & HIKING

Avalon Travel
a member of the Perseus Books Group
1700 Fourth Street
Berkeley, CA 94710, USA
www.moon.com

Editors: Elizabeth Hollis Hansen, Sabrina Young
Series Manager: Sabrina Young
Copy Editors: Valerie Sellers Blanton, Maura
    Brown, Ellie Winters
Graphics and Production Coordinator:
    Domini Dragoone
Cover Designer: Kathryn Osgood
Interior Designer: Darren Alessi
Map Editors: Albert Angulo, Mike Morgenfeld
Cartographers: Mike Morgenfeld, Kat Bennett,
    Brice Ticen

ISBN-13: 978-1-59880-572-7

ABOUT THE AUTHORS

© JOHN BEATH

Tom Stienstra

For 30 years, Tom Stienstra's full-time job has been to capture and communicate the outdoor experience. Tom writes a weekly outdoors column that is distributed across America. He has won more than 100 national and regional writing awards, and has twice been named National Outdoors Writer of the Year. His television show, *The Great Outdoors,* is broadcast weekly on CBS/CW. His first edition of *Pacific Northwest Camping* was acclaimed by the *Portland Oregonian.*

Tom takes part in all facets of the outdoors, and as a pilot and airplane owner, can cover great distances quickly in the pursuit of adventure. He lives with his wife Stephani at their ranch in the "State of Jefferson," near the Oregon border.

You can contact Tom directly via his website at www.tom stienstra.com. His guidebooks include:

Moon Oregon Camping
Moon Washington Camping
Moon Pacific Northwest Camping
Moon West Coast RV Camping
Moon California Camping
Moon California Hiking (with Ann Marie Brown)
Moon California Fishing
Moon California Recreational Lakes & Rivers
California Wildlife
Moon Northern California Cabins & Cottages
Tom Stienstra's Bay Area Recreation

Scott Leonard

© ERIC MELTZER

Scott Leonard spent his childhood fishing, skiing, and hunting in the Oregon outdoors. He began hiking and backpacking when he started college at the University of Puget Sound in Tacoma. He fell in love with the wilderness areas of Washington – and has never grown tired of pounding out miles of trail.

After college, Scott spent several years building and maintaining trails, and teaching others to do the same. He spent a year researching and hiking for *Moon Washington Hiking* and *Moon Pacific Northwest Hiking,* and yet another summer on *Moon Take a Hike Seattle* – never has a job been so easy to get up for each morning.

In addition to writing, Scott works as an attorney in Portland, Oregon, where he has a successful criminal defense practice.

3840014R00089

Made in the USA
San Bernardino, CA
26 August 2013